*The Book of Government
or Rules for Kings*

by Nizām al-Mulk

*translated from the Persian
by Hubert Darke*

The famous Persian vizier Nizām al-Mulk, lifelong friend of Omar Khayyám, wrote this book between the years 1086 and 1091, at the request of Sultan Malikshah of the Saljūg dynasty, which at that time ruled Persia and beyond. In the first part, the author seeks to arouse the interest of his master (who is descended from a wild tribe of Turkish nomads) in the administration of a civilized country and suggests fields to which he should turn his attention. His advice is illustrated by anecdotes about former kings and sayings of philosophers. The tone of bitterness and frustration in the second part suggest that Nizām al-Mulk was out of favor, if not out of office; his advice is now edged with criticism. In the final chapters the author returns to calmer topics and concludes with some general moral precepts.

# RARE MASTERPIECES

## OF PHILOSOPHY AND SCIENCE

### EDITED BY DR. W. STARK

PUBLISHED ON THE LOUIS STERN MEMORIAL FUND

# THE BOOK OF GOVERNMENT
# OR RULES FOR KINGS

*The Siyāsat-nāma
or Siyar al-Mulūk*

of NIZĀM AL-MULK

*Translated from the Persian by*
HUBERT DARKE

NEW HAVEN
YALE UNIVERSITY PRESS
1960

THIS EDITION FIRST PUBLISHED
IN THE UNITED STATES
BY YALE UNIVERSITY PRESS
NEW HAVEN CONNECTICUT
AND PRINTED IN GREAT BRITAIN
BY BUTLER AND TANNER LTD
LONDON AND FROME

UNESCO COLLECTION OF REPRESENTATIVE WORKS
PERSIAN SERIES

*This book has been accepted in the Persian
Translation Series of the United Nations
Educational, Scientific and Cultural
Organization (UNESCO)*

# CONTENTS

# INTRODUCTION

THE author of the present work, Nizām al-Mulk, was for over thirty years the chief minister of two successive rulers of the Seljūq tribes. They came of a race of wiry and relentless warriors inured to the hardships of life in the Kirghiz steppes, whence in the tenth century A.D. they descended upon the softer and more fertile lands of the Oxus. There they embraced Islam 'with all the fervour of their uncouth souls', as Stanley Lane-Poole puts it, and participated in the struggles between other tribes of recent conversion for supremacy and spoils. Eventually, one Seljūq chieftain, Chaghri Beg, accumulated horses, men and equipment enough to venture on an invasion of the huge Persian province of Khurasan. His son and grandson, Alp Arslan and Malikshah—successive masters of Nizām al-Mulk —swept onwards, while his brother Tughril Beg expanded his conquests in neighbouring territories, until at last the Seljūq Empire covered all the lands from the borders of Chinese Turkestan and India to the confines of Egypt, and rubbed against the frontier-posts of the Byzantine Empire.

The Seljūq Empire was presided over by warrior chiefs, whose slaves commanded the armies which kept it in subjection. These slaves were mamlūks, bought as children and reared in the chieftains' own families, so that their fidelity could be relied upon, whereas that of free men might be tainted with personal ambition. It was to cope with such conditions as these that Nizām al-Mulk compiled his manual. He had been compelled at the outset of his career to construct a civil service capable of administering great tracts of territory, sparsely dotted with inhabited towns and villages. Like the Arabs before them in Persia, the Seljūqs employed the local dihqāns, small landowners familiar with the ancient systems of taxation, to perform the only governmental task that mattered to them, namely that of collecting revenue.

These dihqāns may have been more literate than persons carrying

vii

out similar duties in other countries at the time, but it is hardly to be expected that they were more considerate to the humble folk under their screw. After years of ill-treatment and extortion, the complaints of the subject people came at last to the ears of the Seljūq Sultan and he discovered that nothing was going right in his great empire. It was then, when he at last realized his danger, that he commissioned his chief advisers to discover the reasons for things having gone amiss. Nizām al-Mulk, the most experienced of them all, who had held control for decades, coldly and clearly pointed out where the faults lay, though without a word in self-exculpation. He named no names, but stated in general terms who the enemies of the State—and incidentally of himself—were, and in like fashion sketched out the paths which a monarch must follow if he is to keep his subjects contented. The monarch, of course, could only be an absolute monarch, one who could bind and loose, engage and dismiss, at his own sweet will.

Nizām al-Mulk, as is well known, met his death at the hands of one of the Batini assassins whom, as though by some premonition, he had denounced as enemies of the State in his *Siyar al-muluk*. What is certain is that his reforms were never carried out, for his master, Malikshah, died within a month of him, and after that the empire broke into pieces. What survives is the book that lies before us, translated into plain language which admirably reproduces the style of the original Persian.

REUBEN LEVY

# TRANSLATOR'S NOTES

This translation has been made from a revised Persian text, edited by the translator from the following manuscripts:

Bibliothèque Nationale, Paris: Supplément Persan 1571: dated 694/1294.

Islamic Institute, Istanbul: Fārsī 135: dated 730/1330.

King's College, Cambridge: Pote Collection 219: dated 1020/1611.

British Museum, London: Add. 23,516: dated 1032/1623.

Rāmpūr State Library: Akhlāq 121: undated.

Panjāb University, Lahore: Ph III 68: undated.

As a result of the revision the translation does not correspond to previously published Persian texts at some points.

The work has been edited and translated in Europe before by—

Charles Schefer:

Vol. I    Persian text, Paris, 1891
Vol. II   French translation, 1893
Vol. III  Supplement, 1897

   (Historical extracts—see Browne, *Literary History*, II. 212).

B. N. Zakhoder
Introduction and Russian translation, Moscow, 1949.

The Persian text has been printed in Tehran by—

Sayyid 'Abd ar Raḥīm Khalkhālī, 1310/1932
   This text was edited from a manuscript dated 970/1563 existing in Persia.

'Abbās Iqbāl, 1320/1942
   This is an edition for students made from a comparison of the texts of Schefer and Khalkhali.

Murtaḍā Mudarrisī Chahārdihī, 1334/1955

A reprint of Schefer's text with some corrections and notes by Mīrzā Muḥammad Qazwīnī.

Of reference books in English the following are recommended:

*Chahār Maqāla,* translated by E. G. Browne. Gibb Memorial, Old Series XI. 2.

*Classical Persian Literature,* by A. J. Arberry. London, 1958.

*Shorter Encyclopaedia of Islām,* by H. A. R. Gibb and J. H. Kramers. Leiden, 1953.

*Ḥudūd al ʿĀlam,* translated by V. Minorsky. Gibb Memorial, New Series XI.

*Introduction to the Jawāmiʿ al Ḥikāyāt of ʿAufī,* by M. Niẓāmuʾddīn. Gibb Memorial, New Series VIII.

*Kashf al Maḥjūb,* translated by R. A. Nicholson. Gibb Memorial, Old Series XVII.

*The Koran Interpreted,* by A. J. Arberry. 2 vols. London, 1955.

*Landlord and peasant in Persia,* by A. K. S. Lambton. Oxford, 1953.

*The Lands of the Eastern Caliphate,* by G. Le Strange. Cambridge, 1930.

*A Literary History of Persia,* by E. G. Browne. Vols. I and II. Cambridge, 1928.

*A Mirror for Princes* (The Qābūs-nāma), translated by Reuben Levy. London, 1951.

*The Mohammadan Dynasties,* by Stanley Lane-Poole. Paris, 1925.

*Sulṭān Maḥmūd* by Muḥammad Nāzim. Cambridge, 1931.

*Tārīkhʾi Guzīda* of Ḥamd Allāh Mustaufī, abridged translation and indices by Browne and Nicholson. Gibb Memorial, Old Series XIV. 2.

*Turkestān down to the Mongol Invasion,* by W. Barthold. Gibb Memorial, New Series V.

Reference is also made in the footnotes to an important historical work in Persian:

*Rāḥat aṣ Ṣudūr* of ar Rāwandī, edited by Muḥammad Iqbāl. Gibb Memorial, New Series II.

Words in round brackets are in the original Persian, but are to some extent superfluous to the English.

Words in square brackets are not in the Persian, but are added in the translation by way of amplification or explanation.

I should like to thank Professor Reuben Levy for kindly reading the entire manuscript and for making a number of useful suggestions.

To avoid interrupting the text, diacritical marks have been omitted throughout. However, all names have been shown fully pointed in the index.

# RULES FOR KINGS

*In the name of Allah, The Merciful, The Clement*

## PROLOGUE[1]

1. Thanks and praise be to God (to Him be power and glory) who is the Creator of heaven and earth, the Provider of daily food for His servants, the Knower of the hidden and the open, the Pardoner of sins; and blessings upon the best of mortals, The Chosen One (the prayers of Allah and His peace be upon him), who is the greatest of prophets, the elect of the God of the world, the vehicle of the Quran, and the advocate of his people on the day of judgment; blessings too upon the people of his house and his Companions (may Allah give these good and pure men His great peace, and He is a sufficient witness).

2. Thus says the copyist of the books of the Royal Library that the reason for the composition of this book was that The Fortunate Sultan Malikshah (may Allah illumine his proof) in the year 479[2] gave orders to several of the nobles, elders and wise men, instructing each one of them to give thought to the condition of the country, and to consider—'whether there is in our age and time anything out of order either in the divan, the court, the royal palace or the audience-hall—anything whose principles are not being observed by us or are unknown to us; whether there are any functions which kings before us have performed and we are not fulfilling: consider further what have been the laws and customs of past kings, make a digest of them and present them for our judgment; we shall then reflect upon them, so that hereafter affairs religious and worldly may proceed in accordance with their proper rules, every duty may be

[1] The text of the prologue is confused in the MSS.: the translation is a reconstruction and presents a prologue written by 'the copyist', incorporating material from the original of Nizam al Mulk.

[2] This date (A.D. 1086) is given in the Istanbul MS.

I

correctly discharged, and all wrong practices may be discontinued; for since God (be He exalted) has given us His consummate grace, and bestowed the world upon us and subdued all our enemies, there must not be hereafter anything improperly done or anything concealed from us.' This request was addressed to Nizam al Mulk, Sharaf al Mulk, Majd al Mulk and others. Each one wrote what occurred to him on this subject and presented it to The Sublime Judgment. The sultan liked none of their compositions except that of the wazir Nizam al Mulk (may Allah have mercy upon him); he said, 'These chapters have been written exactly as I desired; there is nothing to add to them; I will make this book my guide and follow its precepts.' Thereafter he always went by this book, and gave his commands and wrote his treaties according to these chapters. And now that I, your humble servant, wish to present my case and renew my obligations to The Lord of the Universe, The Helper of the World and the Faith, Muhammad ibn Malikshah (may Allah exalt him), I have made a copy of this volume for the magnificent Royal Library (may Allah prosper it) and I offer it as a humble gift; if Allah wills, it may be approved and accepted.

3. No king or emperor can afford not to possess and know this book, especially in these days, for the more he reads it, the more he will be enlightened upon spiritual and temporal matters, the better he will appreciate the qualities of friends and foes; the way of right conduct and the path of good government will be open to him; the rules for the management of the court, the audience-hall, the divan, the royal palace and the parade ground, and the methods of administering taxes, transacting business and settling the affairs of the people and the army will be clear to him; and nothing in the whole realm whether great or small, far or near, will remain concealed (if Allah wills—be He exalted).

4. This book is composed of fifty chapters in the following order:

### [PART ONE]

5. First of all Nizam al Mulk composed this book ex tempore in thirty-nine chapters and delivered it [to Sultan Malikshah]. Then he revised it, and because of the anxiety that was in his mind on account of the enemies of this dynasty he added another eleven chapters, and in each chapter he set forth what was relevant to it. At the time of his departure he gave the book to me. Then after the calamity that happened to him on the road to Baghdad, when the Batinis revolted and people suffered harm, I did not dare to publish the book until the present time, when justice and Islam have gained strength from the everlasting reign of The Master of the World (may God Almighty preserve this dynasty in perpetuity until the resurrection—through His grace and favour).

[PART ONE]

# CHAPTER ONE

*On the turn of Fortune's wheel and in praise of The Master of the World—may Allah confirm his sovereignty*

1. In every age and time God (be He exalted) chooses one member of the human race and, having adorned and endowed him with kingly virtues, entrusts him with the interests of the world and the well-being of His servants; He charges that person to close the doors of corruption, confusion and discord, and He imparts to him such dignity and majesty in the eyes and hearts of men, that under his just rule they may live their lives in constant security and ever wish for his reign to continue.

2. Whenever—Allah be our refuge!—there occurs any disobedience or disregard of divine laws on the part of His servants, or any failure in devotion and attention to the commands of The Truth (be He exalted), and He wishes to chasten them and make them taste the retribution for their deeds—may God not deal us such a fate, and keep us far from such a calamity!—verily the wrath of The Truth overtakes those people and He forsakes them for the vileness of their disobedience; anarchy rears its head in their midst, opposing swords are drawn, blood is shed, and whoever has the stronger hand does whatever he wishes, until those sinners are all destroyed in tumults and bloodshed, and the world becomes free and clear of them; and through the wickedness of such sinners may innocent persons too perish in the tumults; just as, by analogy, when a reed-bed catches fire every dry particle is consumed and much wet stuff is burnt also, because it is near to that which is dry.

3. Then by divine decree one human being acquires some prosperity and power, and according to his deserts The Truth bestows good fortune upon him and gives him wit and wisdom, wherewith he may employ his subordinates every one according to his merits and confer upon each a dignity and a station proportionate to his

9

powers. He selects ministers and their functionaries from among the people, and giving a rank and post to each, he relies upon them for the efficient conduct of affairs spiritual and temporal. If his subjects tread the path of obedience and busy themselves with their tasks he will keep them untroubled by hardships, so that they may pass their time at ease in the shadow of his justice. If one of his officers or ministers commits any impropriety or oppression, he will only keep him at his post provided that he responds to correction, advice or punishment, and wakes up from the sleep of negligence; if he fails to mend his ways, he will retain him no longer, but change him for someone who is deserving; and when his subjects are ungrateful for benefits and do not appreciate security and ease, but ponder treachery in their hearts, shewing unruliness and overstepping their bounds, he will admonish them for their misdeeds, and punish them in proportion to their crimes. Having done that he will cover their sins with the skirt of pardon and oblivion. Further he will bring to pass that which concerns the advance of civilization, such as constructing underground channels, digging main canals, building bridges across great waters, rehabilitating villages and farms, raising fortifications, building new towns, and erecting lofty buildings and magnificent dwellings; he will have inns built on the highways and schools for those who seek knowledge; for which things he will be renowned for ever; he will gather the fruit of his good works in the next world and blessings will be showered upon him.

4. Since the decree of God was such that this should be the era by which bygone ages are to be dated and that it should crown the achievements of former kings, whereby He might bestow on His creatures a felicity granted to none before them, He caused The Master of the World, the mightiest king of kings to come forth from two nobles' lines whose houses were cradles of royalty and nobility, and had been so from generation to generation as far back as the great Afrasiyab;[1] He furnished him with powers and merits such as had been lacking in the princes of the world before him, and endowed him with all that is needful for a king—such as a comely appearance, a kindly disposition, integrity, manliness, bravery, horsemanship, knowledge, [skill in] the use of various kinds of arms

[1] Primordial king of the Turkish race.

IO

and accomplishment in several arts, pity and mercy upon the creatures of God, [strictness in] the performance of vows and promises, sound faith and true belief, devotion to the worship of God and the practice of such virtuous deeds as praying in the night,[1] supererogatory fasting, respect for religious authorities, honouring devout and pious men, winning the society of men of learning and wisdom, giving regular alms, doing good to the poor, being kind to subordinates and servants, and relieving the people of oppressors. Following all this God gave him power and dominion as befitted his worthiness and good faith, and made all the world subject to him, causing his dignity and authority to reach all climes; all the dwellers on earth are his tributaries, and as long as they seek his favour they are protected by his sword.

5. Now in the days of some of the caliphs, if ever their empire became extended it was never free from unrest and the insurrections of rebels; but in this blessed age (praise and thanks be to Allah) there is nobody in all the world who in his heart meditates opposition to our lord and master, or ventures his head outside the collar of obedience to him—may God perpetuate this empire until the resurrection and keep the evil eye far from the perfectness of this kingdom, so that His creatures may pass their days under the equity and authority of The Master of the World and be ever intent on blessing him.

6. Such is the happy state of this great empire; and in proportion to its greatness it is blessed with an abundance of wise and good institutions. The wisdom of The Master of the World is like a taper from which many lamps have been lighted; by its light men find their way and emerge from the darkness. He has no need of any counsellor or guide; nevertheless he is not without cares, and perhaps he wishes to test his servants, and assess their intelligence and wisdom. So when he commanded his humble servant to write down some of those good qualities that are indispensable to a king, indicating every principle which kings have followed in the past but now do not observe, whether praiseworthy or unpraiseworthy, whatever came to the mind of his humble servant that he had seen, learnt, read or heard, was written down, and The Sublime Command was

[1] i.e. in addition to the five prescribed times of prayer.

fulfilled; these few chapters were composed in the manner of an epitome, and what was proper to each chapter was mentioned in that chapter in a simple style, by the grace of Allah.

# CHAPTER TWO

## *On recognizing the extent of God's grace towards kings*

1. It is for kings to observe His pleasure (His name be glorified) and the pleasure of The Truth is in the charity which is done to His creatures and in the justice which is spread among them. A kingdom which is blessed by its people will endure and increase from day to day, while its king will enjoy power and prosperity; in this world he will acquire good fame, in the next world salvation, and his reckoning will be the easier. Great men have said [in Arabic], 'A kingdom may last while there is irreligion, but it will not endure when there is oppression.' (The meaning is . . .[1])

2. Tradition tells that when Joseph the prophet (the prayers of Allah and His peace be upon him) went out from this world, they were carrying him to Abraham's tomb (upon him be peace) to bury him near his forefathers, when Gabriel (upon him be peace) came and said, 'Stop where you are; this is not his place; for at the resurrection he will have to answer for the sovereignty which he has exercised.' Now if the case of Joseph the prophet was such, consider what the position of others will be.

3. It has come down in a tradition from The Prophet (may Allah bless him and save him) that on the day of the resurrection, when anyone is brought forward who [in his life] wielded power and command over God's creatures, his hands will be bound; if he has been just, his justice will loose his hands and send him to paradise; but if he has been unjust, his injustice will cast him into hell as he is, with his hands bound in chains.

[1] The translation into Persian corresponds exactly to the Arabic.

4. There is also a tradition that on resurrection day whoever had any command in this world over God's creatures, even over the inhabitants of his own house or over his own underlings, will be questioned about it; likewise the shepherd who tended his sheep will be required to answer for that too.

5. They say that at the time of his father's leaving this world 'Abd Allah ibn 'Umar ibn al Khattab (may Allah be pleased with them both) asked, 'O father, where and when shall I see you again?' 'Umar said, 'In the next world.' 'Abd Allah said, 'I would it were sooner.' He said, 'You will see me in a dream tonight, tomorrow night, or the next night.' Twelve years passed by without his appearing in a dream. Then one night he saw him in a dream and said, 'O father, did you not say that within three nights I should see you?' He said, 'O son, I was occupied, because in the country around Baghdad[1] a bridge had become dilapidated and officials had not attended to repairing it. One day a sheep's forefoot fell into a hole on that bridge and was broken. Till now I have been answering for that.'

6. Of a certainty The Master of the World (may Allah perpetuate his reign) should know that on that great day he will be asked to answer for all those of God's creatures who are under his command, and if he tries to transfer [his responsibility] to someone else he will not be listened to. Since this is so it behoves the king not to leave this important matter to anyone else, and not to disregard the state of God's creatures. To the best of his ability let him ever acquaint himself, secretly and openly, with their conditions; let him protect them from extortionate hands, and preserve them from cruel tyrants, so that the blessings resulting from those actions may come about in the time of his rule, if Allah wills.

[1] Baghdad was not yet founded in the time of 'Umar ibn al Khattab.

# CHAPTER THREE

*On holding court for the redress of wrongs and practising
justice and virtue*

1. It is absolutely necessary that on two days in the week the king should sit for the redress of wrongs, to extract recompense from the oppressor, to give justice and to listen to the words of his subjects with his own ears, without any intermediary. It is fitting that some written petitions should also be submitted if they are comparatively important, and he should give a ruling on each one. For when the report spreads throughout the kingdom that on two days in the week The Master of the World summons complainants and petitioners before him and listens to their words, all oppressors will be afraid and curb their activities, and no one will dare to practise injustice or extortion for fear of punishment.

2. I have read in the books of the ancients that most of the non-Arab [Persian] kings used to put up a high platform and sit up there on horseback so that they could see all the complainants gathered round about, and they would redress the grievances of every one. The reason for this was that when the king sits in a place protected by gates, locks, vestibules and screens, self-interested and oppressive persons can keep people back and not let them go before the king.

3. I have heard that a certain king was rather hard of hearing. He was anxious lest those who acted as interpreters might not report the words of the complainants correctly, and that he, not knowing the true facts, might give an order quite unsuitable to the case. So he commanded that all complainants were to wear red clothes, so that he could recognize them; no one else at all was to wear red. This king used to appear on the plain seated upon an elephant, and wherever he saw people in red clothes, he ordered them to be collected in a group. Then he would sit in a place apart and they were brought before him; they stated their cases in a loud voice and he gave them justice.

Men have taken all this care so that they may not be found ignorant when they have to give their answer in the next world.

*The story of The Just Amir and the Saffarids*

4. One of the kings of the Samanid line was called Isma'il ibn Ahmad. He was extremely just, and his good qualities were many. He had a pure faith in God (to Him be power and glory) and he was generous to the poor—to name only one of his notable virtues. His seat was at Bukhara. Khurasan, 'Iraq[1] and Transoxiana all belonged to his ancestors.

5. Ya'qub ibn Laith emerged in revolt from the City of Sistan [Zaranj] and took the whole of Sistan; then he went to Khurasan, and captured that province; from Khurasan he went to 'Iraq, and seized the whole of 'Iraq. Propagandists deceived him and he secretly swore allegiance to the Isma'ilis; he hardened his heart against the caliph of Baghdad. Then he mustered the armies of Khurasan and 'Iraq and prepared to march to Baghdad to kill the caliph and overthrow the house of the 'Abbasids.

6. The caliph received information that Ya'qub was marching upon Baghdad. He sent a messenger to say, 'You have no business at Baghdad; it were better that you should attend to Kuhistan, Khurasan and 'Iraq, and administer them so that no disorder or anxiety may arise. Turn back.' He did not obey the command, but said, 'It is my desire that without fail I should come to the court, and carry out the rites of homage and renew my obligations; until I have done this, I will not turn back.' However many messengers the caliph sent, he gave this same answer. Then he moved his army towards Baghdad. The caliph became suspicious of him; he summoned the nobles of the state and said, 'I see that Ya'qub ibn Laith has withdrawn his head from the collar of obedience to us, and is coming here with treacherous intent, for we have not commanded him to come and yet he is coming; we command him to turn back; he turns not. At all events he has some evil design in his heart and I think he has sworn allegiance to the Batinis;[2] he will not reveal it until he arrives here. We must not neglect to take precautions against him; what is the best way to deal with this matter?'

[1] i.e. Persian 'Iraq: see Le Strange, *Lands*, 185.

[2] 'Esoterics': a term of reproach applied by the Sunnis to the Shi'ites, Isma'ilis and Qarmatis.

They settled on the following plan: that the caliph would not stay in the city, but go into the open country and pitch camp, and the nobles of Baghdad and all of his retinue would be with him; so that when Ya'qub arrived and saw the caliph in the open country with his troops, his plan would misfire and his rebellion against The Commander of the Faithful would become manifest; thereupon men would go to and fro from one camp to the other; for if he were starting a rebellion, not all the nobles and chiefs of 'Iraq and Khurasan would agree with him and assent to his plans: if he openly shewed his rebelliousness they would contend with his troops as best they could, but if they failed and were unable to cope with him in battle, very well—the road would be open before them and they would not be caught like prisoners within four walls; they would betake themselves wherever they could. This plan was acceptable to The Commander of the Faithful. Thus they did. And this caliph was al Mu'tamid 'ala 'llah.

7. When Ya'qub arrived he dismounted opposite the caliph's camp and pitched his tents; and the men of the two armies mingled together. On that very day he bid defiance to the caliph and sent a messenger to him to say, 'Give up Baghdad and go where you like.' The caliph asked for two months grace; Ya'qub refused him. When night came on, the caliph secretly sent someone to the officers of Ya'qub's army to say, 'He has openly revolted, and made common cause with the Shi'ites; he has come on purpose to overthrow our house, and set our adversary in our place. Are you too in sympathy with him in this, or not?' One party said, 'From him we have received our subsistence and by virtue of service to him we enjoy the position and prosperity which we have. Whatever he has done we have done.' The majority said, 'We are not aware of these circumstances of which The Commander of the Faithful speaks; we do not think that he will oppose The Commander of the Faithful; hereafter if he openly rebels, we shall entirely disapprove; and in the hour of battle we shall come to your aid.' This party consisted of the army-commanders of Khurasan.

8. When the caliph heard the words of the chiefs of Ya'qub's army on this wise, he was glad. The next day in a bold spirit he sent a message to Ya'qub, saying, 'Now that you have openly displayed

your ingratitude and have made an agreement with my adversary, the sword is betwixt me and you; I am not afraid because my forces are few and yours are many. God (to Him be power and glory) is the helper of the right, and right is on my side. Those troops which you have really belong to me.' He gave the command, and his troops armed themselves, beat the drums of war and blew the trumpets; they went forth from the camp and drew ranks upon the plain.

9. When Ya'qub heard the caliph's message in those terms, he said, 'I am now attaining my desire.' And he too gave orders for the drums to be beaten; all his troops mounted and went in formation on to the plain and drew ranks opposite the caliph's forces. On the one side the caliph came and took up his position in the centre, and on the other side Ya'qub ibn Laith. Then the caliph ordered a certain man who had a powerful voice to go between the two arrays, and proclaim aloud, 'O assembly of Muslims, know that Ya'qub is a rebel and has come on purpose to overthrow the house of 'Abbas, and to bring the caliph's adversary from Mahdiyya[1] to replace him; he wishes to remove the *sunna* [orthodox tradition] and make heresy rife. Whoever opposes the caliph [successor] of The Prophet of God, has opposed The Prophet himself; and if any man plucks his head out of the collar of obedience to The Prophet (upon him be peace), it is as if he has renounced obedience to God and quitted the circle of Islam; as God (be He exalted) says in His incontrovertible book [Quran 4. 62], "Obey Allah, and obey The Messenger and those of you who are in authority." Who is there now amongst you who will choose heaven instead of hell, and will assist the truth and turn his face from vanity? Then let him be with me, not with my enemy.'

10. When the army of Ya'qub ibn Laith heard these words the commanders of Khurasan turned with one accord and approached the caliph and said, 'We thought that he was coming to your presence in obedience to your command; now that he has declared his opposition and rebellion, we are with you, and as long as we have life, we shall wield the sword on your behalf.'

11. When the caliph had thus acquired strength he ordered his total forces to make an assault. Ya'qub ibn Laith was defeated in

[1] The North African capital of the Fatimid (Isma'ili) caliphs, which was founded in A.D. 915 whereas Ya'qub's revolt took place about A.D. 875.

the first charge, and took to flight in the direction of Khuzistan. His treasury, stores and camp were all plundered, and the caliph's troops became rich with the spoil. When he reached Khuzistan he sent persons in all directions to call up troops; he began to summon his officers and gave orders that they should bring stores and money from the treasuries of 'Iraq and Khurasan.

12. When the caliph received news that Ya'qub had settled in Khuzistan, he immediately sent a messenger with a letter to him saying, 'It is known to us that you are a simple-hearted fellow; you succumbed to the deceits of our adversaries, and you had no regard for the outcome of your venture. You saw how God (be He exalted) displayed his working to you; He caused you to be defeated even by your own troops, and he preserved our family. It was merely a misunderstanding on your part. I know that now you have woken up and are sorry for your deeds. Nobody is more suitable than you to be amir of 'Iraq and Khurasan; we shall not impose a higher authority over you, for by your services you are entitled to many rewards from us. We regard those admirable services as outweighing this your single error.' [The caliph considered that] since he was prepared to forgive his unruliness and regard his action as undone, Ya'qub ought to forget the affair and go with all speed to 'Iraq and Khurasan, and devote himself to administering those provinces.

13. When Ya'qub read the caliph's letter his heart was in no way softened, nor did he repent of his actions. He ordered some leeks, onions and fish to be brought on a wooden tray and put before him. Then he ordered them to bring in the caliph's envoy and make him sit. He turned towards the courier and said, 'Go and tell the caliph that I was born a coppersmith; I learnt that trade from my father, and my victual used to be barley-bread, fish, onions and leeks. The sovereignty, treasure and wealth which I enjoy, I have acquired by my own bold enterprise[1] and daring; I neither have it as an inheritance from my father, nor did I get it from you. I shall not rest until I have sent your head to Mahdiyya and destroyed your family. Either I shall do as I say or I shall go back even to my barley-bread, fish and leeks. Behold I have opened the doors of my treasuries and

---

[1] Pers. ʿayyārī 'knight-errantry' or 'chivalrous brigandage': see Levy, *Mirror for Princes*, 242, note 1.

summoned my troops; and I am coming in the tracks of the bearer of this message.' He despatched the courier. The caliph then sent many couriers and letters but he refused to abandon his project. He collected his army and set his course towards Baghdad. When he had gone three stages the colic gripped him, and his condition reached the point where he knew that he would not be delivered from the pain. He nominated his brother 'Amr ibn Laith as his heir, gave him the treasure-books, and died.

14. 'Amr ibn Laith returned to Kuhistan and stayed there a while. Then he went to Khurasan and reigned as king, keeping allegiance to the caliph. The army and the people liked 'Amr better than Ya'qub, for 'Amr was magnanimous, generous, enlightened and statesmanlike to a degree. His humanity and magnanimity went so far, that four hundred camels were required to transport his kitchen; other things can be inferred by analogy.

15. However the caliph continued to be apprehensive, lest 'Amr too should follow the ways of his brother, and later engage in the same activities. Although 'Amr had no such intentions, still the caliph was anxious on this score. Frequently and secretly he sent messengers to Bukhara to Isma'il ibn Ahmad to say, 'Go out against 'Amr ibn Laith; lead your army and wrest the kingdom from his grasp, for you have more right to govern Khurasan and 'Iraq, seeing that this was the kingdom of your fathers, and they [the Saffarids] have usurped it. Firstly you have the right, secondly your conduct is more acceptable, and thirdly my prayers are behind you. Considering these three points I have no doubt but that God will assist you against him. Regard not the fact that your supplies and troops are few; look at what God says [in the Quran 2. 250]: How many a little company has overcome a great company by Allah's leave! Allah is with the steadfast.'

16. The caliph's words had their effect on Isma'il. He firmly resolved to oppose 'Amr ibn Laith. He gathered all the forces he had, and having crossed to the near [south] side of the Oxus, he counted them with the tip of his whip. They amounted to 2,000 horsemen; one in two had a shield, out of twenty men one had a coat of mail, and of every fifty men one had a lance; and there were men who, for lack of a mount, were carrying their coats of mail

themselves, tied on to saddle-straps. Then he moved off from Amuy [Amul] and came to the city of Marv.

17. ʿAmr ibn Laith was informed that Ismaʿil ibn Ahmad had crossed the Oxus and come to Marv, whose city prefect had fled; Ismaʿil was aiming at capturing the province. ʿAmr ibn Laith, who was at Nishapur, laughed. He paraded 70,000 cavalry, all clad in horse-armour with weapons and full equipment. He set out for Balkh. When the two armies met they joined battle. It so happened that ʿAmr ibn Laith was defeated at the gates of Balkh and his 70,000 horsemen fled without one man being wounded or taken prisoner; of them all ʿAmr alone was captured. When they brought him in front of Ismaʿil, he ordered them to hand him over to his guards. And this is one of the wonders of the world.

18. At the time of afternoon prayers a certain groom belonging to ʿAmr ibn Laith was wandering in the camp. He happened to see ʿAmr; his heart was stricken and he went up to him. ʿAmr said, 'Stay with me tonight for I am left all alone': then he said, 'As long as a man is alive, there is no escaping the need for food; contrive to find something to eat.' The groom procured one maund of meat and borrowed an iron frying-pan from the soldiers. Then he ran around and collected a little dry dung, and he put together two or three clods of earth, intending to make a dry fry. When he had put the meat in the frying-pan, he just went to look for some salt. The day had then come to its close. A dog came and put its head into the frying-pan and took out a bone, so burning its mouth; it raised its head and the ring of the frying-pan fell round its neck. On feeling the heat of the fire it leapt up and carried off the frying-pan. When ʿAmr ibn Laith saw that, he turned towards the soldiers and guards and said, 'Take warning: I am that man whose kitchen in the morning was transported by four hundred camels; at evening a dog took it away. [In Arabic:] I was an *amir* in the morning: I became an *asir* [prisoner] in the evening.' (That means: In the morning I was an amir: at evening I am a prisoner.) And this event too is one of the wonders of the world.

19. In connection with the amir Ismaʿil and ʿAmr ibn Laith, even more remarkable than these two events is the fact that when ʿAmr was captured, the amir Ismaʿil turned to the nobles and chiefs

of his army and said, 'God granted me this success, and to no one am I indebted for this favour except to God (His name be magnified).' Then he said, 'Know that this 'Amr ibn Laith was a man of lofty purposes and great generosity; he was well provided with equipment and supplies, and possessed wisdom and prudence besides. In the conduct of affairs he was vigilant, and he was abundantly hospitable and liberal in his expression of gratitude. It is my idea to see to it that he suffers no harm and is freed from his bonds.' The nobles said, 'The amir's opinion is best; let him command whatever is advisable.' He then sent someone to 'Amr ibn Laith to say, 'Do not fear, because I am planning to ask the caliph for your life to be spared. Even if it costs the whole of my treasury, I shall not mind so long as you suffer no mortal harm and can pass the rest of your life in safety.'

20. When 'Amr ibn Laith heard this, he said, 'I know that there will never be any escape for me from these bonds, nevertheless, thou who art Isma'il, send me a confidant, for I have some words to say; let him report them to you just as he hears them from me.' The man came and told Isma'il. Isma'il at once sent him a confidant, and 'Amr said to him, 'Tell Isma'il: It was not you that defeated me, but it was your piety, faith and character, together with the displeasure of The Commander of the Faithful. God (to Him be power and glory) has taken away this realm from me and given it to you, and you by your goodness are more worthy and deserving of this favour. I have surrendered to God (to Him be power and glory), and I do not wish you anything but good. Meanwhile you have acquired a new kingdom, but you have no wealth or backing. Now I and my brother have many treasures and buried hoards, and the list of them is in my possession; I offer them all to you, so that you may gain backing and power; you should procure supplies and stores, and replenish your treasury.' Thereupon he revealed the treasure-list and sent it to Isma'il by the hand of that confidant.

21. When the confidant came and repeated what he had heard and placed the treasure-list in front of Isma'il, he turned towards the nobles and said, 'This 'Amr ibn Laith is so cunning that he thinks he can escape from our cunning hands and catch us in the traps and snares of eternal ruin.' He picked up the treasure-list and threw it in

front of the confidant, saying, 'Take this treasure-list back to him and say: You with your wiles think you can escape from everything. Whence fell treasure to you and your brother, for your father was a coppersmith and taught you that trade? Through some celestial chance you seized dominion, and by reckless ventures your affairs prospered. This treasure with its dirams and dinars is all that which you have taken from the people by extortion; it comes from the price of thread spun by decrepit old men and widowed women, from the provisions of strangers and travellers, and from the property of weaklings and orphans. Tomorrow you will have to answer for all this before God (to Him be power and glory); so now you promptly want to cast these wrongs about our neck, so that on the morrow at the resurrection when creditors seize you and ask you to give back all the property which you wrongfully took, you will say, "All that we took from you, we gave to Isma'il; seek it from him." You will transfer it all to me and I shall be powerless to answer the creditors and to withstand the wrath and interrogation of God.' Such was his piety and fear of God that he did not accept the treasure-list but sent it back to 'Amr. So he was not deluded by worldly goods.

22. Is that like the amirs of these times who think nothing of condoning ten crimes for the sake of one ill-gotten dinar? They pervert the truth and have no regard for the consequences.

23. Now it was the custom of this Isma'il ibn Ahmad that on days when the cold was severe and snow was falling heavily, he would mount his horse and go alone to the square [of Bukhara], remaining there on horseback until the midday prayers. He used to say, 'It may be that a complainant will come to the court with a petition, and he may not have any money for expenses or anywhere to stay. If we excused ourselves from appearing because of the snow and cold, it would be difficult for such a person to stay and gain access to us. If he knows that we are standing here, he will come and discharge his business and go away in peace.'

There are many stories of this kind; only a few have been repeated here. And all this care has been taken for the sake of the answer in the next world.

# CHAPTER FOUR

*Concerning tax-collectors and constant enquiry into the
affairs of wazirs*

1. Tax-collectors,[1] when they are given a fiscal district, must be
instructed to deal honourably with their fellow creatures, and to take
only the due amount of revenue, and to claim that too with civility
and courtesy, and not to demand any taxes from them until the time
comes for them to pay; because when they demand payment before
the time, trouble comes upon the peasants, and to pay the tax they
are obliged to sell their crops for half [of what they would be worth
when they ripen], whereby they are driven to extremities and have to
emigrate. If any peasant is in distress and in need of oxen or seed,
let him be given a loan to ease his burden and keep him viable, lest
he be cast out from his home into exile.

2. I heard that in the time of King Qubad there was famine in the
world for seven years, and blessings [rain] ceased to come down
from heaven. He ordered the tax-collectors to sell all the grain which
they had, and even to give some of it away as charity. All over the
kingdom the poor were assisted by gifts from the central treasury and
[local] treasuries, with the result that not one person died of hunger
in those seven years—all because the king chid his officers.

3. One must enquire constantly into the affairs of the tax-collector.
If he comports himself in the manner just described, the fiscal district
can be kept in his hands, but if not, he must be changed for someone
suitable. If he has taken more than is due from the peasants, it must
be recovered from him and given back to them; after that if he has
any property left, it must be seized and brought into the treasury.
The officer should be dismissed, and never employed again. Others
will then take warning and give up practising extortion.

4. It is also necessary to enquire secretly into the affairs of ministers
and confidants, especially the wazir, to see if he is fulfilling his
function properly or not, for the good or ill of king and kingdom
depends on him. When the wazir is of good character and sound

[1] Muhammad Nazim, *Sultan Mahmud,* 126–50, describes the functions of most of
the officials mentioned in this book.

judgment, the kingdom is prosperous, the army and peasantry are contented, peaceful and well supplied, and the king is free from anxiety. But when the wazir is bad, irreparable harm is done to the kingdom; the king is constantly perplexed and distressed and the provinces are in a state of disorder.

### The story of Bahram Gur and Rast-ravishn

5. They say that Bahram Gur had a wazir whom they called Rast-ravishn [Right-Conduct]. Bahram Gur had put the whole country in his hands, and placed reliance upon him; he would not hear any word against him. He himself was occupied day and night with entertainments, hunting and drinking. This Rast-ravishn said to a certain person who was the [so-called] 'deputy' of Bahram Gur, 'The peasantry have become unruly and refractory because of our abundant justice; unless they are chastised a catastrophe will occur. The king is busy drinking and is heedless of the condition of his subjects. Chastise them, before a catastrophe occurs; and know at once that chastisement has two aspects—getting rid of the bad, and fleecing the good. Whomsoever I tell you to seize, seize him.' From everyone that the 'deputy' caught and held in custody Rast-ravishn extracted a bribe for himself and then ordered the 'deputy' to let him go; until eventually all the property in the country, whether houses, or pages, or beautiful girls, or estates, or farms, was seized by him. The peasantry were impoverished, the nobility all emigrated, and nothing came into the treasury.

6. When some time had passed after these events, an enemy rose against Bahram Gur. He wanted to provide his troops with money and supplies, and send them against the enemy. He went into the treasury. Not a thing did he see. He enquired after the notables and mayors of the city. People said, 'It is several years since so-and-so and so-and-so emigrated, and went to such-and-such a country.' He said, 'Why?' They said, 'We do not know.' Nobody dared to say anything for fear of the wazir. All day and all night Bahram Gur was in meditation; he could not think what was the cause of the trouble. The next day at crack of dawn, worried and alone, he mounted his horse and set out into the desert. Deep in thought he

24

went along until the day was high. He travelled a distance of seven farsangs without being aware of it. Heat and thirst prevailed over him, and he needed a drink of water. He surveyed the open country; he saw some smoke going up, and said, 'At all events there will be people there.' He made for the smoke. When he got near he saw a flock of sheep sleeping, a tent pitched, and a dog hanging on a gibbet. He was astonished, and went close up to the tent. A man came out and greeted him; he helped him to dismount and brought him something to eat, not knowing that he was Bahram. Bahram said, 'First of all before we eat bread, tell me about this dog; I would like to know what happened to it.'

7. The young man said, 'This dog was my custodian in charge of these sheep; I knew his virtues were such that he could contend with ten wolves, and no wolf would dare to roam near the sheep for fear of him. Many a time I used to go to the city for some business and come back the next day. He would take the sheep to graze and bring them back safely. One day, after some time had passed, I counted the sheep; several were missing; and no thief ever comes here. I could not understand at all why the sheep were getting fewer. The state of my flock reached such a point of diminution that when the collector of [compulsory] alms came and demanded from me the usual amount [assessed] upon the whole flock, [yet to be paid] out of what was left of my flock, that remnant too went to pay the alms. So now I perform the pastoral office for that collector.

8. Now this dog had made friends with a she-wolf and they had mated; and I was ignorant and unaware of what was going on. It so happened that one day I had gone into the fields in search of fire-wood. When I returned, I came up from behind a hill, and saw the flock of sheep grazing and a wolf running around looking at them. I sat down behind a thorn bush and secretly watched. When the dog saw the wolf he went to meet her and wagged his tail. The wolf quietly stood still. The dog mounted and covered her; then he went into a corner and slept. The wolf ran into the midst of the flock. She seized one sheep, tore it to pieces and ate it; and the dog never made a sound. When I saw this commerce of wolf and dog, I realized and knew that the ruin of my affairs was due to the

waywardness of the dog. So I caught him and hanged him on the gibbet because of his treachery.'

9. Bahram Gur was astonished at this story. As he returned, all the way he pondered over this thing, until it crossed his thoughts that, 'Our subjects are our flock, and our wazir is our custodian. I see that the country and the people are in a very distracted and disturbed state, and when I question people, they do not tell the truth but keep it hidden. What I must do is to enquire into the relations between the people and the wazir.'

10. When he came back to his abode, firstly he called for the daily lists of prisoners. From beginning to end he saw the evil hand of Rast-ravishn, and recognized that he had maltreated and oppressed the people. He said, 'This is not *rāst ravishn* [right conduct] but dark falsehood.'[1] Then he repeated the proverb which wise men have spoken truly, that, 'He who is deceived by a good name loses his living; he who uses a good name to deceive loses his life.' 'I have strengthened the hand of this wazir; as long as people see him so dignified and august, they will not dare to speak the truth for fear of him. My plan is that tomorrow when he comes to the court I will disgrace him in front of the nobles; I will detain him and order heavy fetters to be put on his feet; then I will call the prisoners before me and ask about their cases; I will command a proclamation to be read in these terms, "We have removed Rast-ravishn from the office of wazir and ordered his imprisonment; we shall not employ him any more; if any man has suffered injury from him and has a claim, let him come and state his case with his own tongue and make it known, so that we may give him justice." When people hear this they will let us know how things really are. If he has treated people well and practised no unjust extortion, and if they speak well of him, we will bestow favours on him and reinstate him in his post; but if his behaviour has been otherwise, we will punish him.'

11. The next day when King Bahram Gur held his court with the nobles in attendance and the wazir sitting in his usual place, Bahram Gur turned towards him and said, 'What is this confusion which you have spread abroad in the kingdom? You have failed

---

[1] The author apparently mistook the archaic word *ravishn* 'conduct' for *raushan* 'bright': both words appear the same in unpointed Arabic script.

to keep the troops supplied and you have ruined the peasants. We commanded you to provide the people's subsistence in due time, continually to promote the prosperity of the country, and to take no more than what is due in taxes from the peasants; you were required to keep the treasury stocked with supplies; as it is I see the treasury is empty, the army lacks provisions, and the peasants are destitute. You may think that I have been occupied in drinking and hunting, and neglectful of the affairs of the kingdom and the condition of the people.' He ordered Rast-ravishn to be removed with ignominy from his place and to be taken into a certain house; heavy fetters were put on his feet, and it was proclaimed at the doors of the palace that, 'The king has removed Rast-ravishn from the office of wazir and is angry with him and will not employ him any more. If any man has suffered injury from him and has a complaint, let him without any fear of danger come to the court and reveal his case, so that the king may give him justice.' Immediately he ordered them to open the doors of the prison and bring the prisoners before him; one by one he asked them, 'For what crime were you detained?'

12. One said: I had a rich brother and he owned much property and wealth. Rast-ravishn seized him, took all his property away from him and killed him under torture. People asked why he had killed this man. He said, 'He had correspondence with the king's enemies.' So he sent me to prison to prevent me from complaining before the king and to keep the case concealed.

13. Another said: I had a very flourishing and pleasant garden which was left to me as an inheritance from my father. Rast-ravishn had an estate next to it. One day he came into my garden; he was attracted by it and wanted to buy it; I would not sell it. He seized me and put me in prison, saying, 'You are in love with the daughter of such-and-such a person, and it is clear you have committed an offence. Give up possession of this garden and make out a deed certifying that you have relinquished it and have no claim to it, and that it is the rightful property of Rast-ravishn.' I refused to give such a certificate; and it is five years today that I have been in prison.

14. Another said: I am a merchant, and it is my occupation to travel on sea and land. I have only a small amount of capital, and such choice things as I find in one city, I buy and take to the next

city to sell them; I am content with a minimum of profit. Perchance I had a pearl necklace; when I came to this city I put it up for sale. Information reached the king's wazir; he sent someone and summoned me; he wanted to buy that string of pearls from me. Without paying me for it he sent it to his treasury. For several days I kept going to call on him. He shewed no inclination to pay the price of the necklace, nor did he give it back to me. I could not wait any longer and I was destitute. One day I went to him and said, 'If that necklace suits you, command that I be paid for it; if it is not suitable, let it be given back, for I am destitute.' He gave me no answer. When I came back to my tent, I saw an officer with four soldiers, who entered the tent and said, 'Come along, the wazir is calling for you.' I rejoiced and said, 'He is going to pay me for the pearls.' I got up and went with those guards; they took me to the door of the prison and said to the gaoler, 'The order is that you keep this man in prison and put heavy fetters on his feet.' It is now a year and a half that I have been suffering bondage and imprisonment.

15. Another said: I am the mayor of such-and-such a district, and my house always used to be open to guests, strangers and men of learning; I used to give assistance to all kinds of destitute people, and I was constantly dealing out alms and charities to the deserving, a habit which I acquired from my forefathers. I used to spend all the income from my inherited property and estates on acts of charity, generosity and hospitality. The king's wazir seized me on the pretext that I had discovered treasure; he detained me in prison and subjected me to inquisition and torture. Every property and farm which I owned I was obliged to sell at half price and give to him. I have now endured imprisonment and bondage for four years; and I have not a single diram to my name.

16. Another said: I am the son of such-and-such a chieftain. The king's wazir mulcted my father and killed him under rod and inquisition; he put me in prison, and for seven years I have been undergoing the ordeal of incarceration.

17. Another said: I am a military man and for so many years I served the king's father and campaigned with him; and for so many years I have been serving Your Majesty. I have a small salary from the government; last year nothing was paid to me, and this year

I applied to the wazir and said, 'I am a family man and last year my salary was not paid. Please pay it this year, so that I may use some of it for [paying back] loans and spend the rest on my subsistence.' He said, 'The king has no war in view for which he will need troops, and it matters not whether you and the likes of you are in service or not; if you need bread, go and do labourer's work.' I said, 'I am entitled to so much for my services to this government; I ought not to have to do labourer's work. But you need to learn something about administration, for I am more skilled in swords-manship than you are in penmanship; when it comes to fighting I sacrifice my life for the king and do not swerve from his command; but on pay-day you withhold my bread from me and fail to carry out the king's order. Do you not know this much, that to the king you are a servant as much as I am? He has engaged you in one capacity and me in another: the difference between me and you is that I am obedient and you are not. If the king doesn't need the likes of me, he doesn't need the likes of you any more either. If you have an order saying that the king has removed my name from the pay-roll, shew it to me; otherwise continue to pay what the king has ordained for me.' He said, 'Be off! It is I who look after both you and the king; if it were not for me the vultures would have eaten your brains out long ago.' Then two days passed. He sent me into confinement, and now it is four months that I have been in prison.

18. There were more than seven hundred prisoners. Less than twenty men turned out to be murderers, thieves and criminals. All the others were those whom the wazir had detained and imprisoned out of cupidity and cruelty. When the people of the city and the surrounding district heard about the royal proclamation, the next day so many complainants came to the court that they were beyond limit or measure.

19. When Bahram Gur heard these reports of the condition of the people and the illegal, unjust and tyrannous conduct of the wazir, he said to himself, 'The corruption which this man has wrought in the country seems to be beyond description; the defiance which he has displayed towards God and the creatures of God (be He exalted) and against me is too great to be imagined. I must look

deeper into this affair.' He ordered men to go to the house of Rast-ravishn and bring his files of papers and seal up all the doors of the house. Trusted men went and did this. They brought the files and began to look at them. Among them they found one file full of overtures sent to Rast-ravishn by a certain king who had revolted and attempted to usurp Bahram Gur's kingdom; and in Rast-ravishn's writing they found a letter which he had written to this king saying, 'Why are you so slow? The wise have said that negligence is the thief of empire. I have used every possible means to espouse and serve your cause; I have won over several officers of the army and brought them into your allegiance; I have left most of the troops without provisions or equipment, but I have sent a number to a certain station and appointed them to a certain task. I have rendered the people hungry, destitute and homeless; with all that I have acquired in the course of time I have prepared a treasury for you such as no other king today possesses; and I have made ready crown and girdle, together with [a set of] golden and jewelled banqueting dishes the like of which no one has ever seen before. I have had enough of this man; the field is empty and the enemy unaware; hasten as fast as you can before he wakes up from the sleep of negligence.'

20. When Bahram Gur saw these documents, he said, 'Indeed! So it is he who has incited and inveigled the enemy who is at this moment advancing against me; now there remains no doubt about the wickedness and treachery of this man.' He commanded that all his possessions should be brought into the treasury; they took his slaves and animals, and gave back to the owners everything that he had received in bribes or seized by force; his estates and lands were sold or given away, and his house and home was razed to the ground. Then he ordered a gallows to be erected at the gate of the palace, and in front of that thirty other gibbets. First they hanged Rast-ravishn, just as that man had hanged his dog; then they hanged his associates and persons who were in league with him. The king commanded a proclamation to be read for seven days, saying, 'This is the punishment for a man who plots against the king, associates with his enemies, prefers treachery to loyalty, oppresses the people, and defies his God and his sovereign.'

21. On the infliction of this punishment all malefactors became afraid of King Bahram. He removed from office all whom Rast-ravishn had employed, and never engaged them again; and he transferred all the other officials. When news of this reached the king who was attacking Bahram Gur's kingdom, he turned straight back from where he was and regretted his action; he sent much money and many choice gifts in homage to Bahram, making excuses and obeisances, and saying, 'I would never have thought of rebelling against Your Highness; however Your Highness's wazir persuaded me to this course through the many letters and messengers which he sent me; the suspicions of your servant were all the time testifying that he was a criminal who was seeking a refuge.' King Bahram accepted his excuse and pardoned him. He gave the wazirship to a God-fearing man of sound faith and good character. The affairs of the army and the people were all restored to order, and work proceeded again; the world set its face towards prosperity and the population were delivered from tyranny and injustice.

[To return to] the man who had hanged his dog on a gibbet—one day he was outside his tent and was about to go in again, when King Bahram Gur drew an arrow out of his quiver, shot it in front of him and said, 'I ate your bread and salt, and came to know of the troubles and losses you have suffered; so I am indebted to you. Know that I am one of the chamberlains of King Bahram, and all the nobles and chamberlains of his court are my friends and know me well. You must arise and come with this arrow to King Bahram's court; whoever sees you with this arrow will bring you to me, and I will discharge my debt to you in a way that will recompense you for some of your losses.' And Bahram departed.

22. After several days that man's wife said to him, 'Arise and go to the city, and take that arrow with you, for that rider with all his finery was undoubtedly a rich and respected man. Even if he does you but little good, that amount will be much for us in these days. Do not lose time, for such a person's word will not be false.' The man arose and came to the city. He slept that night and next day went to the court of King Bahram. Now Bahram Gur had told the chamberlains and courtiers, 'When such-and-such a man comes to the court, and you see my arrow in his hand, bring him quickly to me.'

23. When the chamberlains saw him with that arrow, they called him and said, 'O noble sir, where have you been? We have been expecting you for several days. Sit here and we will take you to the owner of the arrow.' A time passed. Bahram Gur came out and sat on the throne and gave audience. The chamberlains took the man's hand and led him to the audience-hall; the man's eye fell upon King Bahram and as he recognized him, he said, 'Woe! I am ruined! that rider was King Bahram, and I did not pay him homage as I ought, but I spoke to him rather rudely. May it not be that he has taken a dislike to me!'

24. When the chamberlains led him before the throne he did obeisance to the king. Bahram Gur turned towards the nobles and said, 'This man was the cause of my becoming aware of the state of the country';—and he related the story of the dog to the nobles;—'and I regard him as an omen.' He gave the command and they invested him with a robe of honour, and presented him with seven hundred sheep—as many ewes or rams as he desired; and he ordered that as long as he (Bahram Gur) was alive, they should demand no compulsory alms from him.

25. It is well known how Alexander defeated Darius. The reason for this was that Darius's wazir had secret dealings with Alexander. When Darius was slain, Alexander said, 'The negligence of the amir and the treachery of the wazir have taken away his kingship.'

26. At no time must the king be ill-informed about his officers. He must constantly enquire about their conduct and character, and should any impropriety or treachery be found in any one of them he must not be retained; let him be removed from office and chastised according to his crime, so that others will take warning, and no one will dare to plot any mischief for fear of the king's punishment. Whenever anyone is appointed to a big post, the king must secretly (so that he does not know) put someone to supervise him and report on his actions and affairs.

27. Aristotle thus said to King Alexander, 'If you ever offend one of those who ply their pens in the public service, do not employ that person again because he will combine with your enemies and strive for your destruction.'

28. Parviz the king thus said, 'There are four groups of men whose sins a king should not overlook—firstly those who aim at his kingdom, secondly those who have designs on his haram, thirdly those who do not keep his secrets, and fourthly those who with their tongues support the king, but in their hearts espouse the cause of his enemies and secretly follow their policies.'

29. A man's secrets may be deduced from his actions. If the king is awake to all affairs, nothing will remain concealed from him.

# CHAPTER FIVE

*Concerning assignees of land and enquiry into their treatment of the peasantry*

1. Officers who hold lands in fief[1] must know that they have no authority over the peasants except to take from them—and that with courtesy—the due amount of revenue which has been assigned to them to collect; and when they have taken that, the peasants are to have security for their persons, property, wives and children, and their goods and farms are to be inviolable; the assignees are to have no further claim upon them. If peasants want to come to the court to state their cases, they are not to be prevented from doing so; any assignee who does otherwise must be checked; his fief will be taken away from him and he will be reprimanded as a warning to others. They must know that the country and the peasants belong to the ruling power; assignees and governors are like prefects over the peasants [on their fiefs], in the same relation to them as the king is to other peasants [not on feudal lands]. In this way the peasants will be contented and the king will be secure from punishment and torment in the world to come.

[1] Persian *iqtā*: see Lambton, *Landlord and peasant*, Cap. III.

*The story of The Just King*

2. They say that when Qubad the king died Nushirwan (The Just), who was his son, succeeded to the throne; he was only eighteen years old, yet he reigned as king. He was a youth whose character had been trained in justice right from infancy; he recognized evil things as evil and he knew what was good. He always used to say, 'My father is weak in judgment and simple hearted; he is quickly deceived. He has left the country to the hands of officials and they are doing whatever they please; so the country is being ruined and the treasury emptied; they are embezzling the revenue, and the shame and guilt will be for ever upon his neck.' Qubad completely succumbed to the wiles of Mazdak; similarly he was deceived by two men—a governor and a tax-collector—who together had ruined their province and impoverished the peasantry by illegal extortions; such was his love of money that when they proffered him a purse of dinars he was seduced and satisfied; he had not sufficient discernment to question them and to say [to the one], 'You are the governor and the commander of this province. I assigned you such proportion of the provincial revenue as would suffice for the pay, rations and clothing of you and your retinue; I am sure that you will have extracted the full amount from the people. Then what is this surplus which you have brought to me? I know that you did not inherit it from your father; it is all what you have illegally extorted from the people.' Nor did he speak likewise to the tax-collector, saying, 'The revenue of the province is so much; some of it you have used for [encashing] drafts and some you have sent to the treasury. This surplus which I see you have— where did you obtain that? Is it not part of your illegal extortions?' He never investigated such matters nor took suitable measures against the offenders so that others might have made a practice of honesty.

3. When three or four years of his reign has passed, the assignees and officials were still practising their wonted oppression, and complainants were clamouring at the king's threshold. Nushirwan The Just held court for the redress of wrongs and summoned all the nobles; he sat upon the throne and first gave thanks to God; then

34

he said, 'You know that God (to Him be power and glory) has granted me this kingdom; furthermore I inherited it from my father; and thirdly my uncle rebelled against me and I did battle with him and regained the throne by the sword. As God has bestowed the world upon me, so have I assigned it to you, and to each one have I given authority; I did not leave without a portion anyone who had deserved well of this dynasty; the nobles who had received high rank and command from my father were maintained in their rank and station, and I did not in any way reduce their degree or subsistence. I have constantly exhorted you to treat the people well and to gather only the due amount of taxes; I have guarded your honour but you have cared for nothing and listened to nothing; you do not fear God nor do you spare His creatures. Wherefore I fear retribution; I do not wish that your iniquity and injustice should redound upon the days of my reign. The world is free of enemies; you have prosperity and ease; therefore you ought to concentrate on thanksgiving to God for the benefits which He has bestowed upon you and upon us; for injustice brings about the decline of empires and ingratitude causes the stoppage of benefits. Henceforth there must be no illtreatment of God's creatures; you must keep the peasants lightburdened and never oppress the weak; respect learned men, consort with the good, avoid the bad, and do no harm to those who mind their own business. I call upon God and the angels to be my witnesses that if any man follows a path contrary to this, I will not suffer him further.' All said, 'We will do as you say and obey your command.'

4. A few days later they all returned to their posts. They engaged in the same injustice and oppression; they looked upon Nushirwan as a mere boy and each one in his arrogance imagined that it was he who had set Nushirwan upon the throne, and that he could at his own will regard him or not regard him as king. Nushirwan held his peace and continued to treat them with all external tokens of civility. So five years passed.

5. Now there was a certain army-commander, incomparably wealthy and affluent, whom Nushirwan The Just had made governor of Adharbaygan; in all the kingdom there was no more powerful commander, and nobody could match him in arms, horses and

other paraphernalia. This man was seized with the desire to build a mansion and a garden in the city where he was stationed; in the environs of the city there was a piece of land belonging to an old woman, of such an extent that the income from it sufficed for her to pay the royal quota and for the cultivator to take his share, while enough remained to provide her with four loaves of bread for every day of the year; one loaf she exchanged for other eatables, and one for oil for her lamp; then she ate one loaf for breakfast and one for supper; people took pity on her and gave her clothing; she never went outside her house but passed her life in retirement and poverty. Now it suited this army-commander to include that piece of land in the rest of his property; he sent someone to the wretched old woman to say, 'Sell this piece of land as I have need of it.' The poor old woman said, 'I will not sell it as I need it more; I have only this piece of land in all the world; it gives me my sustenance, and nobody sells his own sustenance.' The man said, 'I will pay you for it or else I will give you in exchange another piece of land which will provide just as much income and produce.' The old woman said, 'This land is my lawful property; I inherited it from my mother and father; the water-supply is near to it, and the neighbours are agreeable and kind to me. Any land which you may give me will not have these particular features. Keep your hands off my land.' The army-commander did not listen to the old woman but he arbitrarily and forcibly seized the land and extended his garden wall around it so that it became part of his estate. The wretched old woman was helpless and reduced to indigence; she resigned herself to accepting payment for the land or else a substitute. She threw herself in front of the man and said, 'Either give me the price or a substitute.' He did not even look at her, but completely ignored her. The wretched old woman gave up hope and went away; and thereafter they did not admit her into his house. But every time the army-commander mounted and went out for recreation or hunting the old woman sat in his way; when he approached her, she called out and demanded payment for the land. He gave no answer but passed by at a distance. If she spoke to his retainers or companions or chamberlains, they said, 'Very well; we will speak to him about it.' But nobody ever did so. Two years passed after this.

36

6. The wretched old woman was reduced to extreme destitution; she found no justice and gave up hope of ever getting it from the man. She said to herself, 'How long shall I hammer cold iron? Over every authority God has placed a higher authority; with all his tyranny this man is but a servant and minion of Nushirwan The Just. I will contrive by whatever means I can, no matter what hardships I may suffer, to make my way to Mada'in, throw myself in front of Nushirwan, and acquaint him of my case; maybe I shall obtain justice from him.' She told no one of her designs, but secretly set out and with great trouble and difficulty went from Adharbaygan to Mada'in; when she saw Nushirwan's palace she said to herself, 'They will never let me go in there; they refused to let me enter the house of the governor of Adharbaygan, and he is a mere servant of this sovereign; so how should they allow me to enter the palace of him who is the lord of the world? I had better find a lodging in this vicinity and enquire when the king will go out riding; perhaps I can throw myself at his feet and present my petition.'

7. By chance the army-commander who had seized the old woman's land came to the court, and King Nushirwan decided to go hunting. The old woman found out that the king was going to a certain hunting-ground on such-and-such a day. She set off and by constant enquiry and strenuous effort made her way to the hunting-ground; she sat down behind a straw [screen] and slept the night. The next day Nushirwan arrived; the nobles and retainers scattered over the country and began the chase. Nushirwan stayed behind with one arms-bearer; he was just riding off to the hunt, when the old woman, seeing the king alone, got up from behind the screen and approached him; she handed him the petition and said, 'O king, if you rule the world, give justice to this poor wretch; read her petition and learn her case.' When Nushirwan saw the old woman and heard her speak, he knew that she would not have come to the hunting-ground except out of dire necessity; he rode towards her, took petition and read it. Tears came into his eyes and he said to her, 'Do not worry any more; up to now this has been your affair; now that we know about it, it has become our responsibility. We shall satisfy your want; then we shall send you home. Rest a few days here as you have come a long way.' He looked round and saw

one of his grooms coming along mounted on a riding-mule; he said, 'Dismount and set this woman on your mule; take her to a village, hand her over to the headman and tell him to look after her; then come back quickly. When we return from hunting take her from the village to the city and keep her in your own house. Allow her two maunds of bread and one maund of meat daily, and let her have five gold dinars a month from our treasury, until such time as I call for her.' The groom did so.

8. As he returned from the chase King Nushirwan spent the whole day pondering how he should contrive a means of examining this case without the knowledge of any of the courtiers. So one afternoon at the time of the siesta, when everyone was asleep and the palace was deserted, he ordered a servant to go to such-and-such a tent and summon a certain page. The servant went and brought the page; the king said, 'O page, you know that I have many worthy pages; I have particularly chosen you to be entrusted with a certain task. You must draw some money from the treasury for your expenses, and go to Adharbaygan; you should lodge in a certain quarter of a certain city and stay for twenty days; you will pretend to the inhabitants that you have come in search of a runaway page. You should associate with all kinds of people, and as you mix with them in drunkenness and sobriety, in the course of conversation enquire about an old woman called so-and-so, who used to live in their district and seems to have disappeared; find out where she went and what she did with the piece of land which she had; listen to what each person says, remember it well and bring back a verified report. This is the true object of your mission; but tomorrow I shall summon you to the court before the nobles and say to you in a loud voice for all to hear: Go, draw money for expenses from the treasury, and travel to Adharbaygan; each city and district that you reach, take note and enquire about the state of the cereals and fruits this year; see whether any celestial calamity has befallen or not, and at the same time look at the condition of the pastures and hunting-grounds. Come back without delay and report what you find without letting anyone know why I sent you.' The page said, 'I will obey your command.'

9. The next day Nushirwan did thus. The page departed and

went to that city. He stayed there twenty days, enquiring about the old woman from everyone he talked to. They all said, 'That old woman was of good family and gentle manners; formerly we used to see her with her husband and children; but the husband and children all died and she was left alone in reduced circumstances with only a piece of land which she inherited. She gave the land to a peasant to cultivate and the produce from it was just enough for her to pay the royal quota and the peasant's share; the portion which remained sufficed until the next harvest to provide her with a ration of four loaves a day; she exchanged one loaf for other eatables and one for oil for her lamp; then she ate one loaf for breakfast and one for supper. Now the governor desired to make a garden with a pavilion and a fine view. He forcibly seized her plot of land and incorporated it in his estate; he neither paid for it nor offered a substitute. For a year the old woman kept going to his house, crying out and demanding payment; nobody listened to her, and now it is some time since anyone saw her in this city; we do not know where she has gone, whether she is dead or alive.'

10. The page returned to the capital. Nushirwan The Just had begun audience; the page entered and bowed; Nushirwan said, 'Ah! tell us what you found.' He said, 'Thanks to Your Majesty the crops are good everywhere this year; no calamity has befallen; the pastures are fresh and the hunting-grounds well stocked.' The king said, 'Praise be to Allah! You have brought good news.' When the people had dispersed and the palace was empty of strangers, the page related the story of the old woman according to what he had heard. Nushirwan was convinced that what the old woman had said was true. All that day and night he could not sleep from anxiety and distress. Next day early he called for the great chamberlain and instructed him that, when the nobles began to arrive, if a certain one came in, he was to keep him in the vestibule until he told him what to do.

11. When all the nobles and priests arrived at the audience-hall, the chamberlain did as Nushirwan had ordered. Nushirwan appeared and gave audience. After some time he turned to the nobles and priests and said, 'I wish to ask you something; answer me truthfully according to your lights and judgment.' They said, 'We will

obey.' He said, 'This man (of such-and-such a name) who is the army-commander of Adharbaygan, how great is his wealth in gold coin?' They said, 'He probably has 2,000,000 dinars which he does not need.' He said, 'How about household furnishings and chattels?' They said, 'He has 500,000 dinars' worth of gold and silver articles.' He said, 'And jewels?' They said, '600,000 dinars' worth.' He said, 'What about landed property, estates and farms?' They said, 'In Khurasan, 'Iraq, Pars and Adharbaygan there is not a district or city where he does not possess a dozen estates, mills, caravanserais, hot-baths and farms.' He said, 'How many horses and mules has he?' They said, 'Thirty thousand.' He said, 'Sheep?' They said, 'Two hundred thousand.' He said, 'Camels?' They said, 'Thirty thousand.' He said, 'Slaves and hirelings?' They said, 'He owns 1,700 Turkish, Rumi and Abyssinian pages and 400 slave-girls.' He said, 'A man who has this amount of wealth and every day eats twenty different dishes of lamb, sweetmeats and rich concoctions, while another human being, a devout servant of God (to Him be power and glory), weak, friendless, helpless, having in all the world only two loaves of dry bread to eat, one for morning and one for evening—supposing the rich man unlawfully seized the other's two dry loaves and deprived him of them, what would he deserve?' All said, 'He would deserve every punishment; whatever penalty he were made to suffer, it would be less than justice.' Nushirwan said, 'I require you immediately to strip the skin from that man's body, throw his flesh to the dogs, stuff the skin with straw and hang it upon the palace gate. Then let it be proclaimed for seven days that hereafter if any man commits oppression, taking even a bag of straw, a chicken or a handful of grass wrongfully from somebody else, and if a complainant comes to the court, the same will happen to him as happened to this man.' They did as Nushirwan commanded.

12. He told the groom to bring the old woman. Then he said to the nobles, 'This is the injured party; and there is the oppressor who has met his reward.' To the page whom he had sent to Adharbaygan he said, 'O page, why did I send you to Adharbaygan?' He said, 'To investigate the case of this old woman and her complaint, and to bring Your Majesty a true and exact report.' Then Nushirwan said to the nobles, 'So that you may know that I have

not inflicted this punishment wantonly, [I warn you that] hereafter I shall not deal with oppressors except by the sword; I shall protect the ewes and lambs from the wolves, I shall restrain grasping hands, I shall remove evil-doers from the face of the earth and fill the world with justice and equity, for this is the task for which I was born. If it were right for men to do as they wished, God would not have created the king and appointed him over them. So now strive to do no act that would lead to your suffering the same fate as this criminal.' All those present were so awed by the king's majesty and authority that they nearly died of fear. He said to the old woman, 'I have punished him who wronged you, and his mansion and the garden which contains your piece of land are now granted to you; I am also giving you animals and money so that you can return home to your own city in safety with my warrant, and I trust that you will remember me in your prayers.' Then he addressed the company, saying, 'Why is it that the door of my palace is open for oppressors and closed to the oppressed? Soldiers and peasants are all my underlings and labourers; nay, the peasants are the givers and the soldiers are the takers; so the door ought to be open wider for the giver than for the taker. Now one of the current irregularities, injustices and unofficial practices is that when a complainant comes to the court, he is not allowed to come before me and state his case. If the old woman had gained access to me here, she would not have needed to go to the hunting-ground.' Then the king commanded that a chain should be set up with bells attached to it, within the reach of even a child of seven years old, so that any complainants who came to the court would not need to see a chamberlain; they would pull the chain and the bells would ring; Nushirwan would hear it and redress their grievances. This was done.

13. When the nobles and army chiefs left the palace and returned to their homes, they straightaway summoned their stewards and underlings and said, 'See how much you have unjustly extorted in the last two years, whose blood you have shed, and whom you have harmed in drunkenness and sobriety; we must all stand together in this and satisfy our creditors before anyone goes to the court and complains against us.' So they all set to and politely summoned their creditors or called at their houses and satisfied every one either

with apologies or indemnities; they also took signed statements to the effect that so-and-so had received satisfaction from so-and-so and had no further claim upon him. By this single exercise of his authority Nushirwan The Just reduced his whole kingdom to order; he eliminated oppression and all the world was so relieved that seven years passed without anyone coming to the court to complain of injustice.

14. Seven years later one afternoon when the palace was empty and everyone had gone, and the guards were asleep, the bells began to ring; Nushirwan heard them and at once sent two servants to see who had come to complain. When they reached the palace gate they saw an old donkey, lean and scabby, which had come inside the gate and was rubbing its back on the chain. The servants went back and said, 'There is no complainant, but only a scabby donkey which is rubbing itself on the chain.' Nushirwan said, 'O fools that you are! it is not as you think; when you look at it well, even this ass has come to seek justice. I desire you both to go, take the ass into the middle of the bazaar; ask everyone about its history and let me know.' The servants went out, took the donkey into the bazaar and asked the people if there was anyone who could tell them about it. All said, 'Yes, by Allah, there is hardly anybody in the city who does not know this donkey.' They said, 'What do you know about it?' They said, 'It belongs to a certain washerman, and for about twenty years we have seen him with it; every day he used to put people's clothes on its back and take them to the washing-place, and bring them back in the evening. As long as the donkey was young and could do its work, he used to feed it; now that it has grown old and incapable of work, he has disowned it and turned it out of his house; it is now a year and a half since he set it loose; night and day it wanders through the streets, bazaars and quarters of the city; people feed it out of charity, but for two days it has failed to get any food and is roaming in vain.'

15. Since the servants heard the same story from everyone they asked, they soon went back and informed the king. Nushirwan said, 'Did I not tell you this ass had come to seek redress? Look after it well tonight and tomorrow bring the washerman to me together with four headmen from his quarter, and I will deal with

him as necessary.' The next day the servants did so; they brought the ass and the washerman together with four headmen in front of Nushirwan at the time of audience; Nushirwan said to the washerman, 'As long as this poor donkey was young and could work for you, you used to feed it and look after it; now that it has grown old and can no longer work, you have cut off its fodder, given it its freedom, and turned it out of your house. So where are his rights for his twenty years service?' He ordered the man to be given forty lashes, and said, 'As long as this donkey is alive, every day in the presence of these four men you must give it as much straw and barley as it can eat, and if you fail and I come to know of it, I shall punish you severely, so that you may know that kings have always been concerned for the rights of the weak and watchful of the doings of officers, assignees and pages, for the sake of their reputation in this world and salvation in the next.'

16. Every two or three years tax-collectors and assignees should be changed lest they become too securely established and entrenched, and begin to cause anxiety. In this way they will treat the peasants well and their provinces will remain prosperous.

# CHAPTER SIX

*Concerning judges, preachers and inspectors (of weights and measures)*
*and the importance of their activities*

1. It is necessary for full information to be available about every single judge in the country. Those that are learned, pious and uncovetous should be retained in their appointments, while any that are not so, should be dismissed, and worthy persons installed in their place. Let each one be paid salary and allowances according to merit, so that he will have no excuse for dishonesty. This is a most important and delicate matter, because they have power over the lives

and property of Muslims. If any judge signs an order or records a sentence capriciously or out of avarice or malice, the other judges must inform the king of this wrong sentence, and that judge must be dismissed and punished.

All other officers must strengthen the hand of the judge and up-hold the dignity of the court. If anyone makes excuses and fails to appear in court, however exalted he may be, he must be forcibly compelled to be present. For in the time of The Companions of The Prophet (upon him be peace and blessings) justice was dispensed by them in person and not delegated to anyone else, so that there could be no scope for injustice or evading the law. In every age from the time of Adam (peace be upon him) until now, in every nation and every country men have practised equity, given justice and striven after righteousness, and where this has been so, dynasties have endured for generations.

2. They say that it was the custom of the non-Arab [Persian] kings to give special audiences for the common people at the festivals of Mihrjan[1] and Nauruz,[2] and nobody was debarred. Several days beforehand proclamations were read telling the people to be ready for a certain day; then they prepared their cases, wrote their petitions and collected their documents, and their opponents did likewise. When the day came the king's herald stood outside the gate of the bazaar and shouted, 'If any man this day impedes another from submitting his needs, the king will be innocent of his blood.' The king then received the people's petitions and laid them all before him; one by one he looked at them, and if amongst them there was one complaining against himself he rose and came from the throne and knelt in supplication before the *mūbad-mūbadān* (this meant chief justice in their language, and he sat on the king's right hand) saying, 'Before all other cases judge between me and this man, impartially and regardlessly.' Then it was announced that all whose suit was against the king should sit on one side as their cases would be dealt with first.

3. Then the king would say to the *mūbad*, 'In the eyes of God (be He exalted) there is no sin greater than a king's sin. The right way

[1] The festival of the autumn equinox.
[2] The festival of the vernal equinox with which the Persian new year begins.

for a king to acknowledge God's grace is by looking after his subjects, giving them justice, and preserving them from oppressors. When a king is a tyrant all his courtiers begin to practise tyranny; they become forgetful of God and ungrateful for His bounty. Verily God abandons them in His wrath, and before long the world goes to ruin and they are all destroyed because of the vileness of their sins. Then the kingship is transferred to another house. O god-fearing *mūbad*, take care that you do not favour me against your conscience, because everything which God (be He exalted) demands of me, I ask of you; so I hereby make you responsible.' Then the *mūbad* considered the case and having decided between the king and his opponent, he awarded judgment in full to the winning party; but if anyone made a false accusation against the king and had no proof, he was severely punished and it was proclaimed that this was the punishment for one who had the audacity to find fault with the king and the state. When the king had finished with these disputes he returned to the throne, put on the crown and turning to his nobles and retainers said, 'For this purpose I commenced the proceedings with myself, namely that if any one of you should have oppressive desires against another they might be suppressed. Now let all of you who have adversaries give them satisfaction.' On that day whoever was nearest to the king was furthest and he who was strongest was weakest.

4. From the time of Ardashir Babakan until Yazdijird this procedure was followed. But Yazdijird changed the customs of his fathers; he made injustice the rule in the world and introduced evil practices. The population suffered distress and their curses upon his name were unceasing. Until one day it happened that a bare-back horse suddenly entered his palace. Its form was such that all the nobles who were present agreed on its excellence, and all tried to catch it. Nobody was successful until it came in front of Yazdijird and stood still at the side of the hall. Then Yazdijird said, 'All stand back, for this is a gift which God (be He exalted) has sent to me.' He got up and gently approaching the horse, caught it by the mane. He stroked the horse's head and patted its back. The horse never moved, but remained quiet. Yazdijird called for saddle and bridle; he bridled the horse and after putting on the saddle and making

the girth tight, he came to the hind quarters to pass the crupper under its tail. Suddenly the horse kicked him right upon the heart and killed him on the spot. Then it bolted out of the door before anyone could stop it. Nobody knew whence it had come nor whither it went. All agreed that it was an angel sent by God to deliver them from that tyrant.

5. It is said that 'Umara ibn Hamza was sitting in the company of Abū Dawāniq[1] on the day for hearing grievances. A man got up—one of the injured parties—and complained that 'Umara had forcibly seized his farm. The Commander of the Faithful said to 'Umara, 'Rise and confront your adversary and plead your defence.' 'Umara said, 'I am not this man's adversary. If the farm is mine, I make him a present of it. I do not wish to leave the place in which the caliph has honourably seated me, nor will I throw my dignity and rank to the winds for the sake of a farm.' All the nobles were impressed by his magnanimity.

6. It must be understood that the king should give judgment in person and hear the words of opposing parties with his own ears. If the king is Turkish or Persian or one who does not know Arabic and has not learnt the precepts of Muslim law, of course he will need a deputy through whom he may perform his function. It is the judges who are the king's deputies, so it is essential for the king to strengthen their hands. Besides, their reputation and dignity must be above reproach because they are the lieutenants of the caliph and bear his standard. At the same time they are appointed by the king and are his agents.

Likewise the preachers who read the prayers in the public mosques should be chosen by the king for their piety and knowledge of the Quran. For it is a crucial point about the prayer of Muslims that it depends upon the *imām* [leader]. When the leader's prayers are invalid the prayers of the whole congregation are ineffectual.

In every city an inspector must be appointed whose duty is to check scales and prices and to see that business is carried on in an orderly and upright manner. He must take particular care in regard to goods which are brought from outlying districts and sold in the

---

[1] 'Father of sixths (of a diram)', nickname of the caliph al Mansur, referring to his noted parsimony.

bazaars to see that there is no fraud or dishonesty, that weights are kept true, and that moral and religious principles are observed. His hand must be strengthened by the king and other officers, for this is one of the foundations of the state and is itself the product of justice. If the king neglects this matter the poor will suffer distress, and the traders in the bazaars will buy as they like and sell as they like, and sellers of short weight will be predominant; iniquity will be rife and divine law set at nought. The post [of inspector] always used to be given to one of the nobility or else to a eunuch or an old Turk, who having no respect for anybody, would be feared by nobles and commoners alike. Thus business was transacted with justice and the precepts of Islam were guarded as the following story shews.

## The story of the drunkenness of 'Ali Nushtgin

7. They say that Sultan Mahmud had been drinking all night with his nobles and boon-companions and at dawn had drunk the morning draught. 'Ali Nushtgin and Muhammad 'Arabi, both generals of Mahmud, were among those present and they had drunk all night and kept awake with Mahmud. By breakfast-time 'Ali Nushtgin was in a state of giddiness and he was suffering badly from lack of sleep and excess of wine. He asked permission to go home. Mahmud said, 'It is not fitting for you to go out in this state in broad daylight. Rest here indoors until the afternoon prayer and then go when you are sober. If the inspector sees you like this he will arrest you and give you the lash. You will be put to shame, and I shall be very embarrassed and unable to help you.' Now 'Ali Nushtgin was a general in command of 50,000 men and the hero and champion of the time, being considered more than a match for a thousand men. He never imagined that the inspector would think of such a thing; he became impatient and quarrelsome, and said, 'I am going all the same'. Mahmud said, 'You know best'; [and to his henchmen] 'loose him and let him go.' 'Ali Nushtgin mounted his horse and with a great crowd of retainers, pages and servants set out for his house.

8. It chanced that in the middle of the bazaar the inspector

appeared with a hundred men, mounted and on foot; when he saw 'Ali Nushtgin in such a drunken state he ordered his men to drag him off his horse. Then he dismounted himself and with his own hand beat 'Ali Nushtgin forty strokes with a stick, without respect or regard, so that he bit the dust, while his servants and followers looked on. Nobody was bold enough to say a word; and that inspector was a Turkish eunuch, old and venerable, who had acquired many rights by his long service.

After he had gone they carried 'Ali Nushtgin home, and all the way he kept saying, 'This is what happens if you disobey the sultan's orders.' The next day when he entered the royal presence, Mahmud said, 'Well, did you escape the inspector?' 'Ali Nushtgin bared his back and shewed it to Mahmud, black and blue. Mahmud laughed and said, 'Now repent [and resolve] never to go outdoors drunk again.'

Since the rules of administration and discipline were firmly established in the country, the workings of justice took this course that we have related.

### The story of the bakers of Ghaznain

9. And I have heard that [one day] the bakers in Ghaznain shut the doors of their shops, and bread became dear and unobtainable. Strangers and poor people were in distress and went to the court to state their grievance, and they complained about the bakers in front of Sultan Ibrahim. He ordered all of them to be brought to his presence; then he said, 'Why have you cut off the supply of bread?' They said, 'Every load of wheat and flour which is brought into the city is bought by your baker and put into his store; he says that this is the order and he does not allow us to buy a single maund.' The sultan gave orders that his private baker was to be taken and thrown under elephants' feet. When he was dead they tied him to an elephant's tusks and paraded him through the city, proclaiming, 'This is what we will do to any baker who does not open the door of his shop.' Then they dealt out his stocks [to all the other bakers]. By evening prayer there were fifty maunds of bread left over in every shop and not enough customers to buy it all.

# CHAPTER SEVEN

*On obtaining information about the conduct of tax-collectors, judges,
prefects of police and mayors, and keeping them in check*

1. Let observation be kept in every city to see who there is in it
who shews interest in religious matters, fears God (be He exalted)
and is not self-seeking. Let such a person be addressed thus, 'We
have now made you responsible for the security of this city and its
district. All that God asks of us, we shall require of you. We desire
that you make constant enquiries and be always well-informed in
matters small and great concerning the conduct of the tax-collector,
the judge, the prefect of police and the inspector (of weights and
measures) towards the people. Make us acquainted with the truth
whether your findings are kept secret or made public, so that we may
give our orders as appropriate.' If persons who are of the right
quality refuse to accept this trust, they must be coerced and however
reluctantly commanded to do it.

2. They say that 'Abd Allah ibn Tahir was a just amir. His
grave is at Nishapur and I have visited it and seen it. It is constantly
thronged with people praying for their needs, and God always grants
their requests. He was a man who habitually appointed devout and
pious men to be his officers, and persons who had no need of worldly
goods and did not busy themselves with their private interests, with
the result that taxes were duly collected, the peasants were not
troubled and he himself was not embarrassed.

3. Abu 'Ali Daqqaq[1] one day called upon the amir Abu 'Ali
Ilyas.[2] The latter was general and governor of Khurasan, and in spite
of his high rank was an extremely virtuous man. When Abu 'Ali
Daqqaq knelt in front of him, Abu 'Ali Ilyas said, 'Give me good
counsel.' He said, 'O amir, I will ask you a question; will you answer
me frankly?' He said, 'I will.' He said, 'Tell me, which do you love

[1] A famous mystic of the tenth century A.D. who lived and preached at Nishapur
in Khurasan: see *Kashf al Mahjub*, 162.

[2] Was amir of Kirman in his day but not of Khurasan: cf. page 68, line 10
below.

more, your gold or your enemy?' He said, 'My gold.' He said, 'Then how is it that that which you love more, you will leave behind you, and your enemy whom you love not, you will take with you to the next world?' Tears came into the eyes of Abu 'Ali Ilyas and he said, 'You have counselled me well and roused me from the sleep of negligence; these words are the sum of all philosophy and they will profit me in both worlds.'

## The story of Sultan Mahmud's ugliness

4. They say that Sultan Mahmud Ghāzī [The Raider] was not handsome; he had a drawn face, his skin was dry, his neck long, his nose high, and his beard was thin. Because he always ate clay, his complexion was yellow. One day after his father Sabuktigin died, and he ascended the throne and Hindustan became subject to him, in the early morning he was sitting on his prayer-mat in his private room; he was praying and in front of him was his mirror and his comb and two private pages were in waiting, when his wazir Shams al Kufat Ahmad ibn Hasan entered the room, and bowed; Mahmud nodded to him to sit down. When he had finished his prayers, he put on his hat and cloak and shoes, and looked at himself in the mirror; he saw his face, then smiled and said to Ahmad ibn Hasan, 'Do you know what is passing through my mind at this moment?' He said, 'My lord knows best.' He said, 'I am afraid that people don't love me because I am not handsome; they always prefer handsome kings.' Ahmad ibn Hasan said, 'Master, do just one thing, and they will love you more than their wives and children and their very selves, and at your command they will go through water and fire.' He said, 'What am I to do?' He said, 'Take gold as your enemy and men will regard you as their friend.' Mahmud was pleased at this and said, 'A thousand meanings and profits are hidden in these words.' Then he opened his hand in generosity and charity. All the world adored him and praised him, and many noble works and great victories sprang from his hands; he went to Somnat and broke the idol and brought it back; he went as far as Samarqand and came also to 'Iraq. Then one day he said to Ahmad ibn Hasan, 'Since I renounced gold, both worlds came

into my hand, and when I repudiated worldly things, I became beloved of both worlds.'

The title of sultan did not exist before him;[1] the first ruler in Islam to call himself sultan was Mahmud. After him it became the general rule. As a king he was just, God-fearing, fond of learning, generous, alert, orthodox in religion and a gallant battler for the faith. The best time is that in which a just king reigns.

5. Tradition says that The Prophet (the prayers of God be upon him) said [in Arabic], 'Justice is the glory of the faith and the power of the government; in it lies the prosperity of nobility and commons.' It is the measure of all good things, as God (be He exalted) said [in the Quran 55. 6], 'He raised up the heavens and He set the Balance'—that is, justice. And in another place [Quran 42. 16] He said, 'Allah it is who sent down the Book with truth, and the Balance.' The person most worthy for kingship is he whose heart is a repository of justice, whose house is a haven for wise and religious men, and whose boon-companions and agents are discreet and God-fearing.

6. Fudail ibn 'Iyad[2] used to say, 'If my prayers were to be granted I should pray only for a just ruler, because the ruler's virtue underlies the well-being of his subjects and the prosperity of the world.'

7. Among the traditions of The Prophet (may God pray for him and give him peace) is the following [in Arabic]: 'Those who do justice in this world for God's sake (to Him be power and glory) [will sit] upon platforms made of pearl on the resurrection day.' (He said: Those who do justice in this world for God's sake will be in paradise on platforms of pearl on the resurrection day.)

8. For the sake of justice and the welfare of the people kings have always put in charge of affairs abstemious and God-fearing men who being without self-interest, will on every occasion report on matters truthfully, as The Commander of the Faithful al Mu'tasim did at Baghdad.

---

[1] See Lane-Poole, *Dynasties*, 286 note.
[2] A famous ascetic and teller of traditions: see *Kashf al Mahjub*, 97.

### *The story of the Turkish amir and the severity of al Mu'tasim*

9. And that was on this wise. Of the 'Abbasid caliphs none had such authority, such dignity, such profusion of wealth as al Mu'tasim; nor did any own as many Turkish slaves as he. They say he had 70,000 Turkish pages; many of his pages he promoted and appointed to governorships. He always used to say there was none like the Turk for service.

10. One day an amir summoned his steward and said, 'Do you know any of the citizens or merchants of Baghdad who would do business with me to the extent of five hundred dinars? I need that sum urgently and would give it back at harvest time.' The steward thought; he remembered a friend of his who traded in the bazaar and possessed six hundred dinars (of *khalifati* [ordinary standard] gold) which he had acquired in the course of time. He said to the amir, 'I have an acquaintance who has a shop in such-and-such bazaar, and from time to time I go to his shop and do business with him. He has got six hundred dinars (*khalifati*). If you sent someone to invite him here, and if you placed him in a seat of honour, favoured him with constant attention, treated him with ceremony at dinner; and then after eating, if you were to mention the financial matter, maybe he would feel abashed at your kindness and not be able to refuse.' The amir did this; he sent someone with the following message, 'Would you trouble yourself for a few moments, as I want to see you about something.' The man got up and went to the amir's house. He was not previously acquainted with this amir. He greeted him when he went in. The amir answered him and turned to his followers, saying, 'Is this the person?' They said, 'Yes.' The amir rose and had him ushered to a good seat. Then he said, 'Sir, I have heard so much about your nobility, morality, honesty and piety that I have been captivated by you without ever having seen you; they say that in all the bazaars of Baghdad there is no one of finer character or fairer business principles than yourself.' He went on to say, 'Why not discard ceremony and let me do something for you; I want you to regard this house as your own and treat me as a friend and brother.' The man bowed at each thing the amir said; while the steward kept saying, 'It is so—a hundred times so.' After some time trays of food

were brought in; the amir seated the man next to himself and was assiduous in his attentions, constantly plying him with titbits.

11. The food was removed, they washed their hands and outsiders departed; only the amir's personal retainers remained. He turned to the man and said, 'Do you know why I troubled you to come here?' He said, 'The amir knows best.' The amir said, 'Know that in this city I have many friends who would not fail to carry out my slightest suggestion; if I were to ask them for five or ten thousand, they would give it at once without grudge, because they have profited much by doing business with me, and never suffered loss in any dealings or relations with me. At the present moment I am anxious that there should be friendship and informality between us. Although I have many creditors, in the present circumstances I would like you to assist me with a thousand dinars for four or five months. I will repay you at harvest time and present you with a suit of clothes for good measure; I know that you have this much and more, and will not refuse.' The man was abashed at the amir's attentions and said, 'It is for the amir to command; but I am not one of those merchants who have a thousand or two thousand dinars. One must speak nothing but the truth to one's superiors; my whole capital is six hundred dinars and with it I manage to scrape a living and do a little trade in the bazaar; it has taken much time and toil to accumulate this sum.' The amir said, 'I have plenty of fine [special standard] gold in my treasury, but it is unsuitable for my present purpose. My object in doing business with you is to gain your friendship. What profit do you get from your slender trade? Let me have the six hundred dinars and I will give you a receipt for seven hundred, witnessed by trustworthy men, and a promise of repayment at harvest time with a handsome present in addition.' Meanwhile the steward was saying, 'You have not got to know the amir yet; of all the pillars of the state there is no one of stricter business principles than he.' The man said, 'It is for the amir to command. As much as I have I will not grudge.' So he gave the amir the gold and took a receipt.

12. Ten days after the expiry of the term the man went to call on the amir. Verbally he made no request; he said to himself, 'When the amir sees me, he will know that I have come for the

money.' He continued to visit the amir in this way until it was two months after the agreed date, and he had seen the amir ten times. The amir appeared not to understand that the man wanted anything or that he himself owed anything to the man. When the man saw that the amir kept silent, he wrote a petition and handed it to him; it said, 'I now need that paltry sum of money, and it is two months after the agreed date. If the amir sees fit could he kindly advise his steward to deliver the money to his humble servant.' The amir said, 'Do you think that I have forgotten your case? Don't worry; be patient for a few days as I am arranging about your money; I will send it to you in a sealed purse by hand of one of my confidants.' The man waited another two months and saw no sign of his money. Once more he went to the amir's house and sent in another petition and also spoke personally. The amir put him off with a few pleasantries; and the man kept pressing his demand every two or three days, but without result. Then eight months passed from the appointed date.

13. The man was in distress. He persuaded people of the city to intercede for him; he went to the qāḍī and summoned the amir to the *shariʿa*[1] court; there was not a single noble or grandee who had not spoken to the amir and interceded on the man's behalf. It had no effect. Even when he took fifty men from the qadi's house, he was unable to bring the amir to court; nor did the amir listen to what the grandees said. Then a year and a half passed. The man was desperate; he resigned himself to forgoing the interest and taking back a hundred dinars less than the full sum. But even that was no use. He abandoned hope of help from the nobles; and he was tired of running hither and thither. Instead he put his trust in God; he went into the Faḍlūmand mosque and performed several *rakʿats*[2] of prayer. He murmured and moaned to God, saying, 'O Lord, hear my prayer and restore me to my rights; extract justice from this oppressor.' Now it chanced that a dervish was sitting in the mosque and heard his wailing and moaning. His heart was moved to sympathy; when the man had finished his supplications, he said,

---

[1] Islamic law.

[2] *Rakʿat* is a cycle of prayers and prostrations; each of the five daily prayers consists of a prescribed number of *rakʿats*.

'O shaikh! what affliction has befallen you that you wail so loud? Tell me what it is.' The man said, 'My distress is such that it will not avail to speak to any mortal; only God (be He exalted) can succour me.' He said, 'Yet tell me, for there must be some reason.' The man said, 'O beggar, there remains only the caliph whom I have not spoken to. I have spoken to all the amirs and nobles, and I have been to the qadi; but it has had no effect. If I tell you, what good will it do?' The dervish said, 'Even if it does you no good to tell me, neither will it do you any harm. Have you not heard what the sages say?—"If you have a pain, you should tell everyone you meet; you may discover the remedy from the humblest of men." If you tell me your case, maybe you will find some comfort, and even if you do not, you will be no worse off than you are now.' The man said to himself, 'He is right.' Then he told him what had happened.

14. When the dervish had heard the story, he said, 'O noble sir, now that you have told me what your trouble is, a remedy has immediately presented itself. Don't worry, for if you do as I tell you, you will get back your gold this very day.' The man said, 'What am I to do?' He said, 'Go at once to a certain quarter of the city where there is a mosque with a minaret; beside the mosque is a gate, and behind the gate is a shop. There is an old man sitting there, wearing ragged clothes and sewing canvas; one or two boys are also doing some sewing with him. Go into that shop and greet the old man; sit down in front of him and tell him your story. When you have attained your object, remember me in your prayers. Do what I have told you without delay.' The man came out of the mosque; he thought to himself, 'Fancy! I appealed to all the nobles and amirs, and they earnestly pleaded on my behalf; but it was of no use. Now this beggar is directing me to a feeble old man and saying that I shall attain my object from him. This seems to me like a trick, but what am I to do? At all events I will go; even if no good comes out of it, things will not be any worse than they are at present.' So he went to the gate of the mosque, went into the shop and saluting the old man, sat down in front of him. Some time passed as the old man was doing some sewing. After putting it down he said, 'Is there anything I can do for you?' The man told him his story from first to last.

15. After hearing all the circumstances the old tailor said, 'It is God (to Him be power and glory) who orders the affairs of His servants. We can do no more than speak; so let me also speak to your debtor on your behalf. I hope that God will put things right and you will get what you want. Sit with your back to that wall and rest a while.' Then he said to one of the two apprentices, 'Put down your needle and go to the house of such-and-such amir. Sit outside the door of his private room, and if anyone goes in or comes out, ask them to tell the amir that a certain tailor's apprentice is waiting and has a message for him. When he calls you in, after greeting him, say, "My master sends his compliments and says that a man has come to him to complain against you; he has a receipt signed by you for seven hundred dinars, and it is now eighteen months after the due date. I request you forthwith to give the man his money in full and satisfy him completely without fail or delay." Bring me back his answer quickly.'

16. The boy went in haste to the amir's house, while I[1] was struck dumb with amazement, for no king would send his own slave such a message as the tailor has just sent to the amir through the medium of a boy. After some time the boy came back and said to his master, 'I did as you said. I saw the amir and delivered the message. The amir got up and said, "Convey my greetings and respects to your master, and tell him that I thank him; I will do as he says. I am coming now bringing the money with me; I shall apologize for my fault and hand over the money in his presence."' An hour had not passed when the amir was on his way with a groom and two attendants. He dismounted from his horse, entered the shop and greeted the old tailor, kissing his hand. Then he sat down in front of him, took a purse of gold from an attendant and said, 'Here is the money. Please do not think that I was going to misappropriate this man's money. What happened was not my fault but my steward's.' He apologized profusely, then said to an attendant, 'Go and fetch an assayer with a balance from the bazaar.' He went and brought an assayer. The gold was assayed and weighed. It came to five hundred dinars (*khalīfatī*). The amir said, 'He will have to take these five hundred dinars today, and tomorrow when I return from

[1] The lapse into the first person is noteworthy.

the court I will summon him and hand over the other two hundred dinars, asking pardon and trying to satisfy him. And I will arrange for an encomiast to call on you tomorrow before the morning prayer.' The old man said, 'Put these five hundred dinars into his bosom, and see that you do not go back on your word.' He said, 'Very well.' He put the money into my bosom, kissed the old man's hand and departed; while I scarcely knew where I was for astonishment and happiness. I put out my hand, took hold of the balance and weighed out a hundred dinars; I laid them before the old man, saying, 'I was prepared to take back a hundred dinars less than the full amount; now that through your good offices I am going to receive my money in full, I freely grant you these hundred dinars as a reward for your efforts.' The old man looked cross and frowned, saying, 'I am content that as a result of what I said a Muslim found release from grief and trouble; but if I allowed myself to take one grain of your money, I should be a worse oppressor than this Turk. Arise and go in safety with the gold you have got; and if he does not send you the other two hundred dinars tomorrow, let me know. Hereafter you had better know who your associates are before you do business with them.' In spite of all my entreaties he would accept nothing; so I got up and went joyfully back to my house. That night I slept free from care.

17. The next day I was sitting in the house, and about the middle of the morning someone came from the amir to see me and said, 'The amir asks you to trouble yourself to visit him for a moment.' I went to the amir's house; when I went in he rose and put me in a seat of honour; then he began to revile his stewards, saying that they were to blame, and that he had been constantly busy in the service of the king. Then he said to his treasurer, 'Bring the purse and the balance.' He weighed out two hundred dinars and put them in my hands. I bowed and got up to go. He said, 'Sit down for a bit.' Food was brought in. When we had finished eating and washed our hands, the amir whispered something in a servant's ear. The servant went out and came back with a robe of honour. The amir said, 'Invest him.' So they invested me with a cloak of great price and put a turban of fine linen on my head. Then the amir said to me, 'Are you now genuinely satisfied?' I said, 'Yes.' He said, 'Then

give me back my receipt and go this very hour to the old man and tell him that you have received your rights and obtained satisfaction from me.' I said, 'Certainly, and in any case he told me to report to him tomorrow.' I rose and went from the amir's house to the tailor's shop. I told him what had happened—how the amir had called me, and treated me well, and paid me the rest of the money, and presented me with the cloak and turban—and I said, 'I know that all this has come about through your good offices. How would it be if you accepted two hundred dinars from me?' Whatever I said he would not take anything, so I got up and returned in good spirits to my own shop.

18. The next day I roasted a lamb and a few chickens, and took them with a plate of sweets and pastries to the old tailor. I said, 'O shaikh, if you will not take money, please accept these few eatables with my best wishes; it is all from my legitimate earnings; I shall be very pleased if you will.' He said, 'I accept.' He put out his hand and ate some of the food and gave some to his apprentices. Then I said to him, 'I have one request to make, if you will permit me.' He said, 'What is it?' I said, 'All the nobles and amirs of Baghdad spoke to this amir on my behalf, and all without avail; he listened to nobody; even the qadi was powerless to deal with him. Why did he listen to you and carry out everything you said and give me my money? How did he come to have such respect for you?' He said, 'Haven't you heard what happened to me with The Commander of the Faithful?' I said, 'No.' He said, 'Listen and I will tell you.'

19. He began: Know that I have proclaimed the hours of prayer from the minaret of this mosque for thirty years. I am a tailor by trade; I have never drunk wine, never indulged in adultery and sodomy, and never approved of improper acts. Now in this street is the house of an amir. One day after the afternoon prayer I left the mosque to come back to this shop; I saw the amir coming along in a drunken state, holding on to a young woman's veil; he was dragging her by force and she was crying for help and saying, 'O Muslims, rescue me; I am not a woman of this sort; I am the daughter of such-and-such and the wife of so-and-so, and my house is in a certain quarter; everyone knows of my chastity and virtue. This Turk

is presumptuously and forcibly carrying me off with mischievous intent. Moreover my husband has sworn to divorce me if I am ever away from the house at night.' She was weeping and nobody went to her assistance, for this amir was too proud and tyrannous; he had 10,000 horsemen, and nobody dared say anything to him. I shouted a bit, but it was useless, and he took the woman to his house. Thus frustrated, my religious ardour was kindled and I could not restrain myself. I went and rallied the elders of the district, and we all went to the amir's house and raised clamorous protests, shouting, 'Islam is no more, for in the city of Baghdad on the caliph's doorstep women are presumptuously and forcibly seized in the street, carried off and raped. If you send this woman outside, well and good; but if not, we shall go at once to al Mu'tasim's court and complain.' When the Turk heard our noise he came out of his house with a party of pages who beat us well and truly and broke our resistance.

20. When this happened we all fled and dispersed. It was the time of the evening prayer. Some time later I got into my night clothes and lay down upon the ground. I was so vexed and roused that I could not sleep. I lay awake till midnight, thinking; and then it occurred to me that if any mischief was going to be done it would have happened by now and could not be helped. What made it worse was that the woman's husband had sworn to divorce her if she went out at night. I had heard that when wine-bibbers get drunk they fall asleep, and when they wake up they do not know how much of the night has passed. I decided immediately to go up the minaret and utter the call to prayer; when the Turk heard it he would think it was daybreak; he would let go of the woman and send her out of his house; inevitably she would pass the door of this mosque; having sounded the call to prayer I would quickly come down from the minaret and stand at the door of the mosque; when the woman appeared I would escort her back to her husband's house, so that at least the poor wretch would not forfeit her husband and her matronage.

21. So I did all this. I went up the minaret and uttered the call to prayer. Now The Commander of the Faithful al Mu'tasim was awake. When he heard the call to prayer at the wrong time he was

very angry, and said, 'A man who sounds the call to prayer in the middle of the night is a miscreant, for whoever hears it will think it is daytime; and as soon as he goes out into the street he will be caught by the night-watch and get into trouble.' He said to a servant, 'Go and tell the porter that I want him to go at once and bring the muezzin who has sounded the call to prayer in the middle of the night; I shall punish him so severely that no muezzin will again utter the call to prayer at the wrong time.' I was standing at the door of the mosque waiting for this woman, when I saw the porter coming with a torch. When he saw me standing there he said, 'Did you sound the call to prayer?' I said, 'Yes.' He said, 'Why did you sound it at the wrong time? The caliph has taken extreme exception to it and is very angry with you; he has sent me to find you so that he can punish you.' I said, 'It is for the caliph to command; but a certain barbarian forced me to utter the call to prayer at the wrong time.' He said, 'Who is this barbarian?' I said, 'One who fears neither God nor the caliph.' He said, 'Who could that be?' I said, 'This is a matter which I can only tell to The Commander of the Faithful. If I did this with evil intent whatever punishment the caliph gives me will be less than my deserts.' He said, 'In the name of Allah, come, let us go to the caliph's palace.'

22. The servant was waiting for us when we reached the palace. The porter repeated to the servant what I had told him. The servant went and told al Mu'tasim. He said, 'Go and bring the man to me.' The servant took me before the caliph. He asked me why I had sounded the call to prayer at the wrong time. I then told him the story of the Turk and the woman from start to finish. After hearing it he told the servant to instruct the porter as follows: 'Go with a hundred horsemen to the house of such-and-such amir and tell him that he is summoned by the caliph; having found him you are to rescue the woman whom he brought to the house yesterday and send her to her husband's house with this old man and two or three lackeys; call her husband to the door and say that al Mu'tasim sends his greeting and wishes to intercede on the woman's behalf and says that she was not at all at fault in what happened; he ought to look after his wife better in future; then bring the amir to me at once.' To me he said, 'Remain here for a while.' An hour later

they brought the amir to al Muʿtasim; al Muʿtasim looked at him and said, 'Wherefore do you suppose that I lack zeal for the Islamic faith? Have you seen me oppress my people? Or is there something wrong with the religion in my time? Am I not the same man who, to save a Muslim who had been taken prisoner by the Rumis [Byzantines], marched from Baghdad, defeated the Rumi army, and put the Caesar to flight, remaining to ravage the lands of Rum for six years and not returning until I had sacked and burned Qustani-niyya [Constantinople], built the Cathedral Mosque and delivered that man from captivity? Today through awe of me and my justice, wolf and sheep can drink together at one place, so how can you dare, here in Baghdad upon my very threshold, to seize a woman by force, take her to your house for a wicked purpose, and then when people protest, to beat them?' He ordered a sack to be brought, the amir to be put into it, and the sack done up tightly. This was done. Then at his behest two clubs were procured, of the kind used for pounding plaster, and he told two men to stand one on each side and beat the amir to pieces. Straightaway the men laid on with the clubs and smashed him to smithereens. They said, 'O Commander of the Faithful, all his bones are minced. What is your command?' He ordered them to take the closed sack as it was and throw it into the Tigris.

23. Then he said to me, 'O shaikh, know that a man who does not fear God (to Him be power and glory) will not be afraid of me, while the man who does fear God will of course not do an act for which he would be brought to book in both worlds. Since this man committed a crime, he has met his just reward. So I command you that in future if anyone wrongs another or unjustly hurts another or holds the religious law in contempt and you become aware of it, you are to sound the call to prayer like this at the wrong time, so that I shall hear it and summon you and ask what is the matter, and deal with any malefactor as I did with this dog, even if it should be my own son or brother.' Then he gave me a present and dismissed me. Now all the nobles and courtiers are aware of this story, so it was not out of respect for me that the amir gave back your money but rather for fear of that sack and the plaster-pounders and the river. For if he had failed, I would immediately have sounded

the call to prayer and the same would have happened to him as happened to that Turk.

24. There are many stories of this kind. I have related this much in order that The Master of the World may know how caliphs and kings have always guarded the sheep from the wolves, how they have kept their officials in check, what precautions they have taken against evil-doers, and how they have strengthened, upheld and cherished the Islamic faith.

## CHAPTER EIGHT

*On enquiry and investigation into matters of religion,*
*religious law and suchlike*

1. It is incumbent upon the king to enquire into religious matters, to be acquainted with the divine precepts and prohibitions and put them into practice, and to obey the commands of God (be He exalted); it is his duty to respect doctors of religion and pay their salaries out of the treasury, and he should honour pious and ab-stemious men. Furthermore it is fitting that once or twice a week he should invite religious elders to his presence and hear from them the commands of The Truth; he should listen to interpretations of the Quran and traditions of The Prophet (may Allah pray for him and give him peace); and he should hear stories about just kings and tales of the prophets (upon them be peace). During that time he should free his mind from worldly cares and give his ears and atten-tion [wholly] to them. Let him bid them take sides and hold a debate, and let him ask questions about what he does not understand; when he has learnt the answers let him commit them to memory. After this has gone on for some time it will become a habit, and it will not be long before he has learnt and memorized most of the precepts of divine law, the meanings of the Quran and the traditions of The Prophet (upon him be peace). Then the way of prudence

and rectitude in both spiritual and temporal affairs will be open to him; no heretic or innovator will be able to turn him from that path. His judgment will be strengthened and he will increase in justice and equity; vanity and heresy will vanish from his kingdom and great works will spring from his hands. The roots of wickedness, corruption and discord will be cut out in the time of his empire. The hand of the righteous shall become strong and the wicked shall be no more. In this world he shall have fame, and in the next world he shall find salvation, high degree and inestimable reward. In his age men will more than ever delight in gaining knowledge.

2. ['Abd Allah] ibn 'Umar (may Allah be pleased with him) says that The Prophet (peace be upon him) said, 'The righteous shall dwell in paradise in palaces [full] of the light of their justice towards their underlings.'

3. The most important thing which a king needs is sound faith, because kingship and religion are like two brothers; whenever disturbance breaks out in the country religion suffers too; heretics and evil-doers appear; and whenever religious affairs are in disorder, there is confusion in the country; evil-doers gain power and render the king impotent and despondent; heresy grows rife and rebels make themselves felt.

4. Sufyan Thauri[1] says, 'The best of rulers is he who keeps company with men of learning, and the worst of learned men is he who seeks the society of the king.'

5. Ardashir says, 'Any ruler who has not the power to check his courtiers will never be able to control his commoners and peasants.' There is a passage in the Quran [26. 214] to this effect, 'And warn thy relatives of near kin.'

6. The Commander of the Faithful 'Umar (may Allah be pleased with him) says 'There is nothing more detrimental to the country and more ruinous to the peasantry than difficulty of access to the king: conversely there is nothing more profitable to the people than ease of access to the king—or more impressive, especially to officers and tax-collectors, for when they know that the king is accessible they will not dare to practise oppression and extortion on the peasants.'

[1] A celebrated scholar of tradition and a contemporary of the first 'Abbasid caliphs.

7. Luqman The Wise said, 'Man has no better friend in this world than knowledge, and knowledge is better than wealth, because you must take care of wealth but knowledge takes care of you.'

8. Hasan of Basra[1] (Allah's mercy upon him) says, 'The wise man is not he who knows more Arabic and is more competent in its grammar and vocabulary; the wise man is he who knows what he ought to know. If he knows languages in addition that is well. If anyone knows the precepts of religious law and meanings of the Quran in Turkish or Persian or Greek, and knows no Arabic whatever, he is still a learned man. If he knows Arabic as well, that is all to the good; for God (be He exalted) sent down the Quran in the Arabic tongue and Muhammad The Elect (the prayers of Allah and His peace be upon him) spoke in Arabic.'

9. But when a king possesses divine splendour[2] and sovereignty, and knowledge withal is wedded to these, he finds happiness in both worlds, because everything he does is informed with knowledge and he does not allow himself to be ignorant. Consider how great is the fame of kings who were wise, and what great works they did; names such as these will be blessed until the resurrection—Afridun, Alexander, Ardashir, Nushirwan The Just, The Commander of the Faithful 'Umar (may Allah be pleased with him), 'Umar ibn 'Abd al 'Aziz (may Allah illumine his resting place), Harun, al Ma'mun, al Mu'tasim, Isma'il ibn Ahmad the Samanid, and Sultan Mahmud (Allah's mercy be upon them all). The deeds and ways of them all are well known for they are recorded in histories and other books; men never cease reading about them and singing their praises and blessings.

### The story of 'Umar ibn 'Abd al 'Aziz and the famine

10. They say that in the days of 'Umar ibn 'Abd al 'Aziz (Allah's mercy be upon him) there was a famine and the people were in distress. A party of Arabs approached him and complained

---

[1] A famous lawyer and ascetic, contemporary of the Umayyad caliph 'Umar ibn 'Abd al 'Aziz: see *Kashf al Mahjub*, 86.

[2] Persian *farr-i ilāhī*: see note on page 120, last line.

saying, 'O Commander of the Faithful, we have consumed our own flesh and blood in the famine (that is, we have become thin), and our cheeks have turned yellow because we have not enough to eat. We need what is in your treasury; and as for that treasure, it belongs either to you or to God or to the servants of God. If it belongs to God's servants it is ours; if it belongs to God, He has no need of it; if it is yours, then [as the Quran 12. 88 says] "be charitable unto us, for Allah will requite the charitable" (the interpretation is . . .); and if it is ours let us have it that we may escape from these straits, for the skin is withered on our bodies.' 'Umar ibn 'Abd al 'Aziz was moved to sympathy for them, and tears came into his eyes; he said, 'I will do as you have said,' and in the same hour he gave orders for their requests to be attended to and their wants to be supplied. When they were about to get up and go, 'Umar ibn 'Abd al 'Aziz (Allah's mercy be upon him) said, 'O men where are you going? As you presented your case and that of the rest of God's servants to me, so do you present my case to God' (meaning: remember me in your prayers). Then those Arab tribesmen lifted their eyes to heaven and said, 'O Lord, by Thy glory [we pray] that Thou wilt do unto 'Umar ibn 'Abd al 'Aziz as he did unto Thy servants.'

11. When they had done praying, immediately a cloud came up and it began to rain heavily; a hailstone fell upon the bricks of 'Umar's palace; it broke in two and a piece of paper fell from inside it. They looked at it and there was written upon it [in Arabic], 'This is a grace from Allah The Mighty to 'Umar ibn 'Abd al 'Aziz [exempting him] from the fire.' (The Persian translation . . .)

12. There are many stories on this subject; but what has been related in this chapter will suffice.

# CHAPTER NINE

*Concerning overlords and their emoluments*

1. Persons who are completely reliable are to be made overlords with the task of keeping themselves informed of all that goes on at the court and making reports as called for and whenever necessary. They will on their own responsibility send lieutenants, who must be upright and honest, to every district and city to supervise the collection of taxes and revenue, and to get to know every event, great or small. Their monthly salaries are not to be a burden upon the peasants and a fresh source of distress, but their requirements must be met from the treasury so that they will have no excuse for corruption and bribery. If they do their work honestly the benefit of them will ultimately prove to be ten or a hundred times what it costs to keep them.

# CHAPTER TEN

*Concerning intelligence agents and reporters and [their importance in] administering the affairs of the country*

1. It is the king's duty to enquire into the condition of his peasantry and army, both far and near, and to know more or less how things are. If he does not do this he is at fault and people will charge him with negligence, laziness and tyranny, saying, 'Either the king knows about the oppression and extortion going on in the country, or he does not know. If he knows and does nothing to prevent it and remedy it, that is because he is an oppressor like the rest and acquiesces in their oppression; and if he does not know then he is negligent and ignorant.' Neither of these imputations is desirable. Inevitably therefore he must have postmasters; and in every age in the time of ignorance and of Islam, kings have had postmasters, through whom they have learnt everything that goes on,

good and bad. For instance if anybody wrongly took so much as a chicken or a bag of straw from another—and that five hundred farsangs away—the king would know about it and have the offender punished, so that others knew that the king was vigilant. In every place they appointed informers and so far checked the activities of oppressors that men enjoyed security and justice for the pursuit of trade and cultivation. But this is a delicate business involving some unpleasantness; it must be entrusted to the hands and tongues and pens of men who are completely above suspicion and without self-interest, for the weal or woe of the country depends on them. They must be directly responsible to the king and not to anyone else; and they must receive their monthly salaries regularly from the treasury so that they may do their work without any worries. In this way the king will know of every event that takes place and will be able to give his orders as appropriate, meting out unexpected reward, punishment or commendation to the persons concerned. When a king is like this, men are always eager to be obedient, fearing the king's displeasure, and nobody can possibly have the audacity to disobey the king or plot any mischief. Thus the employment of intelligence agents and reporters contributes to the justice, vigilance and prudence of the king, and to the prosperity of the country.

*The story of the robbers of Kuch Baluch*

2. At the time of Sultan Mahmud's conquest of 'Iraq it happened that at Dair Gachin[1] robbers stole the chattels of a woman who was travelling by caravan. These robbers came from Kuch Baluch, a district which joins the province of Kirman. The woman went before Sultan Mahmud to complain, saying, 'Robbers stole my chattels at Dair Gachin. Get back my things from them, or else give me compensation for them.' Mahmud said, 'And where might Dair Gachin be?' The woman said, 'Take no more territory than what you can know the extent of, and be responsible for, and look after properly.' He said, 'You are right; but do you know of what tribe these robbers were and whence they came?' She said, 'They were of the Kuch Baluch and had come from the neighbourhood of

---

[1] 'Plaster Convent': see Le Strange, *Lands*, 208.

Kirman.' He said, 'That place is far distant and outside my territory; I cannot do anything to them.' The woman said, 'What sort of administrator of the world are you who cannot administer your own possessions? and what kind of a shepherd are you if you cannot protect the sheep from the wolves? Look at me in my weakness and loneliness and you with all your army and power.' Tears came into Mahmud's eyes and he said, 'You are right; I will give you compensation for your chattels and deal with this matter as best I can.'

3. Then he had some money given to the woman out of the treasury, and he wrote a letter to Abu 'Ali Ilyas[1] who was the amir of Kirman, saying, 'The purpose of my coming to 'Iraq was not conquest, for I was at that time fully engaged in war in Hindustan; but I came because of frequent letters which I received from the Muslims complaining that the Dailamites had spread corruption, oppression and heresy in 'Iraq; that they had set up ambushes on the highways and were seizing every beautiful woman or boy that came along and taking them to their houses where they committed immoral acts, keeping them as long as they liked and releasing them at their pleasure; they were openly cursing The Companions of The Prophet (upon him be peace) and were calling 'Ayisha The Honest (may Allah be pleased with her) an adulteress; the assignees were doing whatever they wished and were taking tribute from the peasants two or three times a year. It was said that a king called Majd ad Daula[2] had nine wives, all in wedlock, and was pleased to be styled King of Kings; moreover the peasants were spreading atheistic and Batini doctrines; they were abusing God (to Him be power and glory) and The Prophet (upon him be peace); they were denying The Creator in public, and repudiating prayer, fasting, pilgrimage and alms; the assignees were unable to restrain them, nor could they say anything about the impiety, tyranny and wickedness of the assignees; both parties were equally steeped in iniquity.

4. 'When I came to know about this state of affairs in 'Iraq, I decided to attend to the matter and give it priority over the war in Hindustan. I detailed Turkish forces, who were all pure Muslims of the Hanafi sect, to oppose the Dailamites and the atheists and the

---

[1] This amir of Kirman was not a contemporary of Sultan Mahmud.
[2] See Levy, *Mirror for Princes*, 134.

Batinis, and they were all exterminated; some fell by the sword, some were taken into bondage, and others were driven into exile. I dismissed all the officials in 'Iraq and gave their posts to civil servants and administrators from Khurasan, who were of the Hanafi or Shafi'i sects; both these sects are orthodox like the Turks, and hostile to the Rafidis, Batinis and other rebels. I did not permit a single 'Iraqi secretary to put pen to paper, because I knew that most of the scribes of 'Iraq belonged to heretical sects and would wreck Turkish interests. Thus in a short time by this process I cleared the country of heretics by the grace of Allah (to Him be power and glory); for God (be He exalted) created me and appointed me over the heads of His creatures for this purpose, that I should remove unbelievers from the face of the earth, protect the people of righteousness, and bring prosperity to the world through generosity and liberality.

5. 'Meanwhile I have been informed that a party of unbelievers from Kuch Baluch have committed highway robbery at Dair Gachin, and carried off some property. I wish you to apprehend them immediately and recover the property; then you may hang them all or send them manacled to the city of Rayy along with the stolen goods; that will teach them not to have the audacity to come from Kirman into my province for highway robbery. Failing this, Kirman is not far from Somnat; I will send my armies and wreak vengeance upon Kirman.'

6. When the messenger delivered this letter to Abu 'Ali Ilyas, he was very much afraid; he entertained the messenger well and sent back some gifts in deference to Mahmud—consisting of jewels of various kinds, choice objects out of the sea and a purse of gold and silver—saying, 'I am your obedient servant; but perhaps the king is not acquainted with the affairs of his servant and the province of Kirman; otherwise [he would know that] his servant has never acquiesced in any disorder, and that the men of Kirman are all Sunnis and righteous men who mind their own business; the mountains of Kuch Baluch are cut off from Kirman by narrow passes and difficult roads; I am driven to exasperation by these people as most of them are robbers and criminals, and they render two hundred farsangs of road unsafe by their activities; moreover they are very numerous and I cannot cope with them. The Sultan of the World

is more powerful; in all the world no one but he can deal with them; my loins are girt for any service he may require of me.'

7. When Mahmud received this reply from Abu 'Ali, he knew that what he said was true. He sent the messenger back again, with a robe of honour and told him to say to Abu 'Ali, 'Concentrate the troops of Kirman and make a circuit of the province; at the beginning of such-and-such month come to the frontier which faces towards Kuch Baluch and wait there. When a messenger comes from me with a certain sign, you should march immediately and attack the province of Kuch Baluch; kill every young man of them that you can find and give no quarter; seize the possessions of their women and old men and send them here so that I may distribute them among those who claim to have lost their property; make a firm agreement and settlement with them and then come back.'

8. Having sent the messenger to Abu 'Ali he made a proclamation that all merchants bound for Yazd and the Kirman road should settle their affairs and pack their loads; he would provide them with an escort and guarantee that if the robbers of Kuch Baluch carried off anyone's goods he would give compensation from the treasury.

9. When this news spread abroad an enormous number of merchants from surrounding parts gathered in the city of Rayy. Then at a definite time Mahmud despatched them with an amir and a hundred and fifty horsemen as escort, and reassured them by saying, 'Do not be anxious, for I am sending a large army in your tracks.' As he dismissed the escort, he summoned the amir in charge by himself and gave him a phial of deadly poison saying, 'When you reach Isfahan stay there for ten days, so that the merchants of that place may settle their affairs and travel in your company; during this time you should buy ten ass-loads of Isfahan apples of the best quality and load them upon ten camels; when you depart you should disperse these among the merchants' camels and keep going until you arrive at the stage after which, on the following day, you will reach the robbers; that night bring the loads of apples into your tent and strew them on the ground; plunge a packing-needle into each apple, sharpen a stick like a needle, dip it into the poison and put it into the hole in the apple; carry on until all the apples are poisoned; then arrange them back in the baskets with their cotton

packing; next day disperse these camels among the others and set out. When the robbers come out and attack the caravan, do not attempt to fight with them as they will be many and you few; retreat immediately taking with you any men that have arms, both mounted and on foot; go about half a farsang away and wait for a good hour; then set upon the robbers and I doubt not but that most of them will have perished from eating the apples; draw your swords and kill them all [on the spot] or pursue them and kill as many as you can. Having finished with them, send ten good riders with one horse apiece to Abu 'Ali Ilyas, taking my ring; inform him what you have done to the robbers of Kuch Baluch and instruct him to attack the province with his own troops in accordance with orders which he has already received, for by then it will be empty of brigands and trouble makers; then bring the caravan in safety to the frontier of Kirman, and join up with Abu 'Ali if you can.'

10. The amir said, 'I will do this, and my heart testifies that by Your Majesty's help the action will be successful, and that that road will remain open to Muslim travellers until the resurrection'; and he left Mahmud's presence. He moved off with the caravan and brought it to Isfahan; there he loaded ten camels with apples and set out for Kirman. The robbers had sent out spies to Isfahan and found out that the caravan was coming with so many thousand animals, bearing such a quantity of luxuries and valuables that God alone knew how much there was; such a caravan had not been seen before in a thousand years and they had an escort of a hundred and fifty Turkish horsemen. The robbers were delighted; they informed and summoned all the youths and brigands from every place in the whole of Kuch Baluch; four thousand fully armed men gathered on the roadside and remained in wait for the caravan.

11. When the amir arrived with the caravan at a certain stage, the residents of the place said, 'So many thousand robbers have blocked your road and have been waiting for you for a number of days.' The amir asked how many farsangs it was from there to the place where they were. They said it was five farsangs. When the people in the caravan heard this they were very anxious. They dismounted there. In the afternoon the amir called all the caravan leaders and men in charge of the freight and reassured them, saying,

'Tell me, which is better, life or wealth?' They all said, 'Life.' He said, 'You are rich men; we are ready to risk our lives for your sakes but we are not worried; so why do you worry about riches which can be replaced? After all, Mahmud has sent us here for a purpose; he is not angry with any of us that he should deliver us to destruction; his plan is to get back from these robbers some property which they stole at Dair Gachin belonging to an old woman; do you think then that he would let them have yours? Be of good cheer! Mahmud is not neglecting you; in fact he told me what he is doing; tomorrow when the sun comes up help will reach us from him, and all will be well, if Allah wills; however you must do everything that I tell you for your welfare lies in that.'

12. When the people heard these words they were pleased and encouraged. They said, 'We will do whatever you tell us.' He said, 'All those of you who have weapons and can fight, let them come to me.' They came and he counted them; with his own troops they came to three hundred and seventy men, both mounted and on foot. He addressed them, 'Tonight we march; those of you who are mounted will be with me at the front of the caravan, and those on foot will be at the rear, for it is the custom of these robbers only to take goods and not to kill anyone except a man who resists them and is killed fighting. Tomorrow by the time the sun reaches the height of two spears, we shall reach them; when they attack the caravan, I shall take to my heels in flight; when you see me turn my back, you all do the same, and I will make some show of fighting until you gain a distance of half a farsang; then I will gallop away and join you; after waiting for an hour we will return all together and fall upon the robbers, whereupon you will behold marvellous things; for thus I have been instructed and furthermore I know something about this which you do not; tomorrow you will see for yourselves; you will come to realize the greatness of Mahmud and understand that what I say is true.' They all undertook to obey and departed.

13. When night came on, the amir undid the loads of apples, poisoned them all and put them back in their baskets; he appointed five of his own men to look after these ten camel-loads of apples and said, 'When we run away and the robbers fall upon the caravan

72

and begin to break open the merchandise, cut the fastenings of the loads of apples, tear off the tops of the baskets and turn them upside down; then get yourselves gone.'

14. At midnight he ordered them to move off and they travelled in the same formation until it was day and the sun was up. The robbers rose up on three sides and ran towards the caravan with drawn swords. The amir made two or three counter-attacks and shot a few arrows; then he turned to flight. When the men on foot saw the robbers they fled; the amir picked them up about half a farsang away and kept them there. When the robbers saw that the escort were few and that they and the travellers in the caravan had fled, they were delighted and began breaking open the loads at their ease and getting busy with the merchandise. When they came to the apples they fell to and plundered the lot, eating them with relish; those who failed to get any were given some by the others and there were hardly any who ate no apples at all. After an hour they fell down one by one and died.

15. Two hours after daybreak the amir went alone to the top of a hill and looked down upon the caravan and the robbers; he saw men lying all over the plain as if they were asleep; he ran down the hill in joy and said, 'Congratulations to you all! Help has come from Sultan Mahmud, the robbers have been killed and scarcely one is left alive. Come on, my hearties, make haste; let us destroy the remnant!' He rode with his men towards the caravan and those on foot ran behind him. When they reached the caravan they saw the whole plain strewn with corpses, shields, swords, bows and arrows; a few of them who were still alive fled when they saw the soldiers. The amir rode after them and the men on foot also joined in the chase; they pursued them for two farsangs and did not turn back until they had killed them all; not a soul remained alive to carry the news of the event back to their own country. The amir ordered all their weapons to be collected and they amounted to several ass-loads. Then he took the caravan on to [the next] stopping place; nobody lost as much as a piece of thread and they could not contain themselves for joy. It was twelve farsangs from there to the place where Abu 'Ali Ilyas was. The amir sent ten pages to him post-haste with Mahmud's ring and informed him what had happened.

16. When Abu 'Ali received the ring he immediately set out for the province of Kuch Baluch with troops who were ready and rested. The amir joined forces with him and together they killed more than ten thousand of the inhabitants, seized several thousand dinars and collected a vast amount of goods, luxuries, arms and animals. Abu 'Ali sent all this booty with the amir to Mahmud. Mahmud issued a proclamation saying, 'Since I came to 'Iraq whoever has had anything stolen by the robbers of Kuch Baluch, let them come and take compensation from me.' Those who had claims came forward and went back satisfied. And for fifty years after that there was no report of any mischief from the Kuchis.

17. Thereafter Mahmud appointed reporters and intelligence-agents in every place, so that if anyone in Ghaznain wrongfully took a chicken from another or struck another man with his fist, Mahmud knew about it at Rayy and ordered amends to be made. From ancient times onwards kings have preserved this system, except for the house of Saljuq[1] who have shown no interest in the matter.

18. Abu 'l Fadl Sigzi[2] once asked The Martyr Sultan Alp Arslan (Allah have mercy upon him) why he had no intelligence-agents. He answered, 'Do you want me to cast my kingdom to the winds and alienate all my supporters?' He said, 'Why so?' The Sultan said, 'If I institute intelligence-agents, my especial favourites, trusting in their special position as favourites, will pay no attention to them nor offer them bribes; while my opponents and enemies will curry favour with them and give them money. Thus obviously the intelligence-agents will always bring to our ears bad reports about our favourites and good reports about our enemies. Now, reports good and bad are like arrows: if you shoot enough of them, at last one will hit the target. In this way we shall become more displeased with our favourites every day and eventually banish them, while admitting our enemies further into our intimacy. In a short time when we look [we shall find that] all our favourites are estranged and their places taken by our enemies. By that time irreparable harm will have been done.'

[1] See *Chahar Maqala*, Translation, 26. 10.
[2] Was amir of Sistan and died in A.D. 1072.

19. All the same it is better that there should be intelligencers, because having intelligencers is one of the rules of state-craft; and when they can be relied upon sufficiently to perform the function we have described, there is no anxiety.

## CHAPTER ELEVEN

*On honouring the sublime commands and edicts*
*which are issued from the court*

1. Letters are constantly being written from the court; the more numerous they become the less respect they command. Unless there is something important, letters should not be sent from The Lofty Throne. When a letter is despatched it should carry such weight that the recipient will not dare to put it out of his hand until he has complied with the order; and if it is known that anyone has not regarded such an order with due respect or has neglected to present himself with instant obedience, that person must be severely punished, even if he is one of the king's intimates. Such is the difference between the king and other men.

*The story of Sultan Mahmud and the disobedient tax-collector*

2. It is related that a woman having a grievance went from Nishapur to Ghaznain. She approached Sultan Mahmud and made her complaint, saying, 'The tax-collector of Nishapur has seized my farm and occupied it himself.' A letter was sent telling him to give back the farm. As it happened the tax-collector possessed the title-deeds to that farm; he said, 'The farm is mine, and I have the deeds; I can explain the situation at the court.' The woman went to Ghaznain a second time and stated her grievance. A page was sent to bring the tax-collector from Nishapur to Ghaznain. The sultan ordered him to be given a thousand strokes at the palace gate. Before they beat him, the tax-collector presented the title-deeds, brought

75

intercessors, and tried to buy off the thousand strokes with a thousand dinars of Nishapur; but it was no use and he suffered the thousand strokes. They rebuked him saying, 'Even if the farm was rightfully yours, why did you not obey the order first and afterwards explain your case? We would then have ordered what was appropriate.'

3. The purpose of this was so that when others heard such cases, no one would dare to disobey or violate the king's command.

4. Whatever concerns the king and falls to him to do or to order, such as castigation, decapitation, mutilation, castration or any other kind of punishment—if anyone does such a thing without the king's permission or command, even to his own servant or slave, the king must not agree to it but have the man punished, so that others may take warning and know their places.

### A story about King Parviz and Bahram Chubin

5. They say that King Parviz treated Bahram Chubin very well in the beginning; he was never without him for a moment. Whether in his cups, in the chase or in the seclusion of his chamber he never dismissed him from his presence. Now Bahram Chubin was unequalled as a horseman and unrivalled in single combat. One day they brought from the (fiscal) districts of Herat and Sarakhs three hundred red-haired camels for King Parviz, each carrying an assload of necessaries and various commodities. He ordered them to take the whole lot as it was to Bahram's palace for the supply of his household and kitchen.

6. The next day Parviz received information that that night Bahram Chubin had struck down his page and beaten him twenty strokes. King Parviz was angry and summoned Bahram. When he came he ordered five hundred swords to be brought from the armoury, and said, 'O Bahram, pick out the best of these swords.' Bahram chose a hundred and fifty. Then the king said, 'Now find the choicest of these you have chosen.' Bahram picked out ten swords. King Parviz said, 'Out of these ten swords choose two.' He selected two. He said, 'Now tell them to put these two swords into one scabbard.' Bahram said, 'O king, two swords will not go into

one scabbard.' Parviz said, 'And how will two commanders be contained in one city?' When Bahram heard this he immediately fell on the ground and did obeisance and asked for pardon, knowing that he had done wrong. King Parviz said, 'Were it not that you have served me well and I do not wish to cast down one whom I have myself raised up, I would not forgive you this sin. Leave this task to us, for God (to Him be power and glory) has appointed us judge over the earth, not you. Whoever has a dispute let him bring the case to us so that we may give the necessary commands with due fairness. After this if one of your underlings or slaves commits any crime, you will first inform us and we will order such punishment as may be suitable, so that nobody suffers unjustly. We pardon you this once.'

Such was the rebuke which was administered to Bahram Chubin who was his general and his favourite.

## CHAPTER TWELVE

*On sending pages from the court upon important business*

1. Pages[1] are frequently sent out from the court, some at the king's behest, some not. They are apt to be a source of trouble to the people and extort money from them. [Supposing there is] a case involving a sum of two hundred dinars, a page goes out and takes five hundred as a perquisite; this causes extreme embarrassment and poverty to the people. Pages should not be sent unless there is an urgent matter, and if they are sent it should be only at The Sublime Command; and they must be given to understand the exact amount due, and they are not to take any more than this by way of perquisite. Then everything will be in order.

[1] Persian *ghulām*. Ghulams were a 'pampered class' of boy-slaves: see Muhammad Nazim, *Sultan Mahmud*, 139. English 'page' corresponds in several respects and this rendering has been adopted consistently here.

# CHAPTER THIRTEEN

*On sending spies and using them for the good of the country and the people*

1. Spies must constantly go out to the limits of the kingdom in the guise of merchants, travellers, sufis, pedlars (of medicines), and mendicants, and bring back reports of everything they hear, so that no matters of any kind remain concealed, and if anything [untoward] happens it can in due course be remedied. In the past it has often happened that governors, assignees, officers and army-commanders have planned rebellion and resistance, and plotted mischief against the king; but spies forestalled them and informed the king, who was thus enabled to set out immediately with all speed and, coming upon them unawares, to strike them down and frustrate their plans; and if any foreign king or army was preparing to attack the country, the spies informed the king, and he took action and repelled them. Likewise they brought news, whether good or bad, about the condition of the peasants, and the king gave the matter his attention, as did 'Adud ad Daula on one occasion.

## The story of 'Adud ad Daula and the unjust judge

2. None of the Dailamite kings was more vigilant, clever and far-sighted than 'Adud ad Daula; he was a great builder and had lofty aspirations and strong authority. One day a reporter wrote to him as follows: On my way to perform the task for which Your Majesty sent me, I had passed through the city gate and gone about two hundred paces, when I saw a youth standing by the roadside with pale cheeks and wounds on his face and neck. He saw me and greeted me; I answered him and said, 'Why are you standing there?' He said, 'I am looking for a companion with whom I may travel to a city where there is a righteous king and a just judge.' I said, 'Do you know what you are saying? Do you want a more righteous king than 'Adud ad Daula, or a more learned judge than the qadi of the city?' He said, 'If the king were righteous and awake to affairs, the judge would be honest: since the judge is not honest the king

must be negligent.' I said, 'What negligence have you seen on the part of the king, or dishonesty on the part of the judge?' He said, 'My story was a long one, but now that I have left this city it is cut short.' I said, 'You must certainly tell me it.' He said, 'Come then; let us shorten our road with the tale.'

3. We set off together and he began, 'Know that I am the son of such-and-such a merchant, and my father's house is in such-and-such district of this city; everyone knows what sort of man my father was and how much money and wealth he had. When he died I spent several years indulging in drinking and debauchery; then I fell seriously ill and gave up hope of recovery. During that illness I vowed to God that if I got better I would go on pilgrimage and holy war; God sent me healing and I got up from my bed safe and sound.

4. 'When I had gained strength I decided to go on the pilgrimage, and later to go to the war. I freed all the slave girls and pages which I had, gave them gold and houses and farms, and betrothed them to one another. Then I sold the remainder of my property, estates and farms, realizing 50,000 dinars in cash. I reflected that the two journeys I had before me were full of danger, and that it would be unwise to take all this gold with me. So I resolved to take 30,000 dinars and leave 20,000. I went and bought two copper ewers and put 10,000 dinars in each one. I wondered with whom I should deposit them. Of all the people in the city I chose the chief qadi; I said to myself, "He is a learned man and a judge; and the king relies upon him and entrusts the lives and property of Muslims to him; he would never cheat me." I went and broached the matter to him. He accepted, and I was glad. I got up in the night, took the two ewers of gold to his house and deposited them with him. Then I set off upon the road and performed the Muslim pilgrimage. From Mecca I went to Medina, and from there I journeyed towards the sea of Rum. I joined up with the warriors and spent several years in holy war; in one battle I was caught in the midst of the infidels and was wounded on face, thigh and hand; I was taken prisoner by the Rumis and remained four years in bondage, until at length the Caesar of Rum fell ill and they set all prisoners free.[1] On gaining

---

[1] A Persian MS. gloss adds: 'for the sake of his recovery'.

my freedom I once more fell in with the irregulars and served with them long enough to save up my travelling expenses. All the time I was fortified by the knowledge that I had 20,000 dinars deposited with the qadi of Baghdad. In expectation of that I set out on the return journey.

5. 'Ten years later I reached Baghdad, destitute; my clothes were worn out and my body was weak from all the hardships and pains I had suffered. I went to the qadi, greeted him and sat before him; two days I called on him like this and he did not speak a word to me. On the third day I called again and gently said to him, "I am so-and-so, son of so-and-so; I have returned from the pilgrimage and holy war; I have borne many hardships and everything that I took with me has gone. I am just as you see me and I have not a single penny left. So I am in need of those two ewers of gold which I deposited with you." The qadi gave not the slightest answer; he did not even go as far as to say, "What on earth are you talking about?" He simply got up and went into his room. Disappointed I went away, and in my wretched and naked state I was too ashamed to go to my own house or to any of my relations or friends. By night I used to sleep in a mosque, and in the daytime I hid in a corner. To cut my story short, I spoke to the chief qadi several times in these terms, but he never answered me. On the seventh day I spoke more strongly. He said to me, "You are suffering from the melancholy; your brain has been desiccated by the dust and toil of travel and your speech is delirious. I do not recognize you nor do I know what you are talking about. As for the man whose name you mention, he was a handsome youth, prosperous and well-dressed." I said, "O qadi, I am that person but I have become pale and thin from hardship, and my face is ugly with wounds." He said, "Be off! don't give me a headache! go away in peace." I said, "O qadi, beware! fear God! for after this world there is another world, and every action has its reward or punishment." He said, "Away with you! don't annoy me!" I said, "Out of my 20,000 dinars 5,000 are yours." He made no reply. I said, "O qadi, I will give you one of the ewers for yourself, freely and willingly, but please give me back the other one, for I am in sore distress. Furthermore I am ready to sign a disclaimer, witnessed by honourable men, to say that I have no

claim upon you." The qadi said, "You are mentally deranged, verging on the point where I shall have to certify you as insane and send you to a lunatic asylum, where you will be put in fetters and never let out for the rest of your life." At this I was afraid, knowing that he intended to keep all my gold and that whatever order he issued would be carried out. I got up quietly and left him, repeating to myself the proverb, "If meat stinks you put salt on it: but what are you to do if the salt is stinking?" All justice is administered by means of the qadi; if the qadi is unjust who is to bring him to justice? If 'Adud ad Daula were a righteous ruler 20,000 gold dinars of mine would not be in the hands of the qadi, nor would I be hungry and destitute as I am, nor would I have abandoned my wealth, my property, my city and my country.'

6. When the reporter heard the man's tale of his experiences and circumstances, he was sorry for him and said, 'My noble friend, all hopes follow after hopelessness; trust in God, for it is God (to him be power and glory) who sets right the affairs of His servants.' Then he said to him, 'I have a friend in this village, a generous and hospitable man, and I am going to visit him. I am very happy to have you with me, so please accompany me; we will stay with my friend today and tonight, and see what happens tomorrow.' So he took him to the friend's house; he offered them what he had to eat, and then the reporter wrote an account of the man's circumstances and gave it to a villager, saying, 'Go to the gate of 'Adud ad Daula's palace, call such-and-such servant and give him this letter. Tell him that so-and-so has sent it and that he should deliver it immediately to 'Adud ad Daula and bring back an answer.' The messenger went and gave the letter to the servant; the servant straightaway delivered it to 'Adud ad Daula.

7. When 'Adud ad Daula read the letter, he bit his fingers [in vexation]; he sent someone at once to the reporter with the command that he should bring the man to him next day in the afternoon. When the reporter heard it he said to the man, 'Come, we must go to the city; 'Adud ad Daula is calling for both of us.' The man said, 'Is that a good thing?' He said, 'It is sure to be a good thing; maybe the wind heard what you were telling me on the road and brought it to the hearing of 'Adud ad Daula. I am hopeful that you will

soon get what you want, and find release from your troubles.' He set out and took the man to 'Adud ad Daula. The king made a place for the youth to sit down and asked him about his troubles. He told him the whole story. 'Adud ad Daula felt pity for him; he said, 'Do not worry; this is now my responsibility, not yours. The qadi is one of my officers, so it is my duty to deal with the matter, for God has given me the guardianship of this country to the end that I should not allow anyone to suffer trouble, least of all from the qadi. I have made him responsible for the lives and property of Muslims; I give him a monthly salary so that he should administer the affairs of the people with rectitude, acting in accordance with the religious law without fear or favour and not taking bribes. If this is the conduct of a venerable and learned man in my own capital, imagine what perfidy may be expected of younger, more reckless judges. In the beginning this qadi was a humble man with a large family, and the monthly payment which he receives consists of his salary and nothing more; today he owns such-and-such amount of landed property in the city of Baghdad; while there is no limit to the sumptuous furnishings which he has. All this wealth could not have been saved from that salary; so it is clear that he has gathered it from the Muslim people.' Then he turned to the man and said, 'I shall not eat happily nor sleep well until I restore you to your rights. Go, draw expenses from the treasury and proceed to Isfahan; remain there with a certain person and I will write and ask him to look after you well until I send for you again.' He then gave him two hundred gold dinars and five suits of clothes, and sent him to Isfahan that very night. The whole night 'Adud ad Daula wondered how he might contrive to extract this money from the qadi. He said to himself, 'If I were to exercise my sovereign power to arrest the qadi summarily and torment him, he would never confess and expose his own villainy; and then the money would be lost; moreover people would begin to wag their tongues and say that 'Adud ad Daula had seized a venerable and learned man like the qadi and was tormenting him to gain possession of his wealth; and the ill repute would spread to the farthest borders of the kingdom. I must devise some method of exposing the qadi's villainy so that this man will get back his money.'

8. A month or two passed after this and the qadi saw no more sign of the owner of the gold. He said to himself, 'I have won 20,000 dinars; but I will wait for another year; maybe I shall hear news of his death, for judging from his condition when I last saw him, I am sure he will soon be dead.'

9. Two months later 'Adud ad Daula sent someone in the hottest part of the day and called the qadi; he gave him a private audience and said, 'O qadi, do you know why I have troubled you to come here?' He said, 'The king knows best.' The king said, 'Know that I have become anxious about the future and because of my melancholy meditations sleep is scared away from my eyes; I have lost faith in the world and my kingdom, and I cannot depend upon further extension of life. There are two alternatives: either some upstart will arise from obscurity and snatch the kingdom from our hands as we snatched it from another—and consider what labours we endured before we could sit securely on this throne—or else The Truth's Command [i.e. death] will overtake us and cut us off, our desires unattained, from throne and kingdom. Nobody can avoid death; and if during our span of life, while our record-book is open, we are good and do good to God's creatures, people will speak well of us as long as the world exists and men are living, and on resurrection day we shall attain salvation and go to paradise; but if we are bad, and do ill to God's servants, people will speak ill of us until the end of time, and at the resurrection we shall be entangled and hell will be our place. Therefore as far as possible we strive after righteousness, we judge the people fairly and we practise charity. However, the reason for this conversation with you is that in the palace I have a handful of wives and children; now the matter of the boys is easy because they take wing like birds and can go from clime to clime; but the lot of the veiled ones is worse for they are weak and helpless; so I am taking thought in their regard now while I can, lest tomorrow death should befall me or the dynasty should change, and then if I wanted to do something for them I could not. Now I believe that in all the kingdom there is nobody more chaste, more lenient, more religious, and more trustworthy than you; therefore I wish to hand over a sum of 2,000,000 dinars in gold currency and jewels to you for safe keeping, so that nobody knows but you and I

and God. Then tomorrow if something were to happen to me and my womenfolk were reduced to poverty and privation you would call them secretly, divide the money amongst them and espouse them to suitable husbands, lest they should suffer the disgrace and distress of begging for their daily sustenance. To this end I propose that you should select a room in the inner apartments of your house and there construct a cellar of baked brick and make it secure; you should inform me when it is ready and one night I will arrange for twenty murderers who are due for execution to be brought out of prison; they will carry this money to your house, place it in the cellar, block up the door, and come back; then I will have them all beheaded so that the matter remains hidden.' The judge said, 'I obey, I will do my utmost to perform this service.' Then the king told a servant to go to the treasury, put two hundred *maghribi* [western] dinars in a purse and bring it to him.

10. When the servant brought the gold 'Adud ad Daula took it and laid it before the qadi saying, 'Use these two hundred dinars for making the cellar; if it is not enough, I will send more.' The qadi said, 'For Allah's sake, O king! I can use my own gold for this service.' 'Adud ad Daula said, 'I cannot agree to your spending your own gold on my affairs; your gold is your lawful property and is not suitable for this purpose. If you strive to carry out the task entrusted to you, you will have performed all the service required of you.' The qadi said, 'It is for the king to command;' he put the two hundred dinars in his sleeve and took leave of the king, congratulating himself and thinking, 'Fortune has befriended me in my old age and my household is going to be full of gold. If anything happens to the king, nobody will have a receipt or any other document and all the money will be left for me and my children. The owner of the two ewers was not able to get a tithe of his 20,000 dinars out of me, and he is alive; when the king is dead, who will be able to take anything from me?' He went and busied himself in building the cellar; within a month he completed a very secure underground chamber. One night about the hour of bedtime prayer he got up and went to 'Adud ad Daula's palace. 'Adud ad Daula gave him a private audience and said, 'What brings you here at this hour?' He said, 'I wanted to inform Your Majesty that what you commanded has

been finished.' 'Adud ad Daula said, 'I am glad to hear it; I knew you were zealous in all things; praise be to Allah that my opinion of you was not mistaken; you have saved me a lot of trouble in this matter. Out of the sum I mentioned to you I have got together 1,500,000 dinars in gold and jewels, and I need 500,000 more; so I have set aside a quantity of robes, incense, ambergris and camphor and I am arranging for sellers to dispose of it bit by bit and bring me the money; in a week's time it will be complete; then I will bring it in one lot to your house. But tomorrow night I wish to come incognito to see the cellar—just to cast an eye over it and see how it has turned out; I do not want you to put yourself out at all as I shall return immediately.' He dismissed the qadi and straight away sent a messenger to Isfahan to bring the owner of the gold. The next day he went to the qadi's house in the middle of the night to see the cellar; he approved of it and said to the qadi, 'You had better come and see me next Tuesday and have a look at what is ready.' He said, 'I will do so.' Having returned from the qadi's house the king ordered his treasurer to put a hundred and forty ewers full of gold into one room and on top of these to place three flasks of pearls, a golden cup full of sapphires, a cup full of rubies and a cup full of turquoises.

11. Tuesday came and the treasurer had carried out this order. 'Adud ad Daula called the qadi, took him by the hand and led him into the room where the valuables were laid out. The qadi was amazed when he saw the ewers. 'Adud ad Daula said, 'You can expect all this treasure to be brought during this week.' Then they came out of the room and the qadi returned to his house in such a state of excitement that his heart was fluttering in his breast. By chance the owner of the two ewers arrived on the next day. 'Adud ad Daula said to him, 'I want you to go and see the qadi straight-away and tell him that you have waited for some time and respected his authority, but you cannot forbear any longer; the whole city knows what wealth and substance you and your father had, and everyone can vouch for your claim; if he gives back your money, well and good, but if not, you will go straight to 'Adud ad Daula to lodge a complaint against him, and you will bring such a disgrace upon his head as will serve as a warning to the whole world.

See what answer he gives; if he gives the gold back, bring it to me as it is; if not, let me know quickly.'

12. The man went to the qadi, sat with him and spoke in these terms. The qadi thought, 'If this man plays a filthy trick on me and goes to 'Adud ad Daula, it may arouse his suspicions about me and he may not send the treasure to my house. The best thing is to give him back his money; after all, a hundred and fifty ewers of gold with all those jewels are better than two ewers.' So he said to the young man, 'Wait a few moments; I have been looking for you everywhere.' After a time he got up and went into a room; he called the man into the room, embraced him and said, 'You are my friend, you are my own son; I have been so very concerned on your behalf and I have been searching for you ever since you went away. Praise be to Allah that I have been able to see you again and discharge my responsibility. Your gold is still there.' He went and brought the two ewers, and said, 'Is this your gold?' The young man said, 'Yes.' He said, 'Receive it now and take it wherever you wish.' The man went out and fetched two porters; he put the ewers on their backs and took them as they were to 'Adud ad Daula's palace.

13. 'Adud ad Daula was holding audience and all the nobles of the state were present, when this young man came in with the two ewers, bowed and placed them in front of 'Adud ad Daula. The king laughed and said, 'Praise be to Allah that you have regained your rightful property and the qadi's treachery has been exposed; you little know what thoughts and schemes occupied me ere you recovered this gold.' The nobles asked to be enlightened. 'Adud ad Daula told them what had happened to the youth and what measures he had taken to help him; they were all astonished. Then he ordered the great chamberlain to go and bring the qadi of the city bareheaded before him, with his turban round his neck. The chamberlain went and brought the qadi in this fashion to 'Adud ad Daula.

14. When the qadi looked and saw the youth standing there with two ewers, he said, 'Woe! I am ruined!' and he realized that all that 'Adud ad Daula had said and done was aimed only at the recovery of those two ewers. 'Adud ad Daula then bellowed forth at him, saying, 'You are an old man, a scholar and a judge, on the brink

of the grave, and you dare to commit such treachery and cheat a man out of his deposit. What then are we to expect of other men? It is now clear that all the wealth which you possess has come from other Muslims' property and from bribes. As far as this world is concerned you will be punished by me; in the next world you will surely meet with due retribution. Considering that you are an old man and a scholar I am sparing your life, but all your money and property is for the treasury.' He confiscated all his wealth and estates and debarred him from ever holding office again: and he gave the two ewers to the noble youth and let him depart in peace.

### The story of Sultan Mahmud and the unjust judge

15. Sultan Mahmud son of Sabuktigin had a similar experience. One day when Sultan Mahmud was travelling a man gave him a petition couched in the following terms: I entrusted to the qadi of the city for safe keeping the sum of 2,000 dinars in a green brocade purse, closed and sealed; and I went on a journey. On the road to Hindustan robbers seized all that I had taken with me. On my return I went to the qadi, recovered my deposit and took it home. When I opened the purse I found it full of copper dirams. I went back to the qadi and said, 'I deposited a purse full of gold with you; now I find it full of copper; how is that?' The qadi said, 'When you handed it over, you did not count it out or shew me any gold at all; you brought me a closed and sealed purse and took it back intact. When I gave it back I asked you if it was your purse; you said it was yours and accepted it. Now you have come with this hollow pretence.' And he drove me away. For the sake of Allah, O sultan, come to my aid for I have not a single piece of bread to eat.

Sultan Mahmud took pity on him and said, 'Do not worry; I must do something about your gold. Go and bring the purse to me.' The man went and brought the purse to the sultan. However closely he examined the purse all over he saw no sign of it having been opened. He said to the man, 'Leave this purse with me, and take three maunds of bread and one of meat daily and one dinar every month from my steward, so that you will not be without provision while I see about your gold.' Then one day about the

time of the siesta Sultan Mahmud laid the purse in front of him and
began to ponder how it could have happened. At last he came to
the conclusion that it was possible for the purse to have been cut
open, the gold taken out, and the purse mended again. He had a
very fine coverlet of cloth of gold which was spread over a mattress.
In the middle of the night he got up and came down from the roof;
he got out a knife, slit about half a yard of the coverlet and went
back to bed. Early next morning he went out hunting for three days.

16. There was a certain palace cleaner who looked after this room.
In the morning he went in there to sweep it, and he saw the coverlet,
with about half a yard of it torn; he was frightened and began to
weep and tremble. In the cleaners' room was an old cleaner who
saw him weeping thus, and said, 'What is the matter?' He said,
'I daren't say.' He said, 'Don't be afraid; you can tell me.' He said,
'Someone has a grudge against me, and has gone into the sultan's
summer-house, and torn about half a yard of his coverlet. If the
sultan sees that he will kill me.' The old man said, 'Has anyone
else seen this besides you?' He said, 'No.' He said, 'Don't worry;
I know what to do and I will teach you. Firstly the sultan has gone
hunting; secondly there is in this city a mender called Ahmad, a
man of middle age, and his shop is in such-and-such quarter; he is
a most expert mender and all the other menders in the city are his
pupils. Take the coverlet to him, give him whatever fee he asks,
and he will do it so that not even an expert will know where it has
been mended.' The cleaner took the coverlet straightaway to the shop
of Ahmad the mender, and said, 'O teacher, how much would you
want for repairing this so that no one will know?' He said, 'I want
half a dinar.' The cleaner said, 'I will give you a whole dinar on
condition that you apply all the skill at your command.' He said,
'Thank you. Don't worry.' The cleaner gave him a dinar and said,
'I need it quickly.' He said, 'Come and take it tomorrow afternoon.'
Next day the cleaner went at the appointed time; the mender gave
him back the coverlet; he looked at it and he could not tell at all
where it had been torn; in good spirits he took it back to the palace
and spread it over the mattress.

17. When the sultan returned from hunting he went into the
summer-house; he looked and saw the coverlet intact. He said,

'Call the cleaner.' The cleaner came. The sultan said, 'This coverlet was torn; who has repaired it?' He said, 'O master, it was never torn; they are telling a lie.' He said, 'O fool, have no fear, for it was I who tore it; I did it for a purpose. Tell me truly; which mender mended this coverlet?' The cleaner said, 'O master, such-and-such mender did it.' The sultan said, 'I want you to bring the man here immediately; tell him the sultan summons him; when he arrives at the palace bring him to me.' The cleaner ran out and called the mender and brought him to the sultan's presence. When he saw the sultan sitting alone he was frightened; the sultan said to him, 'Have no fear, O teacher; tell me, did you repair this coverlet?' He said, 'Yes.' He said, 'You did it extremely skilfully.' He said, 'By the grace of Your Majesty it was done satisfactorily.' He said, 'Is there anyone in this city more expert than you?' He said, 'No.' He said, 'I have something to ask you; answer me the truth.' He said, 'To speak the truth to the king is always the best thing to do.' The sultan said, 'In the last six or seven years have you mended a green brocade purse at any gentleman's house?' He said, 'I have.' He said, 'Where?' He said, 'At the house of the qadi of the city, and he gave me two dinars for my fee.' He said, 'If you saw that purse again would you recognize it?' He said, 'I would.' The sultan put his hand under the mattress, withdrew the purse and gave it to the mender, saying, 'Is this the purse?' He said, 'Yes.' He said, 'Shew me where you repaired it.' The mender laid his finger on the spot. The sultan was amazed at the skill with which it had been done, and said, 'If the need arises could you give evidence against the qadi?' He said, 'Why not?' The sultan sent a man at once to call the qadi, and he ordered the owner of the purse to be brought in.

18. When the qadi appeared he greeted the sultan and sat down in his place as usual. Mahmud turned to him and said, 'You are an old man and a scholar; I have given you jurisdiction over Muslim citizens and committed their lives and property to your judgment; I have trusted you [and preferred you]—are there not two or three thousand men who are more learned than you but unemployed?— is it fair then, that you should deal falsely and disregard the duties of a trustee, by unjustly appropriating a Muslim's property and depriving him of it?' The qadi said, 'O master, what words are these

and who is saying them?' He said, 'Thou hypocrite dog, these deeds are thine, and these words are mine:' and he shewed him the purse and said, 'Do you recognize this purse? This is the one which was deposited with you for safe keeping, and you cut it open, and took out the gold, and put copper in its place, and had the purse mended again; after that you told the owner that he had brought it closed with his own seal and taken it back intact. Do you call this right conduct and honest dealing?' The qadi said, 'I have never seen this purse before nor am I aware of the purport of Your Majesty's discourse.' Sultan Mahmud said, 'Bring in those two men.' A servant went and brought the owner of the purse and the mender. The sultan said, 'Thou liar, this is the owner of the gold, and that is the mender who mended this purse.' The qadi was put to shame; his face turned pale and he began to tremble so much that he was unable to utter another word. The sultan said, 'Lay hands on him and make sure that he gives back this man's gold immediately; if not, I shall order him to be executed.' They dragged the qadi half-dead from the sultan's presence and put him in the guard-house. He called his steward and gave him a sign; the steward went and brought 1,000 Nishapuri dinars, all of fine standard, and gave them to the owner of the purse.

19. Next day Sultan Mahmud held court for the redress of wrongs and publicly declared the perfidy of the qadi. Then at his command the qadi was brought and suspended head downwards from a pinnacle of the palace. The nobles actively interceded for him pleading his age and learning. At length he offered to redeem himself for 50,000 dinars; this was accepted, and the ransom was exacted from him, but never again was he allowed to practise his profession.

20. There are many stories of this kind. These few have been related so that The Master of the World may know how zealous different kings have been in the pursuit of justice and equity; what care they have taken that the oppressed should receive their rights; and what measures they have adopted to remove evil-doers from the face of the earth. Sound judgment is a better thing for a king to have than a powerful army; praise be to Allah that The Master of the

World possesses both these things. This chapter has dealt with spies; and this work must be in the hands of trustworthy people. Let such men continually be procured and sent to all parts.

## CHAPTER FOURTEEN

*Concerning constant employment of messengers and carriers*

1. Messengers must be posted along the principal highways, and they must be paid monthly salaries and allowances. When this is done, everything that happens throughout the twenty-four hours within a radius of fifty farsangs will come [to their knowledge]. In accordance with established custom they must have sergeants to see that they do not fail in their duties.

## CHAPTER FIFTEEN

*On being careful about giving verbal orders in
drunkenness and sobriety*

1. Verbal orders [from the king] reach the divan and the treasury concerning matters of state, fiefs or gifts. It may be that some of these commands are [given] in a state of merriment. Now this is a delicate matter and it needs the utmost caution. Or possibly the bearers of the message may not agree, or have not heard correctly. Such a mission must be entrusted to one person only, and he must deliver the message personally, not through a deputy. And it must be the rule in those cases [where there is doubt about an order] that, in spite of the fact that an order has been delivered, it must not be executed or acted upon until its substance has been referred by the divan back to The Sublime Intellect [for confirmation].

# CHAPTER SIXTEEN

*Concerning the steward of the household and the
importance of his post*

1. The office of steward of the household has fallen into disuse nowadays. This work always used to be entrusted to someone well-known and respected, for a person whose duties concern the royal palace, the kitchen, cellars and stables, the king's children and his retainers, must have daily access to The Lofty Throne for discourse with the sovereign. He must [be free to] present himself at any hour of the day to report on all matters, to ask advice and to render account of all his arrangements and transactions. So he needs to command complete respect in order to be able to do his work and discharge his duties successfully.

# CHAPTER SEVENTEEN

*Concerning boon-companions and intimates of the king and the
conduct of their affairs*

1. A king cannot do without suitable boon-companions with whom he can enjoy complete freedom and intimacy. The constant society of nobles [such as] margraves and generals tends to diminish the king's majesty and dignity because they become too arrogant. As a general rule people who are employed in any official capacity should not be admitted as boon-companions nor should those who are accepted for companionship be appointed to any public office, because by virtue of the liberty they enjoy in the king's company they will indulge in high-handed practices and oppress the people. Officers should always be in a state of fear of the king, while boon-companions need to be familiar. If an officer is familiar he tends to oppress the peasantry; but if a boon-companion is not familiar the king will not find any pleasure or relaxation in his company. Boon-

companions should have a fixed time for their appearance; after the king has given audience and the nobles have retired, then comes the time for their turn.

2. There are several advantages in having boon-companions: firstly they are company for the king; secondly since they are with him day and night, they are in the position of bodyguards, and if any danger (we take refuge with Allah!) should appear, they will not hesitate to shield the king from it with their own bodies; and thirdly the king can say thousands of different things, frivolous and serious, to his boon-companions which would not be suitable for the ears of his wazir or other nobles, for they are his officials and functionaries; and fourthly all sorts of sundry tidings can be heard from boon-companions, for through their freedom they can report on matters, good and bad, whether drunk or sober; and in this there is advantage and benefit.

3. A boon-companion should be well-bred, accomplished and of cheerful face. He should have pure faith, be able to keep secrets and wear good clothes. He must possess an ample fund of stories and strange tales both amusing and serious, and be able to tell them well. He must always be a good talker and a pleasant partner; he should know how to play backgammon and chess, and if he can play a musical instrument and use a weapon, so much the better. He must always agree with the king, and whatever the king says or does, he must exclaim, 'Bravo!' and 'Well done!' He should not be didactic with 'Do this' and 'Don't do that' for it will displease the king and lead to dislike. Where pleasure and entertainment are concerned, as in feasting, drinking, hunting, polo and wrestling—in all matters like these it is right that the king should consult with his boon-companions, for they are there for this purpose. On the other hand in everything to do with the country and its cultivation, the military and the peasantry, warfare, raids, punishments, gifts, stores and travels, it is better that he should take counsel with the ministers and nobles of the state and with experienced elders, for they are more skilled in these subjects. In this way matters will take their proper course.

4. Some kings have in the past made their physicians or their astrologers boon-companions, so that their opinions could always

be sought about what was advisable and what was inadvisable. The physician looked after the king's health, and the astrologer gave warning of good and bad auguries; he kept watch on the time and the hour, and chose the right moment for every enterprise. Other kings have refused to have them and said, 'The physician forbids us to eat the things we like and gives us medicine when we are not ill and bleeds us when we have no pain; likewise the astrologer prevents us from doing what we want to do and hinders us from important business; and when you consider, both of them do nothing but keep us back from the pleasures, appetites and desires of this world, and make our life miserable; so it is better that we should call for them only when we need them.'

5. A boon-companion is more highly esteemed if he is a man of experience and has travelled widely and served great people. When people want to know the character and disposition of the sovereign they judge by his boon-companions; if they are good-natured, affable, liberal, patient, merciful and gracious, they will know that the king has a kindly nature, a pleasant disposition, good morals and acceptable manners; but if his boon-companions are sour-faced, haughty, foolish, miserly and wanton, people will judge that the king is of unpleasant disposition, evil nature, bad temper and bad morals.

6. And further every one of the boon-companions should have a rank and degree; some have sitting status, others standing status. From ancient times this has been the custom at the courts of kings and caliphs; and it is a custom that is still observed. The present caliph has as many boon-companions as his fathers had before him; and the sultans of Ghaznain have always had twenty companions, ten standing and ten sitting; they took the custom and procedure from the Samanids. The king's boon-companions must be given salaries, and treated with the highest respect among the retinue; they must know how to control themselves, be polite and shew affection for the king.

# CHAPTER EIGHTEEN

*On having consultation with learned and experienced men*

1. Holding consultations on affairs is a sign of sound judgment, high intelligence and foresight. Every person has some knowledge and in every branch of knowledge one knows more and another less. One may have knowledge and never have put it into practice or tested it; another has that same knowledge, and has used it and tried it. For example one may have read in medical books the cure of this pain or that sickness and know by heart the names of all the specific medicines, but no more; while another knows these same medicines and has used them in treatment and tried them many times. Never will the first be on a level with the second. Likewise a man who has travelled widely and seen the world and experienced heat and cold and been in the midst of affairs is not to be compared with one who is untravelled and inexperienced. Thus it has been said that one ought to take counsel with the wise, the old and the experienced. Further, some people have sharper wits and quicker perception of affairs; others have duller intellects. The wise have said, 'The counsel of one man is like the strength of one man, and the counsel of ten persons is as the strength of ten.' Everybody in the world agrees that there has never been any mortal wiser than The Prophet (upon him be peace); and with all the wisdom that he had —for he could see behind him as well as in front; and the skies and the earth, the tablet and the pen, the throne and seat [of God], paradise and hell and all things in between were revealed to him, and Gabriel (upon him be peace) often used to visit him, bringing inspiration and giving news of things past and things to come—in spite of all this perfection, in spite of all his miracles, God (be He exalted) said to him [in the Quran 3. 153], 'Consult them in affairs.' ('O Muhammad, when you do any work or when you are confronted with an important matter, confer with your companions.') Since God commanded him to seek advice and even he needed counsel, it is obvious that nobody can need it less than he.

2. Thus when the king does any work or is confronted with urgent business, it is his duty to take counsel with wise and loyal

friends. Each person will say what comes to his mind and the king's opinions will be compared with what everyone else says. When they all hear one another's words and thoughts and discuss them, the right course will stand out clearly, and the right course is that which all agree to be imperative.

A man who does not take counsel in affairs shews weak judgment; a man of this kind is called self-willed. No task can be accomplished without men of the proper skill; no more can any enterprise succeed without deliberation. Praise be to Allah that The Master of the World is endowed with sound judgment and served by men of prudence as well as skill. [I could say more] but I have set down here what comes within the scope of this book.

# CHAPTER NINETEEN

*Concerning special [guards] and their equipment and administration*

1. There should be kept at the court two hundred men called special [guards], men chosen for good appearance and stature as well as for great manliness and bravery. A hundred of them should be Khurasani and a hundred from Dailam and their duty is to be in constant attendance upon the king both at home and abroad. They are permanently attached to the court and must be finely attired. Two hundred sets of weapons are to be kept ready for them and issued to them when duty commences and withdrawn when they are dismissed. Of those weapons twenty sword-belts and twenty shields should be of gold, and a hundred and eighty belts and shields of silver, together with spears of Khat.[1] They should be paid adequate salaries and allowances. There should be a sergeant to every fifty men and his job is to know all about his men and to give them their orders. They must all be good horsemen and be provided

---

[1] According to *Nuzhat al Qulub* (Gibb Memorial, Old Series, XXIII) Khat was 'an island in the Persian Gulf near to India'.

with the necessary trappings, so that upon all important occasions they will not fail to perform their special functions.

2. The names of four thousand unmounted men of all races should always be kept on the rolls. One thousand picked men are exclusively for the king and three thousand are to be attached to the retinues of governors and army-commanders so as to be ready for any emergency.

# CHAPTER TWENTY

*On the provision and use of special weapons studded with precious stones*

1. Twenty special sets of arms, studded with gold, jewels and other ornaments, must always be kept ready and stored at the treasury, so that whenever ambassadors arrive from distant parts of the world, twenty pages finely attired can take these weapons and stand round the throne. And although our sovereign (praise be to Allah The Mighty) has attained such a lofty state that he can do without such ceremonies, nevertheless the pomp and circumstance of the kingdom and kingship must accord with the highmindedness of the king. Today there is no king on earth greater than The Master of the World (may Allah perpetuate his reign) and there is no kingdom more vast than his. So it is fitting that wherever other kings possess one of a thing, our sovereign should have ten; where they have ten he should have a hundred, for he has at his command all spiritual and material resources, coupled with a sound judgment. In fact he lacks nothing of majesty and dominion.

# CHAPTER TWENTY-ONE

### *Concerning ambassadors and their treatment*

1. When ambassadors come from foreign countries nobody is aware of their movements until they actually arrive at the city gates; nobody gives any information [that they are coming] and nobody makes any preparation for them; and they will surely attribute this to our negligence and indifference. So officers at the frontiers must be told that whenever anyone approaches their stations they should at once despatch a rider and find out who it is who is coming, how many men there are with him, mounted and unmounted, how much baggage and equipment he has, and what is his business. A trustworthy person must be appointed to accompany them and conduct them to the nearest big city; there he will hand them over to another agent who will likewise go with them to the next city (and district), and so on until they reach the court. Whenever they arrive at a place where there is cultivation, it must be a standing order that officers, tax-collectors and assignees should give them hospitality and entertain them well so that they depart satisfied. When they return, the same procedure is to be followed. Whatever treatment is given to an ambassador, whether good or bad, it is as if it were done to the very king who sent him; and kings have always shewn the greatest respect to one another and treated envoys well, for by this their own dignity has been enhanced. And if at any time there has been disagreement or enmity between kings, and if ambassadors have still come and gone as occasion requires, and discharged their missions according to their instructions, never have they been molested or treated with less than usual courtesy. Such a thing would be disgraceful, as God (to Him be power and glory) says [in the Quran 24. 53], 'The messenger has only to convey the message plainly.'

2. It should also be realized that when kings send ambassadors to one another their purpose is not merely the message or the letter which they communicate openly, but secretly they have a hundred other points and objects in view. In fact they want to know about the state of roads, mountain-passes, rivers and grazing grounds, to see whether an army can pass or not; where fodder is available and

where not; who are the officers in every place; what is the size of that king's army and how well it is armed and equipped; what is the standard of his table and his company; what is the organization and etiquette of his court and audience-hall; does he play polo and hunt; what are his qualities and manners, his designs and intentions, his appearance and bearing; is he cruel or just, old or young; is his country flourishing or decaying; are his troops contented or not; are the peasants rich or poor; is he avaricious or generous; is he alert or negligent in affairs; is his wazir competent or the reverse, of good faith and high principles or of impure faith and bad principles; are his generals experienced and battle-tried or not; are his boon-companions polite and worthy; what are his likes and dislikes; in his cups is he jovial and good-natured or not; is he strict in religious matters and does he shew magnanimity and mercy or is he careless; does he incline more to jesting or to gravity; and does he prefer boys or women. So that, if at any time they want to win over that king, or oppose his designs or criticize his faults, being informed of all his affairs they can think out their plan of campaign, and being aware of all the circumstances, they can take effective action, as happened to your humble servant in the time of The Martyr Sultan Alp Arslan (may Allah sanctify his soul).

3. In all the world there are only two doctrines which are good and on the right path; one is that of Abu Hanifa and the other that of ash Shafi'i (Allah's mercy be upon them both) and all the rest are vanity and heresy. Now The Martyr Sultan (Allah's mercy upon him) was so strict and exact in his personal religion that he was often heard to say, 'What a pity! if only my wazir[1] were not of the Shafi'i persuasion.' He was exceedingly imperious and awe-inspiring and because he was so fanatical in his beliefs and disapproved of the Shafi'i religion I lived in constant fear of him.

4. Now it chanced that the sultan decided on [an expedition to] Transoxiana[2] because the khan of Samarqand, Shams al Mulk Nasr ibn Ibrahim,[3] was being refractory. He called his troops and

---

[1] Internal evidence of the authorship of the book.

[2] It was on this expedition in 465/1072 that Alp Arslan met his death.

[3] See *Chahar Maqala*, Translation, 52, 126, note XXII; Barthold, *Turkestan*, 314–16; Lane-Poole, *Dynasties*, 134–5.

sent an envoy to Shams al Mulk; and I sent Danishumand Ashtar
on my own behalf with the sultan's envoy to let me know what
happened. The envoy went there and delivered his message. The
khan sent him back here together with an envoy of his own. Now
it is customary for ambassadors to have access to the wazir every now
and then, and to make requests and say things to him which perhaps
they cannot say to the sultan to his face, and the wazir passes them
on to the sultan. About the time of their departure [back to Samar-
qand] I happened to be sitting in my tent in the company of some of
my friends, playing chess, and I had just beaten one of them and
taken his ring as a forfeit. The ring was too big for the [ring-] finger
of my left hand so I had put it on (the finger of) my right hand. It
was announced that the envoy of the khan of Samarqand was at the
door. I said, 'Bring him in,' and ordered the chess to be taken away.

5. The ambassador came in and sat down, and said what he had
to say to me. I was all the time turning this ring on my finger, and
the ambassador noticed both finger and ring. When he had finished
his business he rose and went. The sultan gave orders that the envoy
of the khan was to be dismissed, and himself appointed another
ambassador to convey his reply. I again sent Danishumand Ashtar
with the envoy as he was a clever man. When the envoys reached
Samarqand they presented themselves in front of Shams al Mulk,
and in the course of the interview he asked his own envoy, 'How did
you find the sultan as regards judgment, appearance and conduct?
What is the size of his army? how are they equipped? what is the
organization of his court, audience-hall and divan, and on what
principles is the country ruled?' The envoy said, 'O master, the sultan
lacks nothing in appearance, bearing, manliness, power, dignity
and command. As for his forces, God knows their number; and
there is no estimating the magnificence of their arms and accoutre-
ments. The organization of his court, audience-hall, divan and
household is excellent. Nothing is wanting in their country; but they
have one fault; if it were not for that, there would be no other.'
Shams al Mulk said, 'What is that fault?' He said, 'The sultan's
wazir is a Rafidi.' [1] He said, 'How do you know?' He said, 'Because
one day, after the morning prayer I went to his tent to speak to him.

---

[1] 'Heretic': another pejorative term applied by the Sunnis to the Shīʿites.

There I saw him with a ring on his right hand and he was turning it on his finger as he spoke to me.' Danishumand Ashtar wrote to me immediately saying, 'Such-and-such was said about you in front of Shams al Mulk by his ambassador; I thought you had better know.' I was very much disturbed through fear of the sultan, and said [to myself], 'He disapproves of the Shafi'i religion and he is always reproaching me for it; if by any means he should hear that the Jikilis[1] have described me as a Rafidi and said as much in front of the khan of Samarqand, he will not let me off with my life.' In spite of my innocence I spent 30,000 dinars undemanded and unsolicited, and gave several presents and pensions to prevent this report from reaching the ears of the sultan.

6. Your humble servant has related this story because ambassadors are generally censorious and always on the look out to see what faults there are in kingdom and kingship, and what virtues; then next time they will convey censure and criticism of those things from their kings. With this in mind past kings, when they have been intelligent and alert, have always refined their manners, and adopted good customs, and kept worthy men of pure faith for employment at the court, lest anyone should find fault with them.

7. For an embassy a man is required who has served kings, who is bold in speaking but does not say too much, who has travelled widely, who has a portion of every branch of learning, who is retentive of memory and far-seeing, who is tall and handsome, and if he is old and wise, that is better. If a boon-companion is sent as an envoy he will be more reliable; and if a man is sent who is brave and manly, skilled in arms and horsemanship, and renowned as a warrior, it will be extremely good, for he will shew the world that our men are like him; and if an ambassador be a man of noble family that will be good too, for they will have respect for his ancestry. Very often kings have sent envoys bearing gifts of money, valuables or weapons and shewn themselves weak and submissive; after giving this illusion they have followed up by preparing their forces, sending picked men in to the attack and defeating the enemy. The conduct and good sense of an ambassador are a guide to the conduct and wisdom of his king.

[1] See Barthold, *Turkestan*, 254 note, 317.

# CHAPTER TWENTY-TWO

*On keeping fodder ready at posting houses*

1. When The Exalted Stirrup proceeds on a journey, there may not be fodder and provisions ready at every station where he halts, and so the rations for the day will have to be procured at great trouble and inconvenience, or even seized from the peasants by shares. This a bad procedure. On all the roads by which the king is going to pass, at every village which is a stopping place, if the environs of it are feudal estates or crown lands, supplies should be requisitioned; but in places where there is no village and no inn, there may be some village in the vicinity; [before requisitioning supplies] they must wait while the harvest in the district is being gathered; then if the provisions are required, they will be used; and if the king does not travel in that direction [after all], the produce should be sold and the money brought to the treasury like other revenues. In this way the peasants will suffer no distress, there will be no breakdown in the supply of fodder, and the king will not fail in the important task which he has undertaken.

# CHAPTER TWENTY-THREE

*On settling the dues of all the army*

1. The troops must receive their pay regularly. Those who are assignees of course have their salaries to hand independently as assigned; but in the case of pages who are not fit for holding fiefs, money for their pay must be made available. When the amount required has been worked out according to the number of troops, the money should be put into a special fund until the whole sum is in hand, and it must always be paid to them at the proper time. Alternatively the king may summon the men before him twice a year, and command that they be paid, not in such a way that the

task be delegated to the treasury and they receive their money from there without seeing the king; rather the king should with his own hands put it into their hands (and skirts), for this increases their feelings of affection and attachment, so that they will strive more eagerly and steadfastly to perform their duties in war and peace.

2. The system of the kings of old was such that they used not to give fiefs; every soldier was paid by the treasury four times a year in cash according to his rank, and they were always well supplied and provisioned, and whatever the emergency two thousand horsemen instantly mounted and set out to meet it. The tax-collectors collected the money and sent it to the king's treasury, and once every three months it was paid out to the troops; and they called this *bistgāni*. This system and custom is still followed by the house of Mahmud.

3. Assignees of land must be told that whenever a man becomes absent from their troops through death or any other cause, [the troop-leaders] should at once report the fact and not keep it concealed; and the troop-leaders should be instructed that once they have received their pay they are to keep all their men ready for such exigencies as may arise; and if any man takes leave of absence, they are to report it immediately, so that the vacancy may be filled. If they do otherwise they are to be reprimanded and to suffer stoppage of pay.

# CHAPTER TWENTY-FOUR

## *On having troops of various races*

1. When troops are all of one race dangers arise; they lack zeal and they are apt to be disorderly. It is necessary that they should be of different races. Two thousand Dailamites and Khurasanis should be stationed at the court. Those that exist at present should be retained and the remainder be levied; and if some of these are from Gurjistan [Georgia] and Shabankara (in Pars), it will be suitable because men such as these are all good.

2. It was the custom of Sultan Mahmud (Allah's mercy be upon

him) to have troops of various races such as Turks, Khurasanis, Arabs, Hindus, men of Ghur and Dailam. When he was on an expedition, every night he used to detail several men of each group to go on guard and allotted each group their station; and for fear of one another no group dared to move from their places until daybreak; thus they all kept watch together. And when it was the day of battle, each race strove to preserve their name and honour, and fought all the more zealously lest anyone should say that such-and-such race showed slackness in battle. Thus all races endeavoured to surpass one another. Since the fighting men possessed this esprit de corps they were all valiant and intrepid. Consequently once they had taken up their arms they did not retreat one pace until they had defeated the enemy.

3. When once or twice an army has waxed valiant and gained victory over the enemy, thereafter a mere hundred of their horsemen will be a match for a thousand of the enemy and no force will ever again be able to oppose that triumphant army and all the armies of neighbouring countries will fear that king and submit to him.

# CHAPTER TWENTY-FIVE

### *On taking hostages and keeping them at the court*

1. The rulers of the Arabs, Kurds, Dailamites, Rumis and others who have only recently come to terms of submission must be told that each of them should keep a son or a brother resident at the court; there should be, if not a thousand, never less than five hundred of them. At the end of a year they can send replacements and the first ones can go back home, but they are not to start back until their replacements arrive here. In this way no one will be able to rebel against the king because of the hostages. In the case of the Dailamites and the people of Kuhistan, Tabaristan, Shabankara and suchlike who hold fiefs and land grants, similarly five hundred of them should reside at the court, and then if any need arises the court will never be lacking in useful men.

104

# CHAPTER TWENTY-SIX

## On keeping Turkmans in service like pages

1. Although there has arisen a certain amount of aversion to the Turkmans,[1] and they are very numerous, still they have a long-standing claim upon this dynasty, because at its inception they served well and suffered much, and also they are attached by ties of kinship. So it is fitting that about a thousand of their sons should be enrolled and maintained in the same way as pages of the palace. When they are in continuous employment they will learn the use of arms and become trained in service. Then they will settle down with other people and with growing devotion serve as pages, and the dislike which is generally felt for them on account of their nature will disappear; and whenever the need arises 5,000 or 10,000 of them, organized and equipped like pages, will mount to perform the task for which they are detailed. In this way the empire will not leave them portionless, the king will acquire glory, and they will be contented.

# CHAPTER TWENTY-SEVEN

## On organizing the work of slaves and not letting them crowd together while serving

1. Slaves[2] who stand in attendance are apt to crowd together[3] in the performance of their tasks [both in the palace] and on hunting expeditions; and when they promptly disperse [to perform a task], they just as promptly come back [in a crowd]. But when orders are given in decisive terms and they are told once or twice how they

[1] See Lambton, *Landlord and peasant*, 56; Barthold, *Turkestan*, 309.
[2] Persian *bandagān*, 'unskilled slaves', as distinct from ghulams who were trained slaves.
[3] Persian *zaḥmat mī-kunand*: see *Rahat as Sudur*, 503 (glossary).

are to behave, then they will act accordingly and there will be no need for this inconvenience. Alternatively [pages should be employed and] clear orders should be given how many water-bearers, arms-bearers, wine-bearers, robe-bearers and the like should report for duty every day, and how many of those pages who have reached the rank of amir-chamberlain and great amir [should attend]; then every day they will come for service from each tent in the required numbers; likewise with the private [servants of the king], so that there is no crowding. Moreover in all former times, from the day they were bought until the time of their superannuation pages have been efficiently organized as to their education and training, but in these days the custom and system have fallen into disuse. Your humble servant will mention a little of what is needed to fulfil the purpose of the book, in the hope that it meets with the approval of The Sublime Intellect.

## Concerning the training of pages of the palace[1]

2. This is the system which was still in force in the time of the Samanids. Pages were given gradual advancement in rank according to their length of service, their skill and their general merit. Thus after a page was bought, for one year he was commanded to serve on foot at [a rider's] stirrup, wearing a Zandaniji[2] cloak and boots; and this page was not allowed during his first year to ride a horse in private or in public, and if it was found out [that he had ridden] he was punished. When he had done one year's service, the tent-leader spoke to the chamberlain and informed him; then they gave him a small Turkish horse, with a saddle covered in untanned leather, and plain bridle and stirrup-leathers. After serving for a year with a horse and whip, in his third year he was given a belt to gird on his waist. In the fourth year they gave him a quiver and bow-case which he fastened on when he mounted. In his fifth year he got a better saddle and a bridle with stars on it, together with a handsome cloak and a club which he hung on the club-ring. In

---

[1] Errors in the numbering of chapters began when scribes numbered this sub-heading as Cap. 28.

[2] See Le Strange, *Lands*, 462.

the sixth year he was made a cup-bearer and had a goblet to hang from his waist. In the seventh year he was a robe-bearer. In the eighth year they gave him a single-apex, sixteen-peg tent and put three newly bought pages in his troop; they gave him the title of tent-leader and dressed him in a black felt hat decorated with silver wire and a cloak made at Ganja. Every year they increased his rank and responsibility until he became a troop-leader, and so on until he became a chamberlain. When his suitability, skill and bravery became generally recognized and when he had performed some outstanding actions and been found to be considerate to his fellows and loyal to his master, then and only then, when he was thirty-five years of age, did they make him an amir and appoint him to a province.

3. Alptigin who was the slave and nursling of the Samanids reached the rank of army-commander of Khurasan at the age of thirty-five. He was outstandingly trustworthy, faithful and courageous. He was a Turk, prudent, skilful, popular, devoted to his troops, liberal, hospitable and God-fearing. He had all the good qualities of the Samanids and he governed Khurasan and 'Iraq for many years. He had 1,700 Turkish pages and slaves. One day he had bought thirty Turkish pages; Sabuktigin, the father of Sultan Mahmud, was among them. The first piece of good fortune which happened to Sabuktigin was that he was bought by Alptigin; the second thing was that three days later he was standing among the pages in front of Alptigin, when the chamberlain came up and said to Alptigin, 'Such-and-such a page who was a tent-leader has died; to which page do you desire to hand over his tent and troop and outfit?' Alptigin's eye fell upon Sabuktigin and he uttered the words, 'I grant it to this page.' The chamberlain said, 'O master, it is yet but three days since you bought this slave; he must do seven years' service before he reaches this rank; how is he fit to receive it now?' Alptigin said, 'I have spoken;'—and the page heard this and bowed—'I give him this as an exceptional case; hereafter you must follow the usual rule.' So they gave him the tent, and the fruit of seven years' service was his. Alptigin thought to himself, 'It is possible that this page is of high birth, of a noble family in Turkistan; maybe he will be favoured by fortune and will have a great career.' Then he began to test him, sending him with messages for all and

sundry, and saying, 'Now repeat what I have told you.' Sabuktigin would repeat it all without a mistake. Then Alptigin would say, 'Go and bring back the answer.' He would go and bring back the answer even more efficiently than he had carried the message. When Alptigin found him every day increasing in aptitude he began to feel affection for him in his heart. He made him a water-bearer and ordered him to serve him personally. He gave him a troop of ten pages and continually promoted him further.

4. When Sabuktigin was eighteen years old he had two hundred manly pages in his troop. He had assimilated all the ways of Alptigin, in such matters as etiquette, his habits in eating, drinking and entertaining, in hunting, polo and archery, in shewing kindness to people and treating the members of his troop as brothers. In fact, if ever he had an apple in his hand, he wanted to share it with ten of his fellows; and because of his good qualities everyone loved him.

*The story of Alptigin and Sabuktigin*

5. One day Alptigin detailed two hundred pages to proceed to the Khalaj Turks[1] and the Turkmans to collect some money which was due from them; Sabuktigin was a member of the party. When they arrived the Khalaj Turks and Turkmans refused to pay the dues in full. The pages were enraged and put their hands to their weapons, intending to fight with them and take the money by force. Sabuktigin said, 'I am certainly not going to fight and I dissociate myself from such action.' His comrades asked why. He said, 'Our master did not send us here to fight; rather he told us to go and collect some money. If we fight now and they beat us, it will be extremely humiliating for us and detrimental to the prestige of our master; furthermore our master will blame us for fighting without his order; we shall have no defence or excuse and as long as we live we shall never be absolved from this reproach.' When Sabuktigin said this, most of the pages agreed that it was right; there was some argument amongst them, but in the end they gave up the idea of fighting and returned home. When they reported to Alptigin and told him that the people had resisted and refused to pay the money,

[1] See Minorsky, *Hudud al 'Alam*, III, 347.

Alptigin said, 'Why did you not take up arms and seize the money from them by force?' The pages said, 'We buckled on our armour and were going to fight, but Sabuktigin would not let us; there was a difference of opinion amongst us, so in the circumstances we returned home.' Alptigin said to Sabuktigin, 'Why did you not fight and not allow the pages to fight?' Sabuktigin said, 'Because The Master had not commanded us to fight; if we had fought without The Master's orders, then each one of us would have been a master not a slave, for the mark of a slave is that he does only what his master tells him. If we had been beaten, The Master would inevitably have asked who gave us the order to fight, and what defence should we have had against your wrath? and if we had beaten them, some people would undoubtedly have been killed, and not only should we have received no sympathy or thanks, but we should also have been censured. If you command us to go and fight, then we shall either obtain the money or die in the attempt.' Alptigin was pleased and said, 'He is right.' So Alptigin continued to promote Sabuktigin until he reached a position where he had three hundred pages in his troop.

6. Now when the amir of Khurasan, Nuh ibn Nasr,[1] died at Bukhara, Alptigin was at Nishapur; the courtiers wrote to Alptigin from the capital to inform him of the situation and said, 'The amir of Khurasan has passed away, leaving a brother thirty years old and a son sixteen years old; which of them do you command us to put on the throne, for you are the mainstay of the kingdom?' Alptigin quickly sent the messenger back with a letter, saying, 'Both are worthy of the throne and kingdom; both are princes of my master's family; of the two the king's brother is a man of ripe experience who has known the ups and downs of life; he knows people well and he recognizes and respects everyone's merit, rank and dignity; on the other hand the king's son is an inexperienced boy; I fear he could not control the people nor could he give effective commands on every subject. Perhaps it would be better to put the brother on the throne.' The next day he sent another letter in the same terms. Five

---

[1] These events took place on the death of ʿAbd al Malik: see *Tarikh-i Guzida*, 384. ʿAbd al Malik is also left out of the author's reckoning at p. 160, line 20, and p. 227, line 27.

days later a messenger arrived bearing the news that the king's son had been enthroned. Alptigin then felt uneasy about the two letters which he had sent; he said, 'Ignoble wretches! when all along they were going to do this on their own responsibility, why did they consult me? As far as I am concerned both the princes are as the light of my eyes; however it worries me that I indicated a preference for the brother, because when my letters reach the capital, the king's son will be displeased; he will think that I favoured his uncle; he will be offended with me and harbour resentment in his heart; then interested persons will try to influence the young prince and estrange him from me.' He straightaway sent off five dromedaries and ordered the drivers to try to overtake the two messengers and turn them back before they crossed the Oxus. The drivers made haste and caught one of them in the desert near Amuy [Amul], but the other one had crossed the Oxus.

7. When Alptigin's letter reached Bukhara, the young prince and his supporters were affronted and said, 'He was wrong to choose the king's brother; does he not know that a man's heir is his son not his brother?' They continued to talk in this vein with the result that every day the prince became more displeased with Alptigin, while Alptigin sent a multitude of apologies and presents, but these in no way removed the cloud of vexation from the prince's heart; interested parties carried on their mischief and the prince's resentment and bitterness grew. Now Alptigin had originally been bought [as a slave] by Ahmad ibn Isma'il towards the end of his life; then he served Nasr ibn Ahmad for a number of years; when Nasr passed away, he served Nuh ibn Nasr, and it was during Nuh's reign that he became army-commander of Khurasan. When Nuh died, this young prince Mansur, his son, succeeded his father. Six years after the accession of Mansur to the kingship, when Alptigin had spent a large amount of money and tried every possible device, he was still unable to win his heart because of the malicious utterances of the time-servers. Meanwhile Alptigin's agents wrote and told him of all that went on in the capital.

8. Then the mischief-makers said to Mansur ibn Nuh, 'Until you kill Alptigin you will not become the real ruler of this kingdom; for fifty years he has exercised sovereignty in Khurasan and amassed

great wealth and treasure; all the troops are obedient to his word; when you capture him you will have peace of mind and your treasuries will be filled with his riches. The best plan is to summon him to the court on the pretext that since your accession to the throne he has not appeared at the court to renew his allegiance; moreover you are eager to see him because he is in the position of grandfather to you; although the foundations of the dynasty rest on him and he is the mainstay of government in Khurasan and Transoxiana, nevertheless the matters which are still being discussed all arise from the fact that he never comes to see you; he should come to the court as soon as possible and rectify any faults in the organization of the court and the audience-hall; thus will your confidence in him be increased and the tongues of the self-seekers be silenced. When he comes here, summon him privately and have him decapitated.'

9. Mansur did accordingly and called Alptigin to the court. Alptigin's agents wrote and warned him of the purpose of the summons. He announced that he was going to Bukhara, and ordered his men to get ready and pack their baggage. He set out from Nishapur and came to Sarakhs, accompanied by about 30,000 horsemen and all the amirs of Khurasan. After three days' rest there he summoned the army-commanders and said, 'I have something to say to you; tell me what you think is right, for our welfare and yours depends on it.' They said, 'We obey.' He said, 'Do you know the reason why Mansur has summoned me?' They said, 'He wishes to see you and enter into a new agreement with you, for you are like a father to him.' He said, 'It is not as you think. The king is calling me for the purpose of cutting off my head; he is a boy and knows nothing of men's worth. You know full well that for sixty years I have been sustaining the Samanid dynasty; I defeated several of the khans of Turkistan who attacked their territory; I subdued rebels wherever they arose; and I was never insubordinate in the slightest degree; it was I who kept the boy's father and grandfather on the throne. Now at last this is to be my reward—he wants to destroy me! he does not even know this much, that his kingdom is like a body and I am its head; when the head has gone how will the body survive? What then do you see fit to do? By what means can we deal with this threat?' All the amirs said, 'There is no means

III

but the sword. If he esteems you thus, what can we expect of him?
If anyone else had been in your position he would have snatched
the kingship from their hands fifty years ago. We all recognize you,
not him nor his father, because we, and everyone who has acquired
some standing in the Samanid empire, have all obtained our
livelihood, rank, dignity and suzerainty from you; to you we owe
our positions, and with you we remain; Khurasan, Khwarazm and
Nimruz are yours beyond dispute. Say farewell to Mansur ibn Nuh
and occupy the throne yourself. If you wish, let him keep Bukhara
and Samarqand; if not, take possession of them as well.' On hearing
the amirs speak with such fervour, Alptigin said, 'Allah have mercy
on you; I know that these words of yours have been spoken out of
honesty and sincerity; this is indeed what I would expect of you.
May God (to Him be power and glory) reward you with all blessings. Now return to your quarters for today, and we will see what
tomorrow brings forth.'

10. At this time there were 30,000 horsemen with Alptigin; had
he wanted he could have raised 100,000. The next day all the amirs
came for audience with Alptigin; he came out and sat down. After
a time he faced them and said, 'When I spoke to you yesterday I
wanted to test you, to see whether you are sincerely with me or not;
and whether you will stand by me and support me in the event of
certain circumstances arising. In fact, the things which I heard you
say were all in keeping with your nobility and loyalty; you have
fulfilled the duty of gratitude and I am well satisfied with you.
However you must know and be aware that I cannot now guard
against mischief from this boy except with the sword; he is a mere
child, and knows nothing of his obligations; he listens to the words
of some baseborn villains and cannot distinguish between good and
evil; he abandons a man like me who has all along been the mainstay of his family; and he takes a handful of rogues who only want
to turn the country upside down and could not correct even the
slightest disorder in the country's affairs, and regards them as his
friends; while he tries to do away with me. I could depose him and
put his uncle on the throne, or even take the kingship myself; but
I think people would say that for sixty years Alptigin protected the
house of the Samanids who were his original masters, and in the

end when he was eighty years old he revolted against them and snatched the kingship from their hands by the sword, putting himself in place of his masters and scorning the duty of gratitude. I have done good works all my life and earned a good name; now that I am on the brink of the grave it is not fitting that I should do something that would bring disgrace upon me; however much it is evident to us that the fault is on the amir Mansur's side, nevertheless everyone does not know this, and some would surely say that Alptigin was to blame. And although I do not covet their throne and wish them no harm, as long as I remain in Khurasan this kind of talk will go on and they will antagonize this boy against me more and more; but if I leave Khurasan and go out of his kingdom, the slanderers will have nothing left to say; and moreover, if hereafter I must needs fight to get my daily bread and pass the remainder of my life, very well then, let me draw my sword against the infidels and so gain the spiritual reward. Now you know, O commanders of the army, that Khurasan, Khwarazm, Nimruz and Transoxiana belong to the amir Mansur, and you are all his troops whom I have been commanding on his behalf. Arise and go to the capital; see the king, renew your commissions and place yourselves at his service; for I intend to go to Hindustan and engage in holy war against the infidels; if I am killed I shall be a martyr, and if I am given grace to succeed I shall turn the house of idolatry into the house of Islam, in the hope of paradise and for the sake of God and The Prophet. Whether my past actions have been good or bad, the amir of Khurasan will no longer be troubled by me, and the tongues of the talkers will be silenced. Hereafter Khurasan, its army and people are his concern.'

11. After making this speech Alptigin got up and said to the amirs, 'Come before me one by one so that I may bid you farewell.' The amirs expostulated, but without result, and they began to weep; with tears in their eyes each one came forward, embraced him and withdrew; when he had said goodbye to them all he retired into his pavilion. In spite of all this nobody believed that Alptigin would leave Khurasan and go to Hindustan, because in Khurasan and Transoxiana he possessed estates amounting to five hundred villages, nor was there a city where he did not own houses, gardens and inns;

in addition he had 1,000,000 sheep and 100,000 horses, mules and camels. Then one day the sound of drums was heard and Alptigin was seen to depart with his pages and followers and proceed in the direction of Balkh, leaving behind him all this wealth. The amirs of Khurasan then all went to Bukhara.

12. On arrival at Balkh, Alptigin resolved to stay there for one or two months to allow all intending holy warriors to come together from Transoxiana, Khutlan and the neighbourhood of Balkh; he would then set out for Hindustan. The slanderers and time-servers persuaded the amir Mansur that Alptigin was an old wolf and that he would not be secure until he had destroyed him; he should send troops after him to capture him and bring him to the capital. So Mansur sent an amir with 16,000 horsemen from Bukhara to Balkh, but by the time they reached Tirmidh and crossed the Oxus, Alptigin had set out from Balkh and gone towards Khulm. Between Balkh and Khulm there is a narrow valley four farsangs long which is called the Khulm pass, and in this valley to the left and right there are villages. Alptigin encamped in the valley and set two hundred horsemen at the head of the valley to keep watch. At this time he had 2,200 slave pages of his own, all good fighters, and eight hundred horsemen who had joined him for holy war.

13. When the amir Mansur's troops reached the pass, they encamped on the plain outside and could not enter the valley. They remained like this for two months. Then one day Sabuktigin happened to be in charge of the watch; when he came to the head of the valley he saw the plain full of troops, with advanced guards posted. He thought to himself, 'Our master has left all his goods and riches with the amir of Khurasan and gone forth to holy war. Now they have designs upon his life and ours, but such is his characteristic loyalty, charity and courtesy towards them that I am afraid he will lead himself and us to destruction. This matter can only be settled by the sword, and as long as we remain quiet, they will not desist from following us. God Almighty helps those who suffer oppression; they are the oppressors and we are the oppressed.' He turned to the pages who were in his troop and said, 'Now our turn has come for action; if they win, not one of us will remain alive. Let us try our hand today and see what happens. Whether our master approves or

not, let fate decide.' So saying, he and his three hundred pages attacked the enemy advanced guard, overpowered them at once and fell upon their camp. By the time they had put on their armour and mounted their horses more than a thousand of them had been struck to the ground; when they rallied and shewed their strength Sabuktigin retreated to the head of the valley.

14. News was brought to Alptigin that Sabuktigin had engaged in battle and killed a number of the enemy. Alptigin summoned him and said, 'Why are you so hasty? You should have waited.' He said, 'O master, how could we wait any longer? Our patience is exhausted. Now is the time for us to fight for our lives. This affair cannot be settled except by the sword. As long as we have breath we will fight for our master, come what may.' Alptigin said, 'Now that you have roused the enemy, a better plan will have to be made. Tell the men to strike camp and pack up the baggage; after the bedtime prayer they should decamp and take all the impedimenta outside the pass; Taghan should move with a thousand pages secretly into a certain ravine on the left-hand side and you are to take a thousand pages into another ravine on the right-hand side; I shall move out of the pass with one thousand horsemen and stop on the plain. Next day, when they come to the head of the pass and see nobody there they will think I have fled; they will mount and gallop after us, making their way into the pass; when about half of them have emerged from the pass they will see us standing on the plain; you will then rush out from your ambushes on both sides, brandishing your swords; when the battle-cry goes up, some of the enemy troops who have emerged from the pass face to face with me, will take to their heels, and others will be stopped by you; I will then attack them from the front, and you will assault them from the pass, intercept them in the middle and lay about them with your swords; as long as they resist we will continue to belabour them; when they turn tail, we will leave the way of flight open for them, and then retire ourselves; we will come out of the pass, fall upon their camp and seize the booty.'

15. This plan was followed. The next day Mansur's troops put on their armour and went to the head of the pass, ready for battle. They saw nobody there. They went into the pass for a distance of

about one farsang. They saw no sign of Alptigin's camp; they were convinced that Alptigin had fled. The troops were told, 'Make haste! Let us pursue him. When we get out of the pass on to the plain, we shall overtake them in an hour and capture Alptigin.' So they rode on at speed with all their best men to the fore. As they emerged from the pass they saw Alptigin with about one thousand horse and a few foot arrayed on the plain. As soon as half of them came out of the pass, Taghan rushed out of the ravine on the left-hand side and attacked with his thousand pages; he forced the advancing troops to retreat and put them to flight, killing a number of them; and on the right Sabuktigin also sallied forth and attacked. Taghan and Sabuktigin then joined forces to the rear of the enemy troops who had emerged from the pass, while Alptigin assaulted them from the front; together they engaged the enemy and soon struck a number of them to the ground; the enemy commander was speared in the belly and the lance went right through and came out behind, so that he was killed. At this the enemy were routed and they fled in all directions wherever they could find a way of escape. Then Alptigin's pages came back through the pass and fell upon the enemy camp; they seized all the horses, mules, camels, gold and silver articles, money and slaves that they could find and departed, leaving the tents, carpets and suchlike; and for the next month the peasants of the district were carrying off goods from that camp. They counted the slain, and they came to 4,750 men, not counting the wounded.

16. Then Alptigin set out from Khulm and went to Bamiyan. The amir of Bamiyan took up arms against Alptigin and was captured. Alptigin pardoned him and gave him a robe of honour. This amir of Bamiyan was the one known as Shir Barik. Alptigin proceeded from there to Kabul and defeated the amir of Kabul, capturing his son whom he subsequently favoured and sent back to his father. The amir of Kabul's son was the son-in-law of Lavik. Then Alptigin attacked Ghaznain; the amir of Ghaznain fled and went to Sarakhs. When Alptigin arrived at the gates of Ghaznain, Lavik came out and did battle with him. The amir of Kabul's son was taken prisoner a second time. Lavik was defeated and retired within the city. Alptigin then encamped at the gates and lay

siege to the city. He issued a proclamation [to his own troops] forbidding them to take anything from the people without payment in gold and threatening to punish anyone who was found to have done so. He thus gained the respect of the population of Zavulistan.

17. Now one day Alptigin caught sight of one of his Turkish pages coming along with a nose-bag of hay and a chicken tied to his saddle-straps. He said, 'Bring that page to me.' The page was brought. Alptigin asked him, 'Where did you get this hay and this chicken?' The page said, 'I took it from a peasant.' Alptigin said, 'Do you not receive your pay every month?' He said, 'I do.' Alptigin said, 'Then why did you not pay for these things? This is why I give you monthly wages, in order that you should not harass the poor with extortions; furthermore I forbade you by proclamation to take anything from anybody without paying.' He then ordered that the page was to be cut in two and hung up by the side of the road at that very spot together with the nose-bag of hay and the chicken; and he had it proclaimed for three days that if anybody purloined private property he would suffer the same punishment as this page. The soldiers were afraid and the peasants were safe. Thereafter enormous amounts of provender were brought into the camp every day from the villages of the district; but Alptigin did not allow a single apple to be taken into the city.

18. When the citizens of Ghaznain saw such justice and protection, they said, 'We want a king who will be just and give us security for our lives, property, women and children, no matter whether he be Turk or Persian.' And on the same day they opened the gates of the city and came to Alptigin. On seeing this Lavik shut himself up in the city's fort. After twenty days he came out and went before Alptigin. Alptigin gave him a pension and made Ghaznain his own permanent seat; he did no harm to anyone at all.

From there Alptigin went to Hindustan and brought back plunder. From Ghaznain to the land of the infidels was two days' march. The report spread in Khurasan, Transoxiana and Nimruz that Alptigin had broken open the doors of Hindustan and found so much wealth there, in gold and silver, animals and slaves, that God alone knew the amount thereof. From right and left men came to join Alptigin so that the number of his followers rose to 6,000 horsemen. He captured several provinces and subdued the country as far as Peshawar. The king of Hindustan put into the field a force of 150,000 horse and foot and 500 elephants, with the object of expelling Alptigin from Indian territory or destroying him and his army. From the west Mansur, amir of Khurasan, still smarting from the defeat and slaughter of his troops in the Khulm pass, sent a man called Abu Ja'far with 25,000 horsemen to contend with Alptigin. Alptigin let Abu Ja'far approach to within a farsang's distance of Ghaznain and charged out with his 6,000 horse; he assailed the Khurasani forces and in an hour he defeated their 25,000 horse a thousand times more thoroughly than he had defeated them outside Balkh. Abu Ja'far fled and it happened that he became separated from his men and found himself alone. Peasants caught him and seized his horse, arms and all that he had. He returned to Balkh on foot and in disguise. All the Khurasani army's equipment and stores fell into Alptigin's hands as booty; and the amir of Khurasan was never able to oppose Alptigin again. The alienation and separation of Alptigin severely weakened the position of the Samanids and left them open to attack from the khans of Turkistan.

19. Having thus dealt with Abu Ja'far, Alptigin turned his attention to the king of Hindustan. He wrote letters to Khurasan and elsewhere seeking support. So many men joined him, being attracted by the prospect of booty, that when mustered they totalled 11,000 horse and foot, all young men, fully armed. He advanced to meet the king of Hindustan and made a surprise attack on his advanced guard, killing more than 10,000 men. He did not stop to gather booty but withdrew in haste. The king's army chased after him but failed to find him. There were some high mountains in the midst of which was a pass; and the Indian king's road lay through that pass. Alptigin seized the head of the pass so that when the king arrived he could not enter it; so he encamped there and remained for two months; every now and again Alptigin would sally forth and kill a number of the Hindus. Sabuktigin exerted himself greatly in this war and performed several valiant deeds. The king of Hindustan was in a hopeless position; he could not go forward and it was impossible for him to go back without accomplishing his purpose or reaching a settlement. Eventually the king of Hindustan made a proposal in

these words: 'You have come here from Khurasan through lack of bread; let me give you grants of land, let me provide you with fortresses, and you become part of my army.' Alptigin's troops agreed to this and the two sides came to terms. However, the king had secretly instructed the fortress-commanders not to hand over the fortresses when he withdrew. The king withdrew and the fortresses were not handed over. Alptigin said, 'It is they who have broken the agreement, not I.' Again he resumed his attacks, capturing cities and laying siege to those fortresses. During these operations Alptigin died. His soldiers and pages were left dumbfounded and bewildered, while on all sides they were surrounded by infidel forces.

20. So they sat down and held council together, saying, 'Alptigin has no son to take his father's place and become our leader. Now we have gained the utmost prestige and respect in Hindustan and indeed the Hindus stand in awe of us. If we occupy ourselves with arguments as to who is superior or who is senior, and if each man tries to lord it over the rest, then our prestige will be shattered and the enemy will gain the upper hand over us; and if we disagree amongst ourselves, instead of wielding the sword against the infidels we shall have to use it against one another, and we shall lose the territory which we have acquired. The best plan is for us to choose the most suitable man among us, make him our commander, accept whatever he commands and treat him as if he were Alptigin.' They all said, 'We have no other remedy but this.' Then they enumerated the names of the senior pages; each one was found to have some objection or shortcoming, until they came to Sabuktigin; when his name was mentioned, they all became silent. Then one of them said, 'There are some pages who were bought before Sabuktigin and have seen longer service than him.' Another said, 'As regards intelligence, gallantry, manliness, generosity, hospitality, charity, good nature, piety and fidelity Sabuktigin lacks nothing; moreover he was brought up by our master, and our master was pleased with his work; in fact he has all the virtues, in character and conduct, of Alptigin, and he well knows the measure of our worth and rank. I have said what I know. You do what you think best.' For some time they discussed the pros and cons; at last they agreed to make Sabuktigin their commander. Sabuktigin would not raise his head until they

pressed him; then he said, 'If it is inevitable, I accept this duty on condition that if anyone opposes me, or disobeys me, or neglects to carry out my command, you will support me and put him to death.' All swore their acceptance and vowed their inviolable allegiance. Then they took Sabuktigin and seated him upon Alptigin's cushion, saluting him as amir and scattering gold and silver in celebration.

21. Every enterprise and every expedition that Sabuktigin undertook was successful. He married the daughter of the mayor of Zavulistan and she gave birth to Mahmud. This is why he was called Mahmud Zavuli. When he grew up he went on many expeditions and journeys with his father. After Sabuktigin had performed many great exploits, fought many battles, defeated mighty armies, and conquered many provinces in the land of India, he received from the caliph of Baghdad the title of Nasir ad Din [Helper of the Faith]. When Sabuktigin died, Sultan Mahmud took his father's place. He had learnt all the procedure of government from his father, and he always loved to listen to the history of kings; so all the principles which he adopted were laudable. He went and conquered the province of Nimruz, he subjugated Khurasan, and he advanced far enough into Hindustan to capture Somnat[1] and bring back the idol; he slew the kings of India, and finally attained that peak of eminence which he did attain.

22. My humble purpose in relating this story is that The Master of the World (may Allah perpetuate his reign) may know how to recognize a good slave and not try to wound the feelings of one who has done creditable service, who has never committed any act of treason or perfidy, but has strengthened the throne and blessed the empire; nor should he listen to the words of those who seek to incriminate him; rather he should trust him more and more every day, for dynasties, kingdoms and cities may at any time be dependent upon one man,[2] and when that man is removed from his

[1] Muhammad Nazim, *Sultan Mahmud*, 115 and App. M gives an account of the expedition to Somnat.

[2] Nizam al Mulk supports the old Iranian belief, which goes right back to the Avesta, in the *farr-i kayani* 'royal splendour', mysteriously vested in a person, an animal (as in the story of Ardashir Babakan) or an object (e.g. a ring).

place, the dynasty crumbles, or the city is destroyed, or the country is thrown into confusion. For instance Alptigin was a good slave and he was a pillar of the Samanid kingdom; but they did not realize his worth and sought to destroy him. When he left Khurasan, fortune deserted the Samanid dynasty. A slave whom one has brought up and promoted and esteemed, must be looked after, for it needs a whole lifetime and good luck to find a worthy and experienced slave. Wise men have said that a worthy servant or slave is better than a son. On this subject the poet says:

> One obedient slave is better
> than three hundred sons;
> for the latter desire their father's death,
> the former long life for his master.

# CHAPTER TWENTY-EIGHT

*Concerning the conduct of private and public audiences*

1. It is necessary to have some system for giving audiences. First of all the relatives [of the king] come in, after them distinguished members of his train, then other classes of people. If they all come in at once, [the correct] distinction between humble and noble is not observed. Raising of the curtain is the sign that an audience is in progress; when the curtain is lowered it indicates that there is no audience, except for persons who are summoned. Thus nobles and army officers, by sending a servant to the court, can find out whether there is an audience or not; then if there is an audience and they need to present themselves, they come; otherwise they do not come. For there is nothing more annoying for nobles and officers than to come to the court and have to return without seeing the king. If they come several times and fail to gain audience, they form a bad opinion of the king and begin to plot mischief. When the king is difficult of access the affairs of the people are put into suspense, evil-doers are encouraged, facts remain concealed, the army suffers harm

and the peasants fall into trouble. There is no better rule for a king than to hold frequent audiences. When he gives audience, margraves, amirs, lords and imams should bow as they come in; with regard to commoners, the procedure is that when they have seen the king they and all their followers retire, so that only the select courtiers remain; and the pages who come in with them must retire also, so that none are left but courtiers and those pages who are actually on duty such as arms-bearers, water-bearers, food-tasters and the like, who are of course required to be present. When this system has been in force for some time, it will become habitual and remain established. Then all crowding will be avoided, and there will be no need for drawing the curtain and closing the door. Any arrangements other than these should not be permitted.

## CHAPTER TWENTY-NINE

*Concerning the rules and arrangements for drinking parties*

1. A week is occasionally given over to convivial pleasures and when this is done public audiences should be held on one or two days, so that those whose custom it is to appear, may come forward and nobody will be debarred. People will have been informed which is the day for them to come, and on days reserved for the elite, commoners will know that there is no place for them and of their own accord will stay away, so that there will not be the necessity of admitting one person and refusing another. Those who are admitted to royal parties must be scrutinized to see who they are and it should be a condition of their admission that they do not come with more than one page each. It is intolerable that anyone should bring his own flagon and cup-bearer; such a custom has never existed before and is extremely reprehensible; for in all ages people have taken away eatables, sweetmeats and wines from kings' palaces to their homes, not from their own homes to royal parties, because the sultan is the paterfamilias of the world, and all the human race are his children

and slaves. It is not right that those who are his family and his dependents should take their own wine and food to his parties, for his housekeeping ought to be better, more lavish and cleaner than that of any of the nobles; and if the reason why they bring their own wine is that the king's wine-bearer gives them bad wine, he should be punished, because he is issued with nothing but good wine; there is no reason why he should give bad. Then this excuse will be removed.

2. Suitable boon-companions are indispensable to the king, for if he spends too much time with slaves they become arrogant and it lessens his majesty and spoils his dignity; and it is a sign of weak character too, for they are only fit for serving; and if he consorts too much with nobles, generals and civil governors it injures the king's authority; they grow too familiar and become slack in obeying orders and defraud the state of money. On all matters concerning the provinces, the army, finance, cultivation, dealing with the enemies of the country, and things of this kind, it is fitting that the king should converse with his wazir. Now these things are all such as increase his fatigue and anxiety and torture his spirit, because wisdom and pride will not, for the sake of the welfare of the state, allow him to take liberties and be facetious with men of this order. It is only through his boon-companions that the king's spirit is set free, and if he wants to live more fully, to refresh himself in sport and jest, to tell stories, jokes and curious tales, he can enjoy these things with his boon-companions without detriment to his majesty and sovereignty, because he keeps them for this very purpose. But we have already written a chapter on this subject.

# CHAPTER THIRTY

*On slaves and servants standing in order when they are on duty*

1. The order in which slaves and servants stand must be laid down. Each one must have a definite place, for standing and sitting

in the presence of kings are both alike [in having different degrees]; the same order must be observed in standing as in sitting. The principal members of his private staff stand near and around the throne, such as arms-bearers, cup-bearers and the like; and if anyone tries to stand among them the chamberlain of the court will send him away, and likewise if he sees any stranger or unsuitable person among any group he will shout at him and not let him stand there.

## CHAPTER THIRTY-ONE

### *On preparing arms and equipment for wars and expeditions*

1. Notables who receive large allowances (for clothing) must be told to have arms and equipment ready for war and to buy pages, for their grandeur, nobility and dignity consist in these things, not in the magnificence of their household decorations and furniture. The man who has more of the former will be more acceptable in the sight of the king, and will acquire greater prestige and power among his equals and his subordinates.

## CHAPTER THIRTY-TWO

### *Concerning the requests and petitions of soldiers, servants and retainers*

1. Every request which is made by soldiers must be passed on through the mouths of their troop-leaders and superior officers, so that if a favourable answer is given, it will be received from their hands. By this means they will gain the respect of the men, for when the men state their wants themselves, there is no need for an intermediary and so the troop-leader loses respect. If any member of a

troop is insolent to his superior officer or fails to give him due respect and oversteps his bounds, he must be punished so that the proper distinction between superiors and subordinates is maintained.

# CHAPTER THIRTY-THREE

*On reprimanding those in high positions when they are*
*guilty of mistakes or wrongs*

1. Men who are promoted and elevated to high rank have to spend time and trouble in the performance of their duties, and when, as sometimes happens, they make a mistake, if they are publicly reprimanded they suffer loss of honour and no amount of goodwill or favour will restore them to their positions. It is better that when anyone commits a fault, it should first of all be overlooked; later on he should be summoned and told, 'You did such-and-such, but because we do not wish to bring low one whom we ourselves raised up, nor cast down one whom we promoted, we have pardoned you'; [it may be assumed that] thereafter he will take more care and not make such a mistake again; otherwise he will fall from his position within the retinue, and that will be entirely his own doing.

2. They asked The Commander of the Faithful 'Ali (upon him be peace), 'Who is the bravest of heroes?' He said, 'He who can control himself in time of anger and does no action which he will regret afterwards when he has calmed down and regret is of no avail.'

3. It is the perfection of wisdom for a man not to become angry at all; but if he does, his intelligence should prevail over his wrath, not his wrath over his intelligence. Whoever allows his lusts to prevail over his common sense, if he becomes distraught, his passion veils the eye of wisdom, and he does and says things which are characteristic of madmen; but when a man lets wisdom restrain his lusts, in the time of wrath wisdom will overcome his selfish desires

125

and he will do and say nothing that is not acceptable to all the sages, nor will anyone know that he has been in anger.

4. One day Husain ibn 'Ali (peace be upon them both) was sitting at table with a group of Companions of The Prophet and chiefs of the Arabs, and they were eating bread. He was wearing a costly cloak and had a fine turban on his head. A page was going to put a dish of food in front of him, and was standing right behind him, when the dish chanced to slip from his hand and fall on Husain's head and shoulders, soiling his turban and cloak. Human nature manifested itself in Husain, and his cheeks flushed with rage and confusion; he raised his head and looked at the page. The page seeing him thus, was afraid that he would punish him. He said [quoting the Quran 3, 128], 'And those who curb their wrath and are forgiving towards mankind.' Husain's features brightened and he said, 'O page, I make you free, so that you may be for ever safe from my wrath and my rod.' All those present were amazed and pleased at Husain's clemency, patience and magnanimity in such circumstances.

5. They say that Mu'awiya was extremely forbearing and merciful. One day when he was giving audience and all the nobles were in his presence, a young man came in wearing tattered clothes; he greeted Mu'awiya and sat down impudently in front of him and said, 'O Commander of the Faithful I have come today with an urgent request; if you [promise to] grant it I will tell you what it is.' Mu'awiya said, 'Anything that is possible I will grant.' The youth said, 'Know that I am a poor man and have no wife; and your mother has no husband. Give her to me in marriage, so that I may have a wife, she a husband and you gain the reward.' Mu'awiya said, 'You are a young man and she is an old woman, so old that she has not a single tooth in her head. What do you want her for?' He said, 'Because I have heard that she has a large bottom, and I always like large bottoms.' Mu'awiya said, 'By Allah, my father married her for the very same thing, and it was the only virtue she had. Anyway I will speak to my mother about this and if she is willing, I am certainly the best procurer for your purpose.' Mu'awiya shewed no sign of agitation and remained completely unmoved. All agreed that there was none more forbearing than he.

6. Wise men have said that forbearance is good, but it is better still in time of success; knowledge is good, but with skill better; wealth is good but with gratitude and happiness better; worship is good but with understanding and fear of God better.

## CHAPTER THIRTY-FOUR

*With regard to night-watchmen, guards and porters*

1. The utmost care must be exercised in regard to the king's private watchmen, guards and porters. Those who are responsible for these people must know them all personally and find out about all their affairs private and public; for they are mostly men of mean estate and covetous, and they are quickly seduced by gold. When a new-comer is seen in their ranks let enquiries be made about his circumstances, and every night when they come on guard, they must all be inspected; this important matter must not be neglected, night or day, for it is a delicate business.

## CHAPTER THIRTY-FIVE

*Concerning the arrangements for setting a good table*

1. Kings have always paid attention to having well supplied tables [lit: trays] in the mornings so that those who come to the royal presence may find something to eat there. If the nobles have no desire for it at the time, there is no objection to their eating their own provisions in due course, but it is essential to have the table well spread in the mornings.

2. Sultan Tughril paid the utmost attention to having good tables and various kinds of eatables. If he mounted his horse in the early

morning to go for a ride or to hunt, food was prepared, and when it was served out in the country, there was so much that all the nobles and amirs were astonished. [Almost] the whole system of government of the khans of Turkistan consists in having abundant food in the hands of servants and in their kitchens. When we went to Samarqand and Uzgand[1] certain meddlesome persons were heard to declare that the Jikilis and people of Transoxiana were constantly repeating that never from the arrival of the sultan until his departure did they eat a single morsel at his table.

3. A man's magnanimity and generosity must be [judged] according to [the excellence of] his household management. The sultan is the head of the family of the world; all kings are in his power. Therefore it is necessary that his housekeeping, his magnanimity and generosity, his table and his largesse should accord with his state and be greater and better than that of other kings.

4. It says in a tradition that providing abundant bread and food for the creatures of God (to Him be power and glory) increases the duration of a king's life, his reign and good fortune.

### The story of Moses and Pharaoh

5. It is written in the histories of the prophets (upon them be peace) that The Truth (to Him be power and glory) sent Moses to Pharaoh with many miracles, wonders and honours. Now the daily ration for Pharaoh's table was four thousand sheep, four hundred cows, two hundred camels and a corresponding amount of chickens, fried meats, sweets, and all sorts of other things. All the people of Egypt and all his army used to eat at his table. For four hundred years he had claimed divinity and never ceased providing this food.

6. When Moses (upon him be peace) prayed saying, 'O Lord, destroy Pharaoh,' God answered his prayer and said, 'I shall destroy him in water, and I shall make all his riches and his soldiers your portion.' Several years passed by after this promise, and Pharaoh, doomed to ruin, continued to live in all his magnificence. Moses

---

[1] Malikshah made two expeditions to these parts in the course of his reign, in about 471/1078 and in 481/1088: see *Rahat as Sudur*, 129. 10.

became impatient in his desire that God should destroy Pharaoh quickly, and he could not endure to wait any longer. So he fasted for forty days and went to Mount Sinai, and in his communing with God he said, 'O Lord, Thou didst promise that Thou wouldest destroy Pharaoh, and still he has forsaken none of his blasphemies and pretensions. So when wilt Thou destroy him?' A voice came from The Truth saying, 'O Moses, you want Me to destroy Pharaoh as quickly as possible, but a thousand times a thousand of My servants want Me never to do so, because they partake of his bounty and enjoy tranquillity under his rule. By My power [I swear] that as long as he provides abundant food and comfort for My creatures, I will not destroy him.' Moses said, 'Then when will Thy promise be fulfilled?' God said, 'My promise will be fulfilled when he withholds his provisions from My creatures. If ever he lessens his bounty, know that his hour is near.'

7. It chanced that one day Pharaoh said to Haman, 'Moses has gathered The Sons of Israel about him and is causing us disquiet. We know not what will be the issue of his plans against us. We must keep our stores and treasuries full lest at any time we be without resources. So we must halve our daily rations and keep the saving in reserve.' He deducted two thousand sheep, two hundred cows and a hundred camels, and similarly every two or three days reduced the ration. Moses then knew that the promise of The Truth was near to fulfilment, for excessive economy is the sign of decline. The masters of tradition say that on the day when Pharaoh was drowned only two ewes had been killed in his kitchen.

8. Abraham (upon him be peace) was praised by God for his munificence and hospitality; and God (to Him be power and glory) guaranteed the body of Hatim Ta'i against the fire of hell because of his liberality and hospitality; and as long as the world exists his generosity will be remembered. Then there is the case of The Commander of the Faithful 'Ali (may Allah ennoble his visage), who while he was at prayer gave his ring to a beggar, and so satisfied several hungry persons; The Truth has mentioned him in several passages in the Quran and praised him, and until the resurrection people will speak of his valour and generosity.

9. Nothing is better than generosity, kindness and hospitality. The provision of bread is the beginning of all charity and the substance of all generosity, as 'Unsuri says:

> Generosity is the best of qualities;
> generosity is of the nature of a prophet.
> Two worlds are assured to the generous man;
> be generous and two worlds are yours.

If a man is rich and desires, all uncrowned, to be kingly and princely; if he wants men to humble themselves before him, to revere him and call him lord and prince, then tell him every day to spread a table with victuals. All those who have acquired renown in the world, have gained it mainly through hospitality, while the miserly and avaricious are despised in both worlds.

10. A tradition is preserved which says [in Arabic], 'The miser will not enter the garden' (meaning that misers will not go to paradise). In all ages in paganism and Islam there has never been any quality more esteemed than hospitality.

# CHAPTER THIRTY-SIX

## *On acknowledging the merits of worthy servants and slaves*

1. Whenever a domestic servant performs some praiseworthy service he should at once receive some mark of appreciation and reap the fruits of his zeal; and one who commits an offence, unnecessarily and not by mistake, should be punished according to the gravity of his transgression, so that the other slaves will be more diligent in their service, while the guilty ones will be more afraid. Then work will proceed correctly.

2. A boy of the family of Hashim quarrelled with a certain group of men, and they went to his father and complained. His father was going to punish him, but the boy said, 'O father, I committed a fault and I was foolish; do not you punish me when you are wise.' This pleased the father and he pardoned him.

3. [Ibn] Khurdadbih relates that King Parviz was angry with one of his courtiers and confined him. Nobody dared to go near him except Barbud the minstrel who every day took him food and drink. King Parviz was informed of this. He said to Barbud, 'When we have put a man into confinement, how have you the audacity to attend to him? Do you not know this much, that when we are displeased with a man and confine him, he is not to be paid any attention?' Barbud said, 'O king, that which you have spared him is worth more than what I am doing for him.' He said, 'What have I spared him?' He said, 'His life, and that is better than the things I send him.' The king said, 'Bravo! thou hast said well. Now go and I grant you the man as a gift.'

4. It was the custom of the kings of the Sasanian line that whenever anyone in their presence said any word or shewed any skill which pleased them, and caused them to utter the word 'Bravo', immediately the treasurer gave that person 1,000 dirams. The Chosroes surpassed all other kings in justice, humanity and magnanimity, especially Nushirwan The Just.

5. They say that one day Nushirwan The Just had mounted his horse and was going to the chase with his retainers. Passing by the edge of a village, he saw an old man of ninety years planting walnuts in the ground. Nushirwan was astonished because it takes twenty years after planting for a walnut to give fruit; he said, 'O greybeard, are you planting walnuts?' He said, 'Yes, O sovereign.' The king said, 'Will you live long enough to eat the fruit?' The old man said, 'Others have sown and we have reaped; we sow and others will reap.' Nushirwan was pleased and said, 'Bravo.' Immediately the treasurer gave 1000 dirams to the old man, who said, 'O master, nobody will eat the fruit of these trees sooner than my humble self.' The king said, 'How so?' The old man said, 'If I had not planted these walnuts, and if Your Majesty had not passed this way, and had not asked me that question, and if I had not given that answer, where should I have got these 1,000 dirams from?' Nushirwan exclaimed, 'Bravo, bravo!' And instantly the treasurer gave him another 2,000 dirams because Nushirwan had twice uttered the word 'Bravo'.

6. One day al Ma'mun was holding court for the redress of

wrongs. He received a petition concerning some need. Al Ma'mun gave the petition to Fadl ibn Sahl who was his wazir, and said, 'Fulfil this man's want soon, for this sphere turns too quickly to stay in one position, and the world travels too rapidly to remain constant to any friend. Today we can do a good work, but tomorrow it may be that if we want to do good to someone, we shall be unable to do it for reasons outside our control.'

# CHAPTER THIRTY-SEVEN

*Concerning precautions to be taken with regard to lands held in fief and the condition of the peasants*

1. If reports come in from any district shewing that the peasants are being ruined and scattered abroad, and if it seems likely that the bearers of the report are actuated by self-interest, one of the private staff should be appointed unexpectedly so that no one will guess the purpose of his mission, and sent on some pretext to that place, to tour the district for a month or two and see the state of the towns and villages, whether they are prosperous or ruined; he should listen to what people have to say concerning assignees and tax-collectors and bring back verified reports, because officials [when they are questioned] always bring up the pretext and excuse that those [who accuse them] are their enemies. They should not be listened to or else they will become audacious and do whatever they like; while trustworthy informants will refrain from advising the king or the assignee for fear lest they be thought self-interested. This is even now a cause of decline in population; the peasants are becoming impoverished and uprooted, and taxes are being unfairly levied.

# CHAPTER THIRTY-EIGHT

*On the inadvisability of hastiness in affairs on the part of kings*

1. One should not be over-hasty in matters, and when one hears some news or suspects some possibility, one should act calmly so as to learn the real state of affairs and distinguish the false from the true. For hastiness is a mark of weakness, not a sign of strength. When two contestants come before the king and dispute with one another, the king should not let them know which side he inclines to, for then the man who is in the right may be afraid and not dare to speak, and the one who is in the wrong may increase in audacity and mendacity. It is the command of The Truth (be He exalted) that when somebody makes a statement, until you have verified it, you should not say anything: Allah (be He exalted) said [in the Quran 49. 6], 'O you who believe, if a wicked man brings you tidings, verify it lest you smite some people in ignorance and then repent of what you did.' So one should not be precipitate for precipitancy brings regret, and regret is of no avail.

2. There was a certain scholar[1] in the city of Herat, a man of some renown; in fact he was that man whom Bikrak[2] introduced to The Master of the World. Now it happened that The Martyr Sultan (Allah's mercy be upon him) went to Herat and stayed there for a time, and 'Abd ar Rahman Khal was lodging in the house of this learned old man. One day during a drinking bout he said in front of the sultan, 'This old man has a room into which he goes at night; I am told that he prays all night long. Today I opened the door of that room, and saw a jar of wine and a brazen idol; [evidently] he drinks wine all night and bows down before this idol.' And he had brought the jar of wine and the brazen idol with him. This 'Abd ar Rahman knew that if he told this story in front of the sultan, the sultan would order the man to be put to death that very hour. The sultan sent a page to look for the old man, and another page to

---

[1] This is a sure reference to the famous mystic 'Abd Allah Ansari: see *Chahar Maqala*. Translation, 163 (note XXXI).

[2] According to *Rahat as Sudur*, 117. 3, Bikrak was a chamberlain of Alp Arslan; apparently he served Malikshah also.

me telling me to send someone and call the scholar. I did not know why he was asking for him. But within the hour the messenger came back and said, 'Don't call him.'

The next day I asked the sultan, 'What was the reason for calling that old scholar yesterday and then not calling him?' He said, 'Because of the impudence of 'Abd ar Rahman Khal.' Then he related this story to me and went on to say that he said to 'Abd ar Rahman, 'In spite of what you have told me and although you have produced the jar of wine and the brazen idol, I do not intend to do anything about it without being sure of the truth. So give me your hand and swear by my life that what you say is true—or false.' 'Abd ar Rahman said, 'I spoke falsely.' The sultan said, 'Wretched fellow, why did you speak falsely against this old scholar, and seek to shed his blood?' He said, 'Because he has a fine house and I am lodging there. If you put him to death, you could give me his house.'

3. Elders of religion have said [in Arabic], 'Haste is from Satan, deliberation is from The Merciful.' (Precipitancy is from the devil and slowness is from God.) Works undone can be done but that which is done cannot be retrieved.

Buzurjmihr says, 'Precipitancy comes from light-headedness; he who is hasty and has not calmness, is for ever sorry and sad.'

I have seen several tasks begun well but spoilt through over-hastiness. The hasty man is always reproaching himself; he is continually repenting, begging to be excused, suffering blame, and paying for his mistakes.

The Commander of the Faithful 'Ali (may Allah be pleased with him) says, 'Slowness is to be praised in all actions, except works of charity.'

# CHAPTER THIRTY-NINE

*Concerning commanders of the guard, mace-bearers,
and the instruments of punishment*

1. In all ages the office of commander of the guard was one of
the most important posts; in fact apart from the great amir-chamberlain no one at the court was higher and grander than the commander
of the guard, because his office is concerned with punishment.
Everyone fears the wrath and chastisement of the king, and when the
king is angry with anyone it is the commander of the guard whom
the king orders to cut off his head, to chop off his hands and feet,
to hang him on a gibbet, to give him the bastinado, to put him in
prison, or to throw him into a pit; and to save their skins and lives
people do not hesitate to sacrifice their goods and wealth. The
commander of the guard was always provided with drums and flags
and music, and the people proverbially feared him more than the
king. But in our epoch this post has fallen into disuse and has been
robbed of its prestige. There should be at least fifty mace-bearers
constantly at the court, twenty with golden maces, twenty with silver
ones and ten with large clubs. The equipment and outfit of the
commander of the guard must be of the finest, and he must be
surrounded with the utmost possible pomp. If the present occupant
of the post can manage this it is well; otherwise he must be changed
for someone else.

## The story of al Ma'mun and the two guard-commanders

2. The caliph al Ma'mun one day said to his boon-companions,
'I have two commanders of the guard who are occupied from morning till night in cutting off people's heads, chopping off hands and
feet, giving the bastinado and putting men in prison. One of them
is constantly spoken well of and praised by everybody; the other one
is reviled; people curse when they hear his name, and they are
constantly complaining about him. I do not know what is the reason
for this. I wish I had someone to inform me why, these two men
being alike, people praise one and complain of the other.' A certain

companion said, 'If my lord gives me three days, I will inform him about this matter.' The caliph said, 'Very well.'

3. The boon-companion went home and said to a trustworthy servant, 'I have a task for you. There are this day in Baghdad two guard-commanders, one old and one middle-aged. I want you to get up tomorrow morning while it is still dark and go to the house of the elder of these two, and when he comes out of his room into the courtyard see how he behaves, what he does and what he says; and when people go before him and criminals are brought in, see what happens and what sort of orders he gives. Remember all that you see and come and give me an account of it. The day after to-morrow likewise go early to the house of the middle-aged one and note everything of his speech and behaviour from first to last and then report to me.' The servant said, 'To hear is to obey.'

4. The next day the servant got up early and went to the house of the elder guard-commander and there sat down. Some time passed. Then a servant came and placed a candle on the bench and spread a prayer-mat and put some volumes of the Quran and prayer books on top of the mat. The old man came out and performed several *rak'ats* of prayer; then some people came in and the imam entered and took his place and led the prayers of the company. The old man took up a Quran and read a portion of the scripture and then recited some prayers. When he had finished his litany he took his rosary and telling the beads, chanted 'Praise be to Allah' and 'There is no god but Allah.' People kept coming in and greeting him and sitting down, until the sun rose. Then he asked, 'Have they found any criminals?' They said, 'Yes, they have brought in a youth who has killed a man.' He said, 'Is there any witness against him?' They said, 'No, he confesses it himself.' He said, 'There is no power and no strength except with Allah The Mighty![1] Bring him in; let me see him.' The youth was brought in.

5. When the old man's eyes lighted on the youth, he said, 'Is this the man?' They said, 'Yes.' He said, 'This man has not the countenance of a sinner; rather does the lustre of humanity and the light of Islam shine forth from him. It is unlikely that his hands should commit such a crime. I think people are lying. I will not hear a word

[1] A pious ejaculation (in Arabic) equivalent to 'Bless my soul!' or the like.

against him. Never would this youth do such a deed. See, his whole
face testifies to his innocence.' He said these words so that the youth
could hear. Then someone said, 'O amir, he himself confesses his
guilt.' The amir shouted at the man and said, 'Silence, who asked
you to speak? Have you no fear of God? Do you wantonly seek to
shed the blood of a Muslim? This young man is too intelligent to do
or say anything that would cause his own destruction.' His intention was to try and make the youth contradict himself and renounce
his statement. Then he turned to the youth and said, 'What have
you to say?' The youth said, 'It was decreed by God that such a deed
should come to pass at my hand. This world is followed by another.
I have not the strength to endure God's punishment in the next world.
So bring to effect the judgment of God Himself upon me.' The
guard-commander pretended to be deaf and turning to the people
said, 'I cannot hear what he is saying. Does he confess or no?' They
said, 'Yes, he confesses.' He said, 'My son, you have not the face of
an evil-doer. Perhaps one of your enemies has put you up to saying
this, someone who desires your destruction. Consider well.' He said,
'O amir, nobody has put me up to this; I am a sinner. Carry out
God's judgment upon me.'

6. When the guard-commander realized that the youth would not
withdraw his declaration, and that he had resigned himself to death,
and that his own suggestions were having no effect, he said to him,
'So it is as you say?' He said, 'It is so.' He said, 'Am I to execute
God's judgment upon you?' The youth said, 'Do so.' Then he
turned to the people and said, 'Have you ever seen such a God-
fearing, far-seeing young man as this? I never have at any rate. The
light of blessedness, of Islam, and of nobility radiates from him.
Through fear of God he makes this confession knowing that [in any
case] he must die; he prefers that he should appear before God as a
saint and a martyr. There is but one footstep between him and the
virgins and palaces [of paradise].' To the youth he went on, 'Go,
wash your body clean, perform two *rak'ats* of prayer, and ask for
your [book of] deeds from God; repent and ask forgiveness. Then
come and I will execute God's judgment upon you.' The youth
went and bathed, and came back and asked for a prayer mat to be
spread. He performed two *rak'ats* of prayer, made his repentance and

asked forgiveness. Then he came and stood in front of the amir, who said, 'It seems that this youth will even now look upon [Muhammad] The Elect (upon him be peace) and will go to paradise.' By this recital he had made death so sweet to the young man's heart that he became impatient for them to kill him as quickly as possible. Then the amir ordered them to strip him of his clothes with all gentleness and kindness, and to blindfold his eyes; and all the while he went on talking to him as before. The executioner came in softly with his sword [glistening] like a drop of water, and stood silently behind the youth so that he was unaware of his presence. The guard-commander suddenly gave a sign with his eye, and the executioner deftly brought down his sword and cut off the youth's head with one blow. After that the amir sent to prison several persons arrested for various crimes, until he could verify their charges. Then he rose and went into his room, and the people dispersed. The servant came back to the boon-companion and reported all that he had seen.

7. The next day he got up and went to the house of the other guard-commander. He sat down [to wait]. Policemen and other people came in one by one until the courtyard was full. When the sun rose, the guard-commander came out of his room and held court, with his brows knit and his eyes sodden with drink, looking as if he had been killing angels all night. The policemen stood in front of him. If anyone greeted him with 'Peace', he did not reply with 'Upon you', or if he did, he said it crossly. After some time he asked if anyone had been brought in. They said, 'Last night a youth was arrested so drunk that he was out of his mind.' He said, 'Bring him in.' The youth was brought before the amir, who looked at him and said, 'Is this the one?' They said, 'Yes.' He said, 'I have been looking for him for a long time. He is an ill-begotten, mischief-making, quarrelsome, impious, seditious rogue who has no equal in all Baghdad. It is not the lash for him but the sword. He does nothing but lead the sons of citizens into bad ways, and no day passes without ten people coming to me to complain of him. I have been in search of him for some time.' After all that he had said, the youth was ready for them to cut off his head, in order to escape from his abuses. Then the amir ordered several whips to be brought, and said, 'Strike him down and sit on his head and feet, and give him forty lashes, so that

he bites the dust with his teeth.' When they had finished beating him and were going to take him off to prison, more than fifty heads of well-known families came and gave evidence of his honesty, chastity, generosity, hospitality, morality and piety; they pleaded that he should be released and given some compensation in addition. The amir took no notice of these old and respected householders and sent him to prison. The elders went away mortified and all the people cursed the amir. He for his part rose and went indoors. The servant returned home and recounted to the boon-companion all that had happened.

8. On the third day the boon-companion went to al Ma'mun and described the conduct and behaviour of these two guard-commanders as it was reported to him. The Commander of the Faithful was astonished and said, 'May Allah pardon the old guard-commander, and curses be upon that dog who treated a noble youth so savagely for being drunk. If he had to deal with a murderer (we take refuge with Allah!), what ever would he do?' Then he gave orders that he was to be deprived of the office of guard-commander, that the youth was to be brought out of prison, and that the old guard-commander was to be confirmed in his appointment and decorated afresh with a robe of honour.

[PART TWO]

# CHAPTER FORTY

*On shewing mercy to the creatures of God and restoring all the affairs and customs of the state to their proper order*

1. At any time the state may be overtaken by some celestial accident, or influenced by the evil eye.[1] Then the government will change and pass from one house to another, or the country will be thrown into disorder through seditions and tumults; opposing swords [will be drawn and there will be] killing, burning and violence. In such troubled days men of noble birth will be crushed; evil-doers will gain control and whoever has strength will do what he likes. Men of good-will will have no power or influence; the least of men will be an amir [army-commander], the basest of persons will become a civil governor. Noble and learned men will be dispossessed, and any wretch will not hesitate to take upon himself titles reserved for the king and the wazir; he might give himself ten titles with impunity and nobody would ask whether he is worthy or not. Turks will adopt titles proper to civil dignitaries and the latter will take those belonging to Turks, while Turks and Taziks [Persians] alike will decorate themselves with titles of learned men and issue orders on behalf of the king. The religious law will be held in contempt; the peasants will become unruly and the soldiers oppressive; all discretion and decency will vanish away and no one will be able to remedy matters. If a Turk keeps ten Taziks as administrators, it will pass, and if one Tazik is administrator for ten Turks, it will be allowed. All the affairs of the country will fall short of their proper order and organization, and the king will be so distracted by expeditions, wars and anxieties that he will not have the opportunity to attend to such matters or even consider them.

2. Later, when through celestial good fortune the evil times pass away, and days of peace and security follow, God (be He exalted) will bring forth a just and wise king from princely stock, and will give him the power to vanquish his enemies, and the wisdom and intelligence to judge matters aright—a king who will enquire from

---

[1] As the author takes up his pen again, probably in 484/1091, the year before his death, the ideas and even the very words of Chapter One return to his mind.

people and read books to learn what were the rules by which former kings directed affairs, so that he may restore all the proper forms and rules of government. He will test the merit and estimate the rank of every one; those who are worthy he will reinstate in their positions, and the unworthy he will dismiss [from high rank] and appoint them to their proper tasks and trades. He will exterminate any ungrateful people who abuse their privileges. He will be the friend of religion and the enemy of oppression; he will assist the faith and remove vanity and heresy, with the permission of Allah and by His grace.

3. Let us now expatiate a little on this subject; much will then become clear and it will be a guide to those things which have fallen into disorder, so that when The Master of the World (may Allah perpetuate his reign) reflects upon them he may issue commands and orders to deal with each. One of the principles which kings have observed in all ages, is to preserve ancient families and honour the sons of kings, not allowing them to be neglected and debarred from their rightful position and power. Rather did they give them a portion for their subsistence so that their families continued to flourish; other deserving persons too were given allotments from the treasury, such as learned men, descendants of 'Ali, guardians of the frontiers [of Islam], and people [expositors] of the Quran. Thus in the days of their dominion no one was deprived of his due portion and privilege; so they gained blessings, praises and rewards in both worlds.

## The story of Harun ar Rashid

4. They say that a party of needy persons presented a petition to Harun ar Rashid saying, 'We are servants of God and sons of distinguished men; some of us are scholars and theologians; some belong to noble families; others are sons of men who have deserved well of this dynasty for their past good services; and we too have laboured without stint; and we are all Muslims of pure faith. Our portion is in the treasury under your control because you are the administrator of the world and The Commander of the Faithful. If that money belongs to the faithful, then spend it on us for we have a right to it. Not more than a tenth of it belongs to you as your portion by virtue

of your kingship and treasurership; every day you spend so many thousand dinars on salaries, rations and lustful objects, while we cannot get a loaf of bread to eat.' The extraordinary thing was, [they thought,] that he should imagine that all the contents of the treasury belonged to him alone. 'Unless you assign to us our portion, we will go and complain about you to the court of The Most High and request Him to take the treasury out of your hands and give it to someone else who has some compassion for his fellow creatures and keeps money and wealth for the sake of men, not men for the sake of money.'

5. When Harun ar Rashid read the petition he was disturbed, and he did not answer it the same day. He returned from the audience-hall to his private palace in a state of uneasiness. When Zubaida saw him out of humour she said, 'O Commander of the Faithful, what is the matter?' He told her about the petition which he had received, and said, 'If it were not for the fact that they have threatened me with the name of God I would have had them punished.' Zubaida said, 'You did well not to hurt them. As you inherited the caliphate from your fathers, so they bequeathed you their principles, their qualities and their traditions. Consider what the caliphs before you did for the good of mankind. Do likewise, for nobility and sovereignty are improved by generosity and liberality. There is no doubt that all the money in the treasury belongs to the Muslims, while you spend much of it for yourself. You should take no more liberties with their property than they would with yours. They are quite justified if they complain about you.'

6. That night it happened that they both dreamed that it was the resurrection and people were going to the place of reckoning; one by one they were brought forward, The Elect (the prayers of Allah be upon him) interceded for them and they went towards paradise; an angel took Harun and Zubaida by the hand; someone asked where he was taking them; he said that The Elect (upon him be peace) had sent him and told him, 'As long as I am present do not let them be brought before me, or I shall be ashamed and unable to say anything about them, because they considered the property of Muslims to be their own and deprived them of their rights—and this when they were my lieutenants.' They both woke up as if in a frenzy.

Harun said to Zubaida, 'What has happened to you?' She told him what she had seen in the dream and that she had been afraid. Harun said, 'I too had the same dream.' Then they praised God that it was not the resurrection and that it had all been a dream.

7. The next day they opened the doors of their treasuries and issued a proclamation saying, 'Let all entitled persons present themselves that we may give them their portion from the treasury and fulfil their needs and desires.' Then people flocked to Harun's court and he awarded them gratuities and pensions; these benefactions amounted to 3,000,000 dinars. Then Zubaida said to Harun, 'The treasury is in your hands and you will be required to answer for it at the resurrection, not I. By virtue of your recent acts of grace you have discharged some of your responsibilities, in that all you gave was the property of the Muslims which you restored to them. The things which I am going to do I shall do at my own expense for God's sake (be He exalted) and for the sake of salvation at the resurrection. I know not when I may have to depart from this world and leave behind all this gold and wealth; so let me send something in advance to the next world by way of provision for the journey.'

8. Zubaida withdrew several million dinars from her treasury as well as jewels, silver and raiment; and she said, 'All this must be spent on charitable works such that the effect of them will last until the resurrection and my name will be blessed for evermore.' So she ordered that from the gates of Kufa to Mecca and Medina wells were to be dug at every stage; they were to be made wide at the top and lined from top to bottom with stone, baked brick and mortar; tanks and cisterns were also to be built so that pilgrims should suffer no hardship on their journey, for every year several pilgrims used to perish in the desert for lack of water. After all these wells, tanks and cisterns had been constructed, much money was still left. She ordered that fortified castles were to be built on the frontiers, that arms and horses were to be bought for warriors engaged in holy war, and that sufficient lands and farms were to be purchased so as to provide throughout the year at each castle food and fodder whenever required for one or two thousand warriors.

9. When all this had been done much money still remained. So on the borders of Kashgar, Bulur and Shuknan they built a city with

a strong wall and named it Badakhshan; it is still in existence and flourishing today. Opposite Rasht they built another fortress called ........;[1] and on the borders of Khutlan they built a fortress called Wishgard which is still in existence and flourishing; its armoury and its flocks of animals are still there. Similarly they built several frontier stations and fortified cities, one at Isbijab which is still in existence and flourishing, a fortress on the road to Khwarazm called Farawa, a fortress at Darband and a fortress at Alexandria. In all they built ten fortresses in various places, each one like a city. Still there was a surplus of money. So they arranged for it to be distributed among the inhabitants of Mecca, Medina and Jerusalem.

## The story of 'Umar and the poor woman

10. Zaid ibn Aslam related the following anecdote: One night The Commander of the Faithful 'Umar ibn al Khattab (may Allah be pleased with him) was on patrol in person in Medina, and I was with him. We went out of the city, and in the fields there was a ruined building from which a light was shining. The Commander of the Faithful said to me, 'O Zaid, come, let us go there and see who it is who has a fire burning in the middle of the night.' So we went, and when we got near we saw a woman with two children asleep on the ground beside her and a cauldron set over a fire; she was saying, 'O Lord, assist me to get justice from 'Umar; he has eaten his fill while we are hungry.' When 'Umar heard this he said to me, 'O Zaid, this woman is arraigning me of all people before God. You stay here while I approach her and ask what is the matter.' He went up to the woman and said, 'What are you cooking at midnight out in the fields?' She said, 'I am a poor woman; I have a house and property in Medina but [otherwise] I am penniless; and I feel so ashamed that these two children of mine are weeping and wailing in hunger and I have nothing to give them, that I have come out here into the fields, so that the neighbours should not know why they are crying. Every time they cry because of hunger and ask for food I put this cauldron on the fire and say, "You go to sleep and by the time you wake up the pot will be ready." By this means I set

[1] The name is corrupt and undecipherable in the MSS.

them at rest; they think that I am cooking something, and in expectation of it they go to sleep; when they wake up and find nothing they start howling again. At the moment I have put them to sleep on the same pretence; for two days now they have not had anything but water, and neither have I; and there is nothing else but water in this cauldron.' 'Umar (may Allah be pleased with him) took pity on her and said, 'You are justified in cursing 'Umar and appealing to God.' The woman did not recognize 'Umar. He said to her, 'Wait here for a while until I come back.'

11. 'Umar then came back to me and said, 'Step out, we are going back to my house.' When we reached his house he went in and I sat down at the door. After some time he came out with two leather bags on his back. He said to me, 'Come, let us go back to that woman.' I said, 'O Commander of the Faithful, put those bags on my back and let me carry them.' 'Umar said, 'O Zaid, if you carry this load, who will carry my load of sin on the resurrection day?' And he ran all the way to the woman and put the bags down in front of her; one of them was full of flour and the other full of rice, fat and peas. He said to me, 'O Zaid, go into the fields, collect all the sticks and straws you can find and bring them quickly.' I went to look for firewood. Then 'Umar took a ewer and fetched some water; he washed the rice and peas, put them in the cauldron and threw in a lump of fat; meanwhile the woman made a large flat round of bread, weeping all the time for joy. I brought the firewood; and with his own hands 'Umar heated the cauldron and put the bread under the fire.

12. When the bread and the cauldron were ready the woman awakened the children and 'Umar placed the food in front of them. Then he retired to a distance, spread his prayer-mat and began to pray. After a while he looked; the children had eaten their fill and were playing with their mother. He took the woman and the children to his house and said, 'O woman, be kind and do not curse 'Umar any more; forgive him for he did not know that you were in distress.' The woman wept and said, 'I conjure you to swear by God that you are 'Umar.' He said, 'Yes, I am.' The poor helpless woman said, 'May God forgive you as you saved us from starvation.'

### The story of Moses and the lost sheep

13. They say that when Moses (upon him be peace) was still the shepherd of Shu'aib and had not yet received divine inspiration, he was one day feeding his sheep. By chance one ewe became separated from the others. Moses wanted to bring her back to the flock, but the ewe not being able to see the sheep, ran about in terror and Moses chased her for a distance of two farsangs, until she had no strength left and fell down exhausted and could not get up. Moses looked at her and was moved with compassion. He said, 'O hapless one, whither are you fleeing? Whom do you fear?' He picked her up and put her on his shoulders and brought her back to the flock. When the ewe saw the flock her heart was glad; Moses put her down upon the ground, and she joined the flock. God (be He exalted) called to the angels saying, 'See ye with what tenderness My servant treated that ewe. Because he took trouble and harmed not the ewe, but rather had mercy on her, [I declare] by My glory that I will raise him up and make him My interlocutor; I will grant him prophethood and send him a book, and as long as the world exists, his name will be spoken.' God bestowed all these tokens upon him.

### The story of Mayor Hajji and the mangy dog

14. In the city of Marv there lived a man who was known as Mayor Hajji; he was a distinguished and wealthy man and owned many farms; in fact in his time there was nobody richer than he. He had served Sultan Mahmud and Sultan Mas'ud. At the beginning of his career when he was a young man he was extremely cruel, practising torture and inquisition and overthrowing noble families; there was nobody more merciless than he. In the latter part of his life he found enlightenment; he desisted from tyranny and oppression and began to do good works, like comforting the poor and building bridges and inns; he set free many of his slaves and slave-girls, he gave clothes to orphans and widows, he provided money and necessaries for pilgrims and holy-warriors, he built the Cathedral Mosque at Nishapur, and lastly after performing all these charitable acts he went on the pilgrimage in the time of Chughri (Allah's mercy be

upon him). When he reached Baghdad he remained there for a period of one month. One day he left his house to go to the bazaar. On the way he saw an extremely mangy dog; all its hair had fallen out and the poor thing was distressed by the mange. The man was sorry for it; he said, 'It too is a living being created by God (be He exalted);' and he told a servant to go and fetch two maunds of bread and a rope. He waited where he was till the servant came back. Then he broke the bread with his own hand and threw it to the dog until it had eaten enough; he put the rope round the dog's neck and handed it to the servant, telling him to take the dog home. He himself also departed from the bazaar.

15. When he reached his house he gave order for three maunds of fat to be bought and melted. Mayor Hajji took a stick and wrapped a piece of rag round the end of it; he got up and approached the dog; and with his own hand he dipped the rag into the fat and began to rub it over the dog until all its members were thoroughly anointed. Then he said to the servant, 'You are not more respectable than I am; I thought it no disgrace to do what I did; so you being a servant must do the same every day and not be ashamed. I want you to knock a nail in the wall and tie the dog to it; every day you should give it one maund of bread in the morning and one in the evening; also let it have the leavings from the table; and treat it with fat twice a day until it gets better.' The servant did as he was told and in two weeks the dog got rid of the mange, grew its hair and became fat; it became so attached to the house that even if it had been beaten and whipped five hundred times it could not have been turned out. Mayor Hajji performed the pilgrimage, travelling by caravan, and he spent much money on the journey; he returned safely to the city of Marv and a year later he died. Some time passed.

16. One night an ascetic saw him in a dream, mounted on a Buraq[1] with boys and girls standing before and behind and holding his hands on either side; he was laughing as he rode gently through one of the gardens of paradise. The ascetic ran towards him and greeted him; he drew rein and returned the salutation. The ascetic said to him, 'O Sir, you were once a tyrant, merciless and oppressive; after you found enlightenment you not only desisted from tyranny,

---

[1] The name of the horse on which the prophet Muhammad ascended to heaven.

but also did more good works and gave more charity than anyone before you; you performed the pilgrimage, you constructed bridges and inns, and you built schools and mosques. Tell me what were the acts of piety and worship by which you attained your present state of exaltation?' He said, 'O ascetic, know that I am lost in amazement at God's works (be He exalted); you, too, should take this as a lesson, and put no trust in piety nor deceive yourself by acts of worship. Know that I had been assigned to hell for all the sins I had committed in my youth; all the acts of piety and charity which I did were of no avail; they were all thrown back in my face on the day of judgment—useless and worthless. I became so despondent that I gave up all hope of paradise and resigned myself to the torments of hell. Then suddenly I heard a voice saying, "You were one of the dogs of the earth, so we have matched you against a dog and considered all your sins as cancelled; you have been admitted to paradise and delivered from hell because you threw off the cloak of pride and took pity on a dog." After that I saw the angels of mercy coming like lightning, and they snatched me from the hands of the angels of torment and took me into paradise. So of all my acts of piety that was the only one which saved me at the last extremity.'

17. Your humble servant has called to mind this story so that The Master of the World (may Allah perpetuate his reign) may know what a good habit it is to have mercy upon the creatures of God. Because these men had mercy on a ewe and a dog they acquired high degree and esteem in both worlds. So it can be imagined what favour and reward a man will receive from God if he has mercy on a Muslim who is in distress, and gives him a helping hand. If the king fears God and takes heed for the future, he is bound to be just in every case, and the just man is always merciful. When the king is such, his officers and soldiers will become like him and follow his example. Consequently all humanity will enjoy ease and prosperity, and the king will find reward in both worlds.

18. It has always been the custom of enlightened monarchs to have respect for old and experienced men, and to keep [in office] those who are skilled in affairs and tried in battle, giving each a position and rank; and whenever any matter important for the welfare of the

state required to be executed, such as arranging an alliance, getting information about a [foreign] king, enquiring into religious affairs, and suchlike, they discussed it thoroughly with men of wisdom and worldly experience. On the other hand, whenever an enemy appeared or a battle threatened, they took counsel with men accomplished in warfare and skilled in such arts; with the result that the business was accomplished successfully. If war broke out they despatched to the front a man who had fought numerous battles, broken [enemy] ranks, captured forts and gained renown in the world; but at the same time they always sent with him men of ripe and wide experience so that nothing went amiss. But [nowadays] it happens that when a serious matter arises, they appoint inexperienced men and [even] boys and women [to deal with it], and errors are committed. If they were to give consideration to this question it would be better and less dangerous.

## On the subject of titles

19. There has become an abundance of titles; and whatever becomes abundant loses value and dignity. Kings and caliphs have always been sparing in the application of titles; for it is one of the principles of government to see that titles are kept in relation to each man's rank and importance. When the title of a bazaar merchant or a farmer is the same as that of a civil governor, there is no difference between humble and noble, and the notable and the insignificant are of the same degree. Supposing an imam or a scholar or a judge has the title of Mu'in ad Din [Supporter of the Faith], and a student or a Turk who knows not the first thing about religious law—nay, cannot even read or write, also has the same title of Mu'in ad Din, then what is the difference in rank between judges and students, learned and ignorant? Both have the same title and this is not right.

20. Amirs and Turks have always been given the titles Husam ad Daula [Sword of the Empire], Saif ad Daula [Sabre of the Empire], Amin ad Daula [Trustee of the Empire], Shams ad Daula [Sun of the Empire], and suchlike; while civil dignitaries, civil governors and officials have received titles like 'Amid al Mulk [Pillar of the Kingdom], Zahir al Mulk [Protector of the Kingdom],

Qiwam al Mulk [Support of the Kingdom], and Nizam al Mulk [Harmony of the Kingdom]. Nowadays all discretion has vanished and Turks give themselves the titles of civil officials, and Taziks take those of Turks, and think it no wrong. But titles always used to be dear.

### The story of Sultan Mahmud and his titles

21. On his accession to the sultanate Sultan Mahmud asked The Commander of the Faithful, al Qadir bi'llah, for a title. He was granted the title of Yamin ad Daula [Right hand of the Empire]. Then after he took possession of the provinces of Nimruz, Khurasan and Hindustan—capturing cities without number, going to Somnat and bringing back the idol, conquering Samarqand and Khwarazm, coming to Kuhistan and 'Iraq and taking Rayy, Isfahan and Hamadan, and bringing Tabaristan to submission—he sent a messenger to The Commander of the Faithful bearing many gifts and asking for more titles. He received no answer and it is said that he sent messengers ten times without result. Now the khaqan of Samarqand had been given three titles—Zahir ad Daula [Protector of the Empire], Mu'in Khalifat Allah [Supporter of the Vicar of Allah], and Malik ash Sharq wa's Sin [King of the East and China]; and this was a constant cause of jealousy to Mahmud. Once again he sent a messenger and said, 'I have gained so many victories in heathen lands, I have established control over Hindustan, Khurasan and 'Iraq, I have captured Transoxiana, and I am continually wielding the sword in your name; yet on the khaqan, who is one of my subjects and vassals, you have conferred three titles and on me, your devoted servant, only one, after all my services and favours.'

22. The reply came back in these words: 'Titles are an honour by which a man's dignity is increased, and by which he is known to the world; know also that a man's [first] name is that which his father and mother give him, his *kunya* [surname of relationship] he chooses for himself, and his title is that which the king gives him. Anything beyond these three is superfluous and a mockery, and no wise man submits himself to mockery and vanity. When a person is small, he is called by his first name and this pleases his mother and

father because they chose that name for him; when he grows up and acquires discretion he chooses a *kunya* for himself in keeping with his intelligence and wisdom, as the saying is [in Arabic], "Appellations and aspirations go together." Thereafter people treat him like a man and call him by his *kunya* in order to gladden him. Later, when he has shewn merit and skill in public life, the king bestows upon him the honour of a title suitable to his rank, in order to distinguish him from his fellow men and exalt him above them. Therefore this name which the king or the caliph grants him is better than the one his parents give him and better than the one he chooses himself. So out of respect for his rank and dignity people call him by the name given to him by the king and known as his title. Apart from these three any other designation is superfluous. However because the khaqan is an ignorant, outlandish Turk, I have granted his request in order to swell his reputation and make up for his lack of wisdom. As for you who are learned in every science and situated close to me, my intentions concerning you are worthier and my trust in you and your honesty is nobler than that you should ask me for something merely spoken or written, and aspire after the same objects as ignorant men.'

23. When Mahmud heard these words, he was confounded. Now there was a certain woman of Turkish birth who often used to come to Mahmud's palace; she was educated, well-spoken and knew several languages; she would talk, joke and play with Mahmud, sometimes reading him books and stories; in fact she was on most familiar terms with him. One day she was sitting with Mahmud and amusing him; he said, 'However much I try to get the caliph to increase my titles, it is of no use; while the khaqan who is a vassal of mine, has received several titles. I wish I had somebody who could steal from the khaqan's treasury or otherwise procure the charter which the caliph sent him; if he were successful I would give him anything he demanded.' This woman said, 'O Master, I will go and get that charter, but you must keep your word and give me whatever I want.' He said, 'I will.' The woman said, 'I have not enough money to devote to the attainment of The Master's desire; if you will give me some assistance from the treasury I will do all in my power to achieve your object.' The sultan said, 'Ask for whatever you need

and I will give it.' So he supplied her with whatever she demanded
in the way of money, jewels, robes, ornaments, animals and provisions. This woman had a son fourteen years old who was being
educated at the hands of a teacher; she took the boy with her and
set out from Ghaznain to Kashghar. There she bought some Turkish
pages and bondmaids, as well as a large supply of choice goods
imported from Cathay and Khotan, such as musk and various kinds
of silk. Then she travelled in the company of merchants to Uzgand,
and went from there to Samarqand.

24. Three days after her arrival she went to pay her respects to the
khatun, offering a very handsome Turkish bondmaid as a gift
together with many choice things from India, Khotan and Cathay;
and saying, 'My husband was a merchant; he used to travel throughout the world and take me with him; we were going to Cathay, but
when we reached Khotan he died. I turned back and came to Kashghar. I offered a present to the khaqan of Kashghar and told him how
my husband had been one of His Excellency's servants and I was
an attendant to the khatun; they had set me free, given me to him as
a wife and I had had this child by him; he had recently died at
Khotan and all that he had left me was some capital which the
khatun had given him; I hoped that His Excellency in his charity
and nobility would extend the hand of succour over the heads of his
humble servant and this orphan and despatch us in good company
towards Uzgand and Samarqand, for which act of kindness I should
thank him and bless him as long as I lived. The khatun treated us
very kindly and so did the khaqan; he gave us a guide and ordered
the khan of Uzgand to look after us and send us in good company
to Samarqand. Now by your grace and favour we throw ourselves
at Your Excellency's feet, knowing that in all the world there is
nowhere such justice and equity as at Samarqand. My husband
always used to say that if ever he reached Samarqand he would never
leave it. It is your name and fame that have brought us here. If you
will accept me as your thrall and extend the hand of succour and
lordship over my head, then I will settle down here, sell the ornaments which I possess and buy a house and farm large enough to
provide me with subsistence; then I will constantly wait upon you
and continue the education of this boy, in the hope that with the

aid of your blessings God (to Him be power and glory) will prosper him.'

25. The khatun said, 'Do not worry at all. I will do everything possible to treat you well and look after you; I will give you a house and a grant of land; I will do whatever you desire, and I will not suffer you to be away from me for an instant. I will also tell the khaqan to fulfil all your needs and requests.' The woman bowed to the khatun and said, 'Now you are my mistress. Since I do not know anybody here I should be grateful if you would bring my presence to the notice of His Excellency the khaqan and introduce me to him, so that I may acquaint him with my case and let him hear my story personally.' The khatun said, 'I will take you to see him any time you like.' The woman said, 'I will present myself tomorrow.' She said, 'All right.' The next day she went to the khatun's house; the khatun had already spoken about her to the khaqan; she took her into his presence. The woman bowed to him and offered presents of a Turkish page, a handsome horse, and all sorts of choice things; and she said, 'Your humble servant has explained something of her circumstances to the khatun. In brief, when my husband died— may Your Excellency live for ever!—his partner advised me not to carry back the goods which we were taking to Cathay; so I gave some of them to the khan of Kashghar, I used some for travelling expenses, and now there is nothing left but your humble servant, this orphan boy, a small quantity of ornaments and a few animals. If Your Excellency will accept me as a thrall, as the khatun has accepted me, then I am ready to spend the rest of my life in your esteemed service.'

26. The khaqan spoke very kindly to her and accepted her. Thereafter she laid a gift before the khatun every two or three days; she entertained them both with pleasant tales and romances, and so captivated them that they could not bear to be without her. She waited upon them so attentively that they began to feel embarrassed, and whenever they offered her villages and farms she declined to accept. Every few days she left the house in which she was lodging and went three or four farsangs outside the city ostensibly for the purpose of buying a farm and estate; she would stay out for three or four days inspecting a farm; then she would find some fault with it,

excuse herself from buying it, and return home. When the khatun and khaqan sent someone to find out why she had forsaken them and ceased coming to see them, they were told that she was buying an estate is such-and-such a village and had been gone for two or three days. They were delighted and assumed that she had decided to stay there. This went on for a period of six months; and the khatun said to her several times, 'The khaqan is constantly saying that whenever he sees you he feels ashamed, because you do so many things for us; every few days you bring us presents, and whatever we offer you, you decline to accept; he has never met a woman as kind as you; and he wonders what we should do for you after all this; and I feel a thousand times more ashamed than he.' The woman said, 'For me the greatest blessing in the world is the sight of my master and mistress, whom God (to Him be power and glory) has made the providers of my daily bread. I see you every day, and I cannot do without you; so when I need something I will not hesitate to ask for it.' Thus she went on deceiving them. Meanwhile she secretly gave the gold, jewels and robes which she had to a merchant who habitually travelled between Samarqand and Ghaznain on business; and she sent out five good horses and five riders on to the road to Balkh and Tirmidh with instructions that one rider with horse was to remain at each stopping place until she arrived.

27. Then she approached the khatun at a time when she and the khaqan were sitting together; after regaling them both with much eulogy and flattery, she said, 'Today I have come with a request; I do not know whether I should ask you or not.' The khatun said, 'This is a strange thing to hear from you. It would have been fitting if by this time you had made a hundred requests and we had fulfilled them. But tell us what it is that you require.' She said, 'You know that this boy is all that I have in the world; I am devoted to him and I am looking after his education; he has already learned the whole of the Quran, and now he is studying secretaryship and reading treatises in Arabic and Persian; I hope that by the grace of my master and mistress he will be fortunate. Now after the writ of God and The Prophet there is nothing on the face of the earth more venerable than the writs of The Commander of the Faithful which are received by kings; the person who composes these documents is

157

the most learned of all secretaries; so the language and purport which they contain should surely be of the most exquisite. If Your Excellencies think it fit, would you kindly allow your humble servant for two or three days to take the document known as the caliph's charter, so that this boy may read it a few times with his tutor; if he learns only five words from it, it may be that he will win good fortune through its influence.' The khaqan and khatun said, 'What a request is this to put to us! Why do you not ask for a city or a district? You have asked for something of which we have fifty put away in the treasury, all rotting under a layer of dust. What virtue is there in a piece of paper? If you like we will make you a present of all those papers.' The woman said, 'Just the document which the caliph sent will be enough.' A servant was ordered to go with her to the treasury and give her any papers she wanted.

28. So the woman went to the treasury, received the charter and took it back home. The next day she had all her horses saddled and her mules loaded, giving out that she was going to such-and-such a village to buy a farm and would be away for a week. She rode away and went straight to that village; before leaving she had taken a safe-conduct stating that wherever she went in the province of Samarqand and Bukhara, whether buying a farm or acquiring an estate or taking up abode, she was to be treated with respect and given hospitality; tax-collectors and other officials were instructed to afford her all assistance within their power and to provide her with anything she might require.

29. Then one night she stole away from the village in the middle of the night, and after halting at a point three farsangs away from the city [of Samarqand] she rode forth. In five days she reached Tirmidh; whenever the need arose she presented the safe-conduct and she had a constant supply of fresh mounts. The khatun was not aware of her going until she had crossed the Oxus and reached Balkh. From Balkh she went to Ghaznain and laid the charter in front of Sultan Mahmud. Mahmud sent it by the hand of a certain scholar to The Commander of the Faithful al Qadir bi'llah together with many presents; he also sent a letter in which he wrote as follows: 'One of my servants was walking in the bazaar at Samarqand, and he passed by a school; there he saw this writ of The Commander of

the Faithful in the hands of some small boys; without the slightest respect or regard they were passing it from one to the other and rolling it in the dust. My servant recognized that illustrious document and wished to rescue it. So he gave a few raisins to the boys and took the charter from them; he brought it to Ghaznain and shewed it to me. I now respectfully forward it for the attention of The Master of the World, and would humbly point out that after all my deference and devotion to duty, whereby I ever hold your decrees dearer than my own eyesight, regarding them as the crown on my head and giving them the most honourable place in my treasury—in spite of all my past services and future expectations you refuse to grant me any titles, and yet you give them to persons who fail to understand the solemnity of your decrees, who treat all honours and patents with contempt, and who merely despise the titles which they receive.'

30. When this scholar arrived at Baghdad and delivered the presents and the letter the caliph was very surprised, and ordered a letter of reproach to be written to the khaqan. Mahmud's envoy remained for six months on the caliph's doorstep, continually sending in petitions and requesting titles on behalf of Mahmud; but he got no decisive answer. So one day he wrote a proposition in the following terms for the decision of the chief judge [of Baghdad]: 'If a king were to emerge, and wield the sword for the sake of Islam, and make war on infidels and pagans who are the enemies of God and The Prophet, and make idol-temples into mosques, and turn the abode of unbelief into the abode of Islam; and supposing he were distant from The Commander of the Faithful, being separated by great waters, lofty mountains and fearful deserts, and were unable at all times to report the events which happen, and all his requests met with no response from the caliph; then would it be lawful for him to install a nobleman of 'Abbasid stock as the caliph's deputy and to submit to his authority, or not?' He gave this proposition to somebody to hand to the chief judge of Baghdad. The judge read it and pronounced judgment that it was lawful. The scholar took a copy of this judgment, and enclosed it with a petition which he wrote to the caliph, saying, 'Your humble servant's stay has become protracted; Mahmud with a hundred thousand acts of devotion and service entreats the favour of one or two titles; but The Master of the World withholds

them from him, disappointing The Warrior King's hopes and cruelly wounding his feelings. If hereafter Mahmud acts in accordance with the chief judge's decree, will he be excused, or not?'

31. As soon as the caliph read this petition, he sent the chamberlain to the wazir with instructions that Mahmud's envoy was to be summoned immediately and set at ease with assurances; then he was to be given such robes of honour, banners, charters and titles as the caliph authorized, and sent on his way satisfied. In spite of all Mahmud's services and attempts to curry favour with the caliph, and despite the clever advocacy of the scholar, he received only one additional title—Amin al Milla [Trustee of the Nation]; and as long as he lived Mahmud's only titles were Yamin ad Daula and Amin al Milla.

In these days the lowest official is angry and indignant if he is given less than seven or ten titles.

32. The Samanids who for so many years were the [greatest] kings of their time and ruled over Transoxiana, Ghaznain, Khurasan, Khwarazm, Nimruz and the two 'Iraqs, each had one title. Nuh was called Shahanshah [King of Kings]; Nuh's father, Mansur, was called Amir Sadid [The Good Commander]; Mansur's father, Nuh, was called Amir Hamid [The Praised Commander]; Nuh's father, Nasr, was called Amir Sa'id [The Fortunate Commander], and Isma'il ibn Ahmad was known as Amir 'Adil [The Just Commander] and in the history books as Amir Madi [The Past Commander], and so on. Titles must suit the persons who hold them. Judges, imams and scholars have had titles like Majd ad Din [Glory of the Faith], Sharaf al Islam [Honour of Islam], Saif as Sunna [Sword of the Ordinance], Zain ash Shari'a [Ornament of the Religious Law], and Fakhr al 'Ulama [Pride of Scholars]; because scholars are concerned with 'the religious law' and 'the faith'. If anyone who is not a scholar takes these titles upon himself, not only the king but all men of discretion and learning should refuse to countenance it, and that person should be punished so that everyone observes his station. Likewise the titles of army-commanders, amirs, assignees and commissioners have been distinguished by the word *daula* [empire], for instance, Saif ad Daula [Sabre of the

Empire], Husam ad Daula [Sword of the Empire], Zahir ad Daula [Protector of the Empire], Jamal ad Daula [Grace of the Empire] and suchlike; while civil governors, tax-collectors and officials have been given titles with the word *mulk* [kingdom], like 'Amid al Mulk [Pillar of the Kingdom], Nizam al Mulk [Harmony of the Kingdom], Jamal al Mulk [Grace of the Kingdom], Sharaf al Mulk [Honour of the Kingdom] and so on. It was never the rule that Turkish amirs should take upon themselves the titles proper to civil dignitaries or vice versa. But after the time of The Fortunate Sultan Alp Arslan (may Allah have mercy upon him) customs changed, discretion disappeared and titles became mixed up; the smallest person demanded the biggest title and was given it, with the result that titles became cheap.

33. Of the Buwaihids, who were the kings of Dailaman and the most powerful rulers of 'Iraq, one had the title Rukn ad Daula [Pillar of the Empire] and another 'Adud ad Daula [Right arm of the Empire], while their wazirs had the titles Ustad Jalil [Illustrious Master] and Ustad Khatir [Honoured Master]. The wazir who was the greatest and most learned in 'Iraq and Khurasan was The Sahib [Isma'il] ibn 'Abbad and his title was Kafi 'l Kufat [Capability of Capabilities] and the title of Sultan Mahmud's wazir was Shams al Kufat [Sun of Capabilities].

Previously the words *ad dunyā wa 'd dīn* [the world and the faith] had not occurred in the titles of kings. The Commander of the Faithful al Muqtadi (bi amri'llah) introduced into the titles of Sultan Malikshah (Allah's mercy be upon him) that of Mu'izz ad Dunya wa 'd Din (Glorifier of the World and the Faith], and after his death[1] it became regular—Bargiyaruq, Rukn ad Dunya wa 'd Din [Pillar . . . ]; Mahmud, Nasir ad Dunya wa 'd Din [Helper . . .]; Isma'il Muhyi 'd Dunya wa 'd Din [Reviver . . .]; and Sultan Muhammad, Ghiyath ad Dunya wa 'd Din [Rescuer . . .]. The words *dunyā* and *dīn* are also written in the titles of the wives of kings, and the same decoration was extended to the titles of kings' sons. For them this title is suitable because the welfare of the faith and of the world

[1] These references to the death of Malikshah and to his successors could not of course have been written by Nizam al Mulk. The whole of paras. 32–6 may be considered the maximum extent of an interpolation, which is perhaps the work of 'the copyist'.

depends on their welfare, and the excellence of the kingdom and empire is bound up with the permanence of the dynasty.

The extraordinary thing is this, that the most insignificant Turkish students or pages, as irreligious as can be, who have committed a thousand crimes and wrongs against religion and state, give themselves the titles of Mu'in ad Din [Supporter of the Faith] and Taj ad Din [Crown of the Faith].

34. The first wazir who was given a title with the word *din* was Nizam al Mulk who received the title Qiwam ad Din [Support of the Faith]. But nowadays any ignorant, uneducated upstart is given titles with the words *din, daulat* and *mulk*.

We have already said that titles including the words *din* and *Islam* are suitable to four classes of persons: kings, wazirs, scholars, and fourthly amirs who are constantly engaged in war [against infidels] and defending Islam. Apart from these whoever introduces the words *din* and *Islam* into his titles should be punished, so that others may take warning.

35. The object of titles is that people may be recognized by them. For example, there may be a hundred persons in a certain company or gathering; of that number perhaps ten may be called Muhammad. Suppose someone calls, 'O Muhammad'; all ten Muhammads will have to answer *'Labbaik'* [Here I am], for each will think that he alone is being called. But if one Muhammad is called Mukhtass [Special], another Muwaffaq [Successful], another Kamil [Perfect], another Rashid [Correct], and so on, then when they are called by their titles, they will know at once who is meant.

36. Apart from the wazir, the head of the correspondence department, the accountant-general, the head of the military department, the head of the secret intelligence department, and the civil governors of Baghdad and Khurasan, nobody else in the country should be given titles other than those without the word *mulk*, such as Khwaja Rashid [The Correct Chief], Khwaja Mukhtass [The Special Chief], Khwaja Sadid [The Good Chief], Ustad Amin [Trusted Master], Ustad Khatir [Honoured Master], and Ustad Tagin [Brave Master] and the like; thus the degrees and ranks of high and low, great and small, nobles and commons will be distinct, and the prestige of the administration will remain undiminished. When

there is stability in the country, when the king is just and vigilant, when he gives diligent attention to affairs, and seeks to learn about the customs and manners of his predecessors, and when he has a successful, knowledgeable and skilful wazir, then he will restore all matters to good order, he will reinstate the proper rules with regard to titles, and he will abolish all bad customs through the exercise of his judgment, his authority and his sword.

## CHAPTER FORTY-ONE

*On not giving two appointments to one man; on giving posts to the unemployed and not leaving them destitute; on giving appointments to men of orthodox faith and sufficient merit, and not employing men of perverse sects and evil doctrines; keeping the latter at a distance*

1. Enlightened monarchs and clever ministers have never in any age given two appointments to one man or one appointment to two men, with the result that their affairs were always conducted with efficiency and lustre. When two appointments are given to one man, one of the tasks is always inefficiently and faultily performed; and in fact you will usually find that the man who has two functions fails in both of them, and is constantly suffering censure and un-easiness on account of his shortcomings. And further, whenever two men are given a single post each transfers [his responsibility] to the other and the work remains forever undone. On this point there is a proverb which runs, 'The house with two mistresses remains unswept; with two masters it falls to ruins.' One of the two thinks to himself, 'If I take pains to do the work expediently, and take care not to let anything go wrong, our master will think that this is due to the capability and skill of my partner, not to my own diligent and patient efforts.' The other one has the same idea and thinks, 'Why should I take trouble for nothing when it will go without praise or thanks? Whatever efforts and exertions I make, my master will suppose that my partner has done it.' Actually there will

be constant confusion in the work, and if the manager says, 'What is the cause of this inefficiency?' each man will say that it is the other's fault. But when you go to the root of the matter and think intelligently, it is not the fault of either of them. It is the fault of the man who gave one appointment to two persons. And whenever a single officer is given two posts by the divan it is a sign of the incompetence of the wazir and the negligence of the king. Today there are men, utterly incapable, who hold ten posts, and if another appointment were to turn up, they would spend their efforts and money to get it; and nobody would consider whether such people are worthy of the post, whether they have any ability, whether they understand secretaryship, administration, and business dealings, and whether they can fulfil the numerous tasks which they have already accepted. And all the time there are capable, earnest, deserving, trustworthy, and experienced men left unemployed, sitting idle in their homes; and no one has the interest or judgment to enquire why one unknown, incapable, base-born fellow should occupy so many appointments, while there are well-known, noble, trusted, and experienced men who have no work at all, and are left deprived and excluded, particularly men to whom this dynasty is greatly indebted for their satisfactory and meritorious services. This is all the more extraordinary because in all previous ages a public appointment was given to a man who was pure alike in religion and in origin; and if he was averse and refused to accept it, they used compulsion and force to make him take the responsibility. So naturally the revenue was not misappropriated, the peasants were unmolested, assignees enjoyed a good reputation and a safe existence, while the king lived a life of mental and bodily ease and tranquillity. But nowadays all distinction has vanished; and if a Jew administers the affairs of Turks or does any other work for Turks, it is permitted; and it is the same for Christians, Zoroastrians and Qarmatis. Everywhere indifference is predominant; there is no zeal for religion, no concern for the revenue, no pity for the peasants. The dynasty has reached its perfection; your humble servant is afraid of the evil eye and knows not where this state of affairs will lead.

2. In the days of Mahmud, Mas'ud, Tughril and Alp Arslan (may Allah have mercy on them) no Zoroastrian or Jew or Rafidi

would have had the audacity to appear in a public place or to present himself before a great man. Those who administered the affairs of the Turks were all professional civil servants and secretaries from Khurasan, who belonged to the orthodox Hanafi or Shafiʿi sects. The heretics of ʿIraq were never admitted as secretaries and tax-collectors; in fact the Turks never used to employ them at all; they said, 'These men are of the same religion as the Dailamites and their supporters; if they get a firm footing they will injure the interests of the Turks and cause distress to the Muslims. It is better that enemies should not be in our midst.' Consequently they lived free from disaster. Now things have reached such a state that the court and the divan are full of them, and every Turk has ten or twenty of these individuals running after him, and their object is to prevent even a few Khurasanis from entering the service of this court and earning a living here. One day the Turks will realize the iniquity of these people and recall my words, when the divan becomes empty of Khurasani secretaries and officials.

In former times if a man offered himself for service to a Turk as an administrator or in any other capacity, and said that he was of the Hanafi or Shafiʿi sect and from a Sunni city, he was accepted; but if he said that he was a Shiʿite from Qum, Kashan or Aba[1] he was refused and told, 'Be gone; we kill snakes not nourish them.' Even if money and presents were offered, the Turk would not accept them, but would say, 'Go in safety; take these gifts back to your own house and use them for yourself.' If ever Sultan Tughril and Alp Arslan (may Allah illumine their graves) heard that a Turk or an amir had admitted a Rafidi into his presence, they would reprimand him for the error.

3. One day it was reported to The Martyr Sultan Alp Arslan (may Allah sanctify his soul) that Ardam was going to appoint a certain village headman as his secretary. He was enraged to hear it, because the headman was known to be of the Batini sect. He spoke to Ardam in the audience-hall and said, 'Are you my enemy and the foe of the state?' When Ardam heard this, he fell on the ground and said, 'O Master, what is this you say? I am the least

[1] These places were noted for their fanatical Shiʿite population; see Le Strange, *Lands*, 209–11, and *Rahat as Sudur*, 30. 20.

of your slaves; what fault have I committed in service and loyalty to my lord?' The sultan said, 'If you are not my enemy why have you taken my enemy into service?' Ardam said, 'Who is that?' He said, 'The headman of Aba who is your secretary.' He said, 'What in the world is wrong with him? and even if he turned into a venomous [serpent] what could he do to this empire?' He said, 'Go and bring this man here.' He was brought in immediately. The sultan said, 'Thou wretch, thou sayest that the caliph of Baghdad is not the lawful caliph; thou art a Rafidi.' The wretched man said, 'O Master, your slave is not a Rafidi; I am a Shi'ite.' The sultan said, 'O cuckold, what is so good about the Shi'a that you give it precedence over the Batini sect? The one is bad; the other is worse.' He commanded the mace-bearers to beat the man, and they threw him half dead out of the palace.

4. Then the sultan turned to the nobles and said, 'It was not this wretched man's fault; it was Ardam's fault for taking an infidel into his service. I have often said that in this country we are foreigners; we conquered this country by force; we are all orthodox Muslims and these 'Iraqis are heretics, and partisans of the house of Dailam. Today God (be He exalted) has favoured the Turks because they are orthodox Muslims and do not tolerate vanity and heresy.' He then asked for some horse hair; he gave one hair to Ardam and said, 'Break it.' Ardam broke it. Then he gave him ten hairs and he broke them. But when he twisted many hairs together and said, 'Break these,' Ardam could not do so. The sultan said, 'So it is with enemies; in ones and twos they can be broken but when they become numerous it is impossible. This is the answer to your question, "What power does this wretched fellow possess and what can he do to the state?" If they infiltrate one by one amongst the Turks, and are allowed to administer their business and get to know about their affairs, then the very moment that revolt breaks out in 'Iraq, or if the Dailamites attack this country, all these people will secretly and openly make common cause with them and seek to destroy the Turks. You are a Turk, and an officer of the Khurasan army; your administrators, secretaries and officials should all be Khurasanis; and the same should apply to all the Turks, if their interests are not to be damaged. When you make an alliance with

your enemy, it is a treason committed against your person and against the king; and even if it is permissible to do what you like to your own person, it is impossible for the king to relax his vigilance and caution, and to spare the traitor. I must protect you; do you then protect me, for God (to Him be power and glory) has made me chief over you not you over me. Know this, that whoever makes friends with the king's enemies, is himself an enemy of the king; and he who has converse with thieves and evil-doers is to be reckoned one of their number.'

5. On this occasion when the sultan was uttering these words Khwaja Imam Mushattab[1] and Qadi Imam Abu Bakr were present. He turned to them and said, 'What is your opinion about what I have been saying?' They said, 'You have said what God and The Prophet say.'

6. Then Mushattab said: 'Abd Allah ibn 'Abbas says that one day The Prophet (upon him be prayers and peace) said to 'Ali (may Allah be pleased with him) [in Arabic], 'If you meet a people called Rafidis casting off Islam, slay them for they are polytheists.' (The Persian translation is as follows: If you find a people called Rafidis, they will have abandoned Islam; when you meet them you must kill them all for they are unbelievers.)

7. Qadi Abu Bakr said: Abu Umama relates that The Prophet (upon him be peace) said [in Arabic], 'At the end of time a people called Rafidi [will arise]; when you meet them, kill them.' (The Persian translation . . .)

8. Then Mushattab said: Sufyan ibn 'Uyaina called the Rafidis infidels and he adduced this verse [Quran 48. 29], 'That the unbelievers may be enraged at them . . . [They are] most vehement against the unbelievers.' And he used to say that whoever slanders The Companions of The Prophet (may Allah bless him) is an unbeliever, on the authority of this verse which has been quoted. And The Prophet (upon him be peace) said [in Arabic], 'Allah (be He blessed and exalted) has given me companions and ministers and kinsmen; whoever abuses them, upon him be the curses of

---

[1] There was a lawyer of the Hanafi school called Mushattab ibn Muhammad Farghani, who was contemporary with Nizam al Mulk, but this conversation is obviously invented only for the purpose of introducing the traditions.

Allah, of the angels, and of all the human race. Allah will not accept their requital nor their repentance.' (The Persian translation . . .) God says [in the Quran 9. 40] concerning Abu Bakr (may Allah be pleased with him), 'The second of two, when they two were in the cave, and he said to his companion: Grieve not; verily Allah is with us.' (The interpretation of this is as follows: If no one helps us, O Abu Bakr, do not grieve for God is with us.)

9. Qadi Abu Bakr said: 'Uqba ibn 'Amir relates that The Prophet (upon him be peace) said [in Arabic], 'If there were a prophet after me, it would be 'Umar ibn al Khattab.' (The Persian . . .)

10. Mushattab said: Jabir ibn 'Abd Allah (may Allah be pleased with him) related [in Arabic] that The Prophet of Allah (may Allah bless and save him) was present at a funeral and did not pray over the corpse; they said, 'O Prophet of Allah, we never saw you omit to pray over any but this.' He said, 'He hated 'Uthman and Allah hates him.' (The Persian translation . . .)

11. Qadi Abu Bakr said: Abu 'd Darda relates (may Allah be pleased with him) that The Prophet (upon him be peace) said concerning 'Ali (may Allah be pleased with him) [in Arabic], 'They who rebel against you are the dogs of hell.' (The Persian . . .)

12. Mushattab said: 'Abd Allah ibn 'Abbas and 'Abd Allah ibn 'Umar (may Allah be pleased with them both) say that The Prophet (upon him be peace) said [in Arabic], 'The Qadaris and the Rafidis have no portion in Islam.' (The Persian . . .)

13. Qadi Abu Bakr said: Isma'il ibn Sa'd relates (may Allah be pleased with him) about The Prophet (upon him be peace) that The Prophet said [in Arabic], 'The Qadaris are the Magians of this community; if they are ill, do not visit them; and when they die be not present at their funerals.' (The Persian translation . . .) And all Rafidis hold the same doctrines as the Qadaris.

14. Mushattab said: Umm Salma relates about The Prophet (upon him be peace) as follows: One day The Prophet (upon him be peace) was with me; Fatima and 'Ali (may Allah be pleased with them) came to him to ask after his health. The Prophet (upon him be peace) raised his head and said, 'O 'Ali, greeting to you, for you and your kinsmen will be in paradise. But after you a people will rise up and they will be called Rafidi. If you overtake them kill

them for they are unbelievers.' 'Ali said, 'O Prophet of Allah, what shall be their sign?' The Prophet said, 'They will not be present at the Friday prayers; they will not congregate [for worship]; neither will they pray at funerals; and they will slander their forefathers.'

15. On this subject there are many traditions and verses [of the Quran]. If I were to mention them all, it would be a book in itself. At all events such are the characteristics of the Rafidis. As for the Batinis, which are worse than the Rafidis—just consider how [vile] they must be. At whatever time they may appear, the ruler of that time will have no more obligatory duty than to wipe them from the face of the earth and make his country free and clear of them.

16. The Commander of the Faithful 'Umar (may Allah be pleased with him) was sitting in the mosque at Medina; Abu Musa Ash'ari (may Allah be pleased with him) was sitting in front of him, and was presenting the accounts for Isfahan—written in a fair hand and exactly reckoned, so that all who saw admired them. Abu Musa was asked, 'Whose writing is this?' He said, 'My secretary's.' They said, 'Send someone to bring him here for us to see him.' He said, 'He cannot come into the mosque.' The Commander of the Faithful 'Umar said, 'Is he unclean then?' He said, 'No; he is a Christian.' 'Umar gave Abu Musa a slap on the thigh—so hard that he said he thought his thigh was broken—and said, 'Have you not read the command of The Lord of Majesty where He speaks [Quran 5. 56]: O ye who believe, take not Jews and Christians as friends; they are friends to one another.' Abu Musa said, 'This very hour will I dismiss him and give him his leave.'

> 'Tis right to beware of friendly enemies;
> friendship with friendly friends is better.
> Be not heedless of two kinds of men—
> hostile friends and friendly foes.

17. After that Sultan Alp Arslan did not speak to Ardam for a whole month but only looked severely at him; until at last the nobles interceded, and he was pleased with him again.

Now let us return to our discourse.

18. Whenever appointments are given to ignoble, unknown and untalented persons, while famous men, learned scholars and Sunnis

are left unemployed—when five or six posts are vested in a single man while another receives none at all, this is a sign of the ignorance and incompetence of the wazir. He is one of the worst of enemies who gives ten appointments to one man and leaves ten men without employment. In such a country there are many people frustrated and idle; finding no work and no attention, they may busy themselves with an activity that has irreparable consequences. But when the wazir is competent and learned, the token of this is the fact that he does not try to damage the king's interests.

19. Now in actual fact there is just such a one[1] who is seeking to ruin this country. At every opportunity he recommends economies; to The Master of the World he alleges that the world is subdued; that there is nowhere any enemy or opponent who can withstand him; that he has nearly 400,000 horsemen on his pay-roll; that 70,000 would be enough and he could detail them to deal with any emergency; let him suppress the pay and allowances of the remainder; this would represent an economy of so many thousand dinars a year, and in a short time the treasury would be full. When The Master of the World spoke in these same terms I knew whose words they were—the words of one who wishes to ruin the country. I replied: It is for The Master to command; but if he gives pay and allowances to 400,000 men, then it follows that Khurasan, Transoxiana, Kashghar, Balasaghun, Khwarazm, Nimruz, 'Iraq, Pars, Syria, Adharbaygan, Armenia, Arran, Antioch, Jerusalem—all these will continue to be his. It were better that instead of 400,000 he had 700,000, because if his men were more, his domain would be greater; then Sind, India, Turkistan, China and Machin [Indo-China] would belong to The Master, and Abyssinia, Barbary, Rum, Egypt and the West [N. Africa] would be in his sway. For the more troops a king has, the wider his realm; the fewer troops he has, the smaller his dominion. Moreover The Sublime Intellect is aware that if he keeps 70,000 men in place of 400,000 the names of 330,000 must be erased from the register. Obviously 330,000 men are more than 70,000, and those 330,000 are all men of the sword. When they have nothing more to hope for from this empire, they

---

[1] This is probably a reference to Nizam al Mulk's rival Taj al Mulk, who was patronized by Turkan Khatun, wife of Malikshah: see *Rahat as Sudur*, 133. 13.

will get out of control. They will find some other master and make him their leader. Then they will attack on every side and cause such confusion that the riches of many years will all be dissipated and still, maybe, the matter will not be put to rights. For countries are held by men, and men by gold. If someone says to the king, 'Take gold, and leave men', that person is in truth the king's enemy and is seeking to destroy the country, for gold is acquired only by men; his words must not be heeded.

20. The case of deprived and destitute civil officials is exactly the same. When people have performed great works and difficult tasks for this empire, have achieved celebrity and fame, and deserved reward from this imperial house for their services, it is not proper to disregard their claims, to leave them ruined, disappointed and dispossessed; to keep them unemployed is not right, nor is it compatible with humanity. The proper thing is to offer them appointments, or allow them some livelihood according to their capabilities, so that at least a part of their dues of service will be paid, and they will not remain without any portion from this empire. Now in fact there is a certain body of men—doctors, scholars, noblemen and men of valour—whose portion lies in the treasury. They are entitled to consideration and remuneration, yet no one offers them any work, and they get neither remuneration nor consideration. Now if they remain deprived of their livelihood and disappointed of their portion from the empire, a time may come when the king's agents, being ignorant and graceless, fail to represent the cases of these deserving people to the king, neglect to give these officials any work and omit to provide salary and sustenance to such noble and learned men; in that time this party, cutting off their expectations from this empire, will become disaffected to the government; they will try to expose whatever faults the king may have—or the scribes, or the tax-collectors or the Turks. Then, whoever amongst them is best provided with lands, instruments and resources and has troops and funds, will be put at their head, and they will cause disturbances and rise against the king, throwing the country into confusion, just as they did in the time of Fakhr ad Daula.

*The story of Fakhr ad Daula*

21. They say that in the city of Rayy in the time of Fakhr ad Daula, whose wazir was the [celebrated] Sahib Isma'il ibn 'Abbad, there was a fire-worshipper, a rich man, who was called Buzurjumid Diru. He had built a tower of silence[1] for himself on the hill of Tabarik,[2] and it is still in existence today; now it is called The Generals' Look-out, and it is situated above The Dome of Fakhr ad Daula. Buzurjumid took great pains and spent much money in completing this two-storied tower on top of that hill. But there was a certain inspector (of weights and measures) whose name was B'akhir-asan [Easy-at-the-end]. On the day that the tower was finished, he went up it on some pretext and proclaimed the [Muslim] call to prayer; the tower was thus desecrated. Thereafter it came to be known as The Generals' Look-out.

22. It so happened that in the latter part of the reign of Fakhr ad Daula couriers reported that thirty or forty people were leaving the city every day and ascending that tower; they would stay up there until sundown and then come down and disperse in the city; if anyone asked them why they were going there every day, they said it was for recreation. Fakhr ad Daula ordered that the men were to be brought before him along with any others who were seen to accompany them. A party of courtiers went and climbed the hill; they shouted at the foot of the tower. The men heard them and looked down; they saw the chamberlain of Fakhr ad Daula with a small party. They let down ladders for the party to ascend. When they got to the top they saw a chess-board laid out, and a backgammon board; there were pens, ink and paper; there was a table cloth with food set on it, a pitcher of water and a rush mat spread out. The chamberlain said, 'Fakhr ad Daula summons you.' The men were brought in front of the king; The Sahib was present. Fakhr ad Daula asked them who they were and why they went up the tower every day. They said they were having an outing. The king said, 'An outing may be for one or two days; you have been carrying on

---

[1] A tower open to the sky and supplied with gratings, upon which Zoroastrians expose their dead.

[2] See Le Strange, *Lands*, 216, 217 note.

this secret business for a long time. Tell me the truth.' They said, 'There is no secret about the fact that we are not robbers, or murderers, or highwaymen, or seducers of women and children; nor has anybody ever complained to Your Majesty about us on account of any objectionable or unreasonable behaviour. If Your Majesty will guarantee our lives, we will tell you who we are.' Fakhr ad Daula said, 'I give you security for your lives and property;' and he took an oath upon it.

23. When they had been assured of security for their lives, they said, 'We are a group of secretaries and officials who have been left unemployed in Your Majesty's reign and deprived of a portion from your government; nobody offers us any work and nobody pays any attention to us. We hear that in Khurasan a king has appeared whom they call Mahmud, and he welcomes men of learning and talent, and does not allow them to be wasted; abandoning all hope in this country we have now pinned our faith upon him. Every day we go up this tower and condole with one another upon our misfortune; whenever anyone arrives from a distance we seek information about Mahmud, and we constantly write letters and overtures to our friends in Khurasan, explaining our circumstances and inquiring after companions for the journey to Khurasan; for we are all family men, and being reduced to poverty we are compelled by necessity to leave the land where we were born and go abroad in search of work. Now we have explained our circumstances; it is for The Master to command.'

24. When Fakhr ad Daula heard these words he turned to The Sahib and said, 'What is your opinion? what ought we to do?' The Sahib said, 'Your Majesty has given them security, and moreover they are learned, distinguished and respected men; I know some of them and some are related to me. Leave the matter of their employment to me; I will do all that is required to provide for them adequately and will ensure that a report reaches you tomorrow.' So the king ordered the chamberlain to conduct the men to The Sahib's house and leave them there. The chamberlain did so and came back to Fakhr ad Daula's palace. Meanwhile the men were quaking in fright for their lives, wondering what punishment he would give them. When The Sahib returned from the palace he took a look at

them. Some time elapsed; then a servant entered and led them all into another room decked out like paradise and strewn with costly carpets. The servant said, 'Go and sit wherever you like.' So they went and seated themselves on the mattresses prepared for them. Sherbet was brought in; when they had drunk that, trays of food were set out; and when they had eaten the food and washed their hands, wine was served; and as they drank the wine minstrels played and sang. Apart from the three servants who were serving them nobody was allowed into that room, and nobody outside knew what had happened to them; throughout the city men and women were worried about them and their children wept.

25. A little later in the day one of The Sahib's chamberlains entered the room and said, 'The Sahib says you are to understand that he does not wish his house to become a prison; today and tonight you are his guests. If they had wanted to do you any harm they would not have sent you to his house; be at ease and make yourselves at home, for tomorrow when The Sahib comes back from the office he is going to attend to arrangements for your employment.' He then fetched a tailor, and ordered twenty brocade cloaks and twenty silk turbans; he also called for twenty horses saddled and caparisoned. At sunrise the following day everything was ready. The Sahib summoned all the men; he invested each with a cloak and turban, gave every one a horse with trappings, and appointed them all to various official posts; some were given pensions and all were given presents; then they were sent to their homes satisfied. The next day they all came to call on The Sahib; The Sahib said, 'Now complain no more; send no more ingratiating letters to Mahmud and stop trying to bring about the decline of our country.'

26. When next Fakhr ad Daula received The Sahib, he asked him what he had done with that group of men. He said, 'O Master, I gave each one a horse with trappings, a suit of clothes and money for expenses; and wherever I found one man holding two posts in the administration, I relieved him of one and gave it to one of these men, so when I sent them back home they had all become government officials.' Fakhr ad Daula was pleased and approved his action, saying, 'If you had done otherwise it would not have been right; would that what you have done this year you had done several years

ago, and then they would not have had recourse to our enemies. Hereafter one man is not to be given two posts; everyone is to have one post only, so that all potential civil servants may be employed and the prestige of all the posts may be maintained. Moreover, when two or three posts are allotted to one man, it becomes difficult for all the officials to make a living; and foreigners and critics will say that we have no men left in our cities and our country because we give two posts to one man; so they will infer that we are incompetent. Do you not know that wise men have said [in Arabic], "There are men for every work." (That is to say: for every work there is a man.) In our country there are high, low and middle grade appointments; and each official and professional civil servant should be given one appointment according to his capacity, knowledge and suitability; if anyone who has an appointment asks for another, his request should be disregarded and refused; then this improper practice will be discontinued, and when there are no officials unemployed, the country will become prosperous.'

27. Furthermore the kingdom is kept in order by its tax-collectors; and the head of all the tax-collectors and other officials is the wazir. Whenever the wazir is corrupt and unjust, the officers are all likewise, nay worse. An officer may be well versed in his duties, he may be a secretary, an accountant or a man of business such that he has no peer in all the world; but if he is a member of a bad sect, such as Jew, Christian or Zoroastrian, he will despise the Muslims and afflict them with hardships on the pretext of taxes and accounts. If the Muslims are oppressed by that infidel and complain about him he must be dismissed and punished. One must not be concerned with what his intercessors may say—they may say there is no secretary or accountant in the world like him; they may say that if he is removed from office, the work will all come to grief, and there is nobody to take his place. This is all lies and such words must not be heeded; it is imperative to change that man for another, as The Commander of the Faithful 'Umar once did (may Allah be pleased with him).

*The story of 'Umar and the Jewish tax-collector*

28. It so happened that in the days of Sa'd [ibn Abi] Waqqas in the neighbourhood of Baghdad, Wasit, Hit, Anbar and other districts as far as Basra and the boundary of Khuzistan, there was a Jewish tax-collector. Now the people of these districts wrote a petition to The Commander of the Faithful 'Umar (may Allah be pleased with him) and complained against that Jewish collector, saying, 'This man on the pretext of tax-collection is humiliating and mocking us; we cannot endure it further. If there is no other alternative, appoint a Muslim collector over us; being of the same religion as ourselves perhaps he will not exceed his authority and oppress us; if however he does so, at least we would prefer to suffer such injustice and indignity from a Muslim than from a Jew.' When 'Umar read the petition he said, 'Is it not enough for a Jew that he should be alive in the world? Does he also expect preference over the Muslims?' He immediately ordered a letter to be written to Sa'd Waqqas telling him to dismiss the Jew and give the appointment to a Muslim.

29. On reading the letter, Sa'd Waqqas detailed a horseman to go and bring the Jewish collector to Kufa, and he sent several other riders to summon all the Muslim tax-collectors in the province of Persia. The Jew arrived and the other tax-collectors. On inspection none of the Arabs was found to possess the knowledge to fulfil the post, and of the Persian collectors who were Muslim not one was discovered who had the same ability as the Jew, nor did anybody understand as well as he the various aspects of the work, such as collecting revenue, developing the country, dealing with people, and keeping up with taxes and arrears. Sa'd Waqqas was at a loss to know what to do. Of necessity he kept the Jew in the appointment and wrote to The Commander of the Faithful saying, 'I attended to your command and brought the Jew here and assembled together all the tax-collectors and civil officials, both Arab and Persian; but there was nobody among the Arabs who was acquainted with Persian affairs, and no one at all who understood the duties of tax-collection and administration as well as the Jew. I was obliged to keep him at his post to prevent disorganization of business

and breakdown in the collection of taxes. What is your command?'

30. When the letter reached 'Umar (may Allah be pleased with him) he was amazed, and said, 'This is most extraordinary, that a man should overrule my authority and countermand my order.' He took up his pen and wrote at the top of the letter, 'The Jew is dead!' and sent it back to Sa'd Waqqas. What he meant was, 'Every man has to die; and death may dismiss the tax-collector. Know that if a tax-collector dies or is dismissed, his work cannot be allowed to lapse. You should appoint someone else at once; why are you so weak and helpless? Suppose the Jew is dead.' When Sa'd received the letter and saw 'Umar's postscript upon it, he immediately recalled the Jew, dismissed him, and gave the post to a Muslim. After a year had passed it was observed that the Muslim discharged his duties even more efficiently than the Jew; the same revenue came in, the peasants were contented, yet public works increased. Sa'd Waqqas then said to the Arab nobles, 'What a great man is The Commander of the Faithful 'Umar! We wrote a long letter on the subject of that Jew; he gave the answer in two words; and it turned out as he said, not as we thought.'

31. Two persons spoke two sayings; both were applauded and among Arabs and non-Arabs will be cited as proverbs by Muslims until the resurrection. One was that saying of The Commander of the Faithful 'Umar (may Allah be pleased with him): 'The Jew is dead!' Whenever it is desired to dismiss a tax-collector or other official who knows well the duties of a secretary, but is extortionate and unjust or a heretic, and some people support him saying, 'Don't, for he is a good secretary and a clever official, and nobody knows more about business than he', and suchlike, then the ruler must say at once, 'The Jew is dead!' All their arguments will be confounded by these (two) words, and the collector will be dismissed. When The Prophet (upon him be peace) went out from the world, not one of his Companions dared to say that The Prophet was dead; after Abu Bakr (may Allah be pleased with him) was installed in the caliphate, he mounted the pulpit to preach, and said [in Arabic], 'Whoever used to worship Muhammad, verily Muhammad is

dead; whoever used to worship Muhammad's Lord, verily He is living and immortal.' (The interpretation is as follows: If you are worshipping Muhammad, Muhammad is dead; and if you are worshipping the God of Muhammad, He is in existence and ever shall be; He it is who has never died and will not die.) The Muslims approved this speech, and it became a proverb among the Arabs; and whenever any great affliction befalls the Arabs or a dear one passes away, and they want to ease the burden of suffering for the unfortunate relative, people cry out, 'Muhammad is dead!'; for of all mankind had it been possible for one man not to die, then that person should have been Muhammad The Elect.

Now let us return to our discourse.

32. We said that tax-collectors and their work are the concern of the wazir. The good wazir enhances the fame and character of his sovereign; and the kings who have become great and whose names will be blessed until the resurrection, have all been those who had good wazirs, and the same is true of the prophets (the prayers of Allah be upon them all): Solomon (upon him be peace) had one like Asaf ibn Barkhiya, Moses (upon him be peace) had his brother Aaron (upon him be peace), Jesus (upon him be peace) had Simon, and The Elect (upon him be prayers and peace) had Abu Bakr as Siddiq (may Allah be pleased with him). Among great kings there was Kai Khusrau who had a wazir like Gaudarz, Manuchihr had Sam, Afrasiyab had Piran Wisa, Gushtasp had Jamasp, Rustam had Zawara, Bahram Gur had Khuraruz, and Nushirwan had Buzurj-mihr; while the 'Abbasid caliphs had such ministers as the Barma-kids [Barmecides], and the Samanids had the Bal'amis, Sultan Mahmud had Ahmad ibn Hasan, Fakhr ad Daula had The Sahib Isma'il ibn 'Abbad, Sultan Tughril had Abu Nasr Kunduri, Alp Arslan and Malikshah had Nizam al Mulk;[1] and there are many more like these.

33. Now a wazir needs to have sound faith and to belong to a pure sect—either Hanafi or Shafi'i, and he must be efficient, shrewd, a good pen-man, and loyal to his king; if he also be the son of a

---

[1] It is conceivable that the author might have included his own name in a list of famous wazirs, but it is less likely that he would have mentioned his old enemy Kunduri: see *Rahat as Sudur*, 117. 12–17: so para. 32 must be considered suspect.

wazir so much the better, for from the time of Ardashir Babakan
to Yazdijird ibn Shahryar (the last of the kings of Persia) wazirs
needed to be sons of wazirs just as kings had to be sons of kings.
When the kingship passed out of the house of the kings of Persia,
the wazirship departed from the house of the wazirs.

*The story of Sulaiman ibn ʿAbd al Malik and Jaʿfar ibn Barmak*[1]

34. They say that one day Sulaiman ibn ʿAbd al Malik was
giving audience and all the nobles of the state and all his boon-
companions were present. [In the course of the proceedings] the
caliph voiced the following idea: 'If my dominion is no greater than
that of Sulaiman ibn Davud [Solomon son of David] (upon them
both be peace) it is not less, except for the fact that he had command
over winds, demons, fairies, wild beasts and birds, and I have not;
as for wealth, magnificent equipage, territorial possessions, military
strength and personal authority, who in all the world now has, or
who before me has ever had, the equal of what is mine at this
moment? In this kingdom of mine do I lack anything which I
ought to have?' One of the nobles said to him, 'The most important
thing which countries need and kings have always had, Your
Majesty has not.' Sulaiman said, 'What is that?' He said, 'You have
not a wazir who is worthy of you.' He said, 'How so?' He said,
'You are a king, born of royal stock; you should have a wazir who
is sprung from a line of wazirs, besides being blessed with talents
and good fortune.' Sulaiman said, 'Can there be found in all the
world a wazir such as you have described?' He said, 'Yes.' He said,
'Where?' He said, 'At Balkh.' He said, 'Who is he?' He said,
'Jaʿfar ibn Barmak, whose ancestors back to the time of Ardashir
Babakan have been wazirs and sons of wazirs; the ancient fire-
temple at Nau-bahar [near] Balkh[2] is a pious foundation vested in

---

[1] This story with almost identical wording is found in the opening pages of an
earlier book, the *Tarikh-i-Baramika* 'History of the Barmakids', and this is undoubtedly
the source from which our author drew it; the important difference is that there the
wazir is Barmak not Jaʿfar; Nizam al Mulk has gratuitously altered the name and
thereby perpetrated an anachronism, probably for no other reason than to introduce
a more celebrated name. [2] See Le Strange, *Lands*, 421.

that family. When Islam spread and fortune deserted the dynasty of the kings of Persia, Barmak's ancestors settled at Balkh, and remained there. Wazirship is hereditary in their family and they possess books about the functions and duties of a wazir; when their children had learnt writing, literature and secretaryship, then they used to be given these books to read and learn; thus sons assimilated the character of their fathers in all respects. Ja'far is the most suitable man in the world to be Your Majesty's wazir. Hereafter Your Majesty knows best.' Yet of the Umayyads and Marwanids there was no greater or more powerful ruler than Sulaiman ibn 'Abd al Malik.

35. When he heard these words he determined to bring Ja'far ibn Barmak from Balkh and give him the wazirship. He wondered whether he might not still be a fire-worshipper; he made enquiries and when he found out that he had been born a Muslim he was glad. He sent a letter to the governor of Balkh instructing him to send Ja'far to Damascus, and even if it cost 100,000 dinars to equip him for the journey he was to spend the money and send him with all possible pomp to the capital. So Ja'far was sent to Damascus. The nobles of every city on the way came out to meet him and gave him hospitality. When he reached Damascus, all the highest officers of state and army, apart from Sulaiman ibn 'Abd al Malik himself, went to welcome him; they escorted him into the city with the utmost pomp and circumstance and installed him in a most palatial residence. After three days he was taken before Sulaiman ibn 'Abd al Malik; when Sulaiman first saw him as he came into the palace, he was pleased with his appearance and bearing. Ja'far entered the hall and the chamberlains conducted him gradually towards the throne; having shewn him to his seat they retired. The moment that Ja'far sat down, Sulaiman looked sharply at him; then he scowled and said angrily, 'Be gone from my sight!' The chamberlains hurriedly seized him and whisked him away; nobody knew what the reason was; until later in the day after the forenoon prayer there was a drinking party attended by nobles and boon-companions; several rounds were drunk and there was general merriment.

36. When it was seen that Sulaiman had recovered his temper,

one of the courtiers said, 'Your Majesty commanded Ja'far to be brought from Balkh with all this dignity and ceremony for a high office. When he appeared before Your Majesty for the very first time you immediately looked coldly upon him; what was the reason for that? We your humble servants were struck with amazement.' Sulaiman said, 'Had it not been for the fact that he is of noble birth and has come from afar, I would have had him executed there and then, because he had deadly poison with him—the very first time he came into my presence he brought poison as a gift!' One of the nobles said, 'Would you permit me to go and question him about this, to see what he says—whether he confesses or denies?' He said, 'You may go.' So he got up and left the company to go and see Ja'far; he asked him, 'When you came before Sulaiman today, did you have poison with you?' He said, 'Yes, and I still have it; here it is, underneath the gem of my ring. My forefathers had similar rings and this one came to me from my father. I and my ancestors have never harmed so much as an ant with this ring, let alone a human being. Rather we kept it for prudence and precaution's sake, for my ancestors were many times subjected to hardship and torture for financial ends; and in this case when Sulaiman summoned me, I did not really know the reason for the call; I considered that if he were to ask for treasure-lists or make some other demand which I could not fulfil, and if then he molested me in any way that I could not endure, I would remove the gem of the ring with my teeth and swallow the poison in order to escape from all the suffering and misery.'

37. Having listened to this explanation from Ja'far, the courtier immediately went back and told Sulaiman what had transpired; he was amazed at his prudence, vigilance and foresight; he had no more doubt about him, and accepted his explanation. Then he ordered all the nobles to take his private horse, go to the door of Ja'far's house and bring him with honour and dignity to the court. The next day this was done. When Ja'far came before Sulaiman, Sulaiman held out his hand to him, enquired about his journey, and welcomed him warmly; he made him sit down and invested him there and then with the robe of the wazir's office; then he placed the inkpot in front of him for him to sign a few official documents

in his presence. Sulaiman had never been seen in such a good humour as he was on that day; after the audience was over, he held a drinking party and the presence-chamber was decorated with gold, jewels and carpets woven with gold thread, the like of which had never been seen before.

38. So they settled down to their drinking; and in the course of the merry-making Ja'far asked Sulaiman, 'How did Your Majesty know that I, out of so many thousand people, had poison with me?' Sulaiman said, 'I have with me something more precious to me than all my treasuries and all my possessions, and I never go without it; this is a couple of beads, like onyx but not in fact onyx; I acquired them from the treasury of the kings and I wear them fastened on my arm; they have this property, that wherever poison may be, whether with a person or in food or drink, as soon as the smell of it reaches them, they immediately start moving and knocking against one another restlessly; then I know that there is poison somewhere in the room and take steps to guard against it. When you set foot inside the hall the beads began to move; the nearer you came the more their agitation increased; by the time you sat down in front of me they were rattling together. I had no doubt at all that you were carrying poison, and had anyone else been in your place I would not have spared him. When they took you away the beads calmed down, but they did not cease moving altogether until you had left the palace.' Then he loosed the beads from his arm and shewed them to Ja'far saying, 'Have you ever seen anything more wonderful than this?' Ja'far and all the nobles looked at the beads in astonishment. Then Ja'far said, 'In the course of my life I have seen two unparalleled marvels; one is this which I now see with Your Majesty; the other is something I saw with the king of Tabaristan.' Sulaiman said, 'What was that? Tell me; I would like to hear.'

39. Ja'far related the following story: When Your Majesty's decree reached the governor of Balkh instructing him to despatch your humble servant to Damascus, I packed my things for the journey and bent my steps towards your presence. From Nishapur I took the road to Tabaristan because I had some goods there. When I reached Tabaristan, the king of Tabaristan came out to meet me and escorted me to his palace in the city of Amul where I

was entertained. Every day the king and I used to eat and sit together, and we made daily excursions to different places. One day in a jovial mood he said to me, 'Have you ever taken a trip on the sea?' I said, 'No.' He said, 'Tomorrow you are my guest for a sea trip.' I said, 'It is for you to command.' He ordered boatmen to prepare boats and hold themselves ready. On the following day the king took me down to the sea and we got into a boat; minstrels struck up a tune and the boatmen rowed us out to sea, while cup-bearers plied us all the while with wine. The king and I were sitting close to one another with nobody in between us; on his finger he had a ring the gem of which was a red ruby of the most exquisite beauty and brilliance that I had ever seen; and on account of its splendour I could not keep my eyes off it.

40. When the king noticed that I was constantly looking at the ring, he took it off his finger and tossed it into my lap. I bowed to him, kissed the ring and laid it in his lap. The king picked it up and gave it to me again, saying, 'A ring which has left my finger by way of being a present freely given does not come back on my finger again.' I said, 'This particular ring is worthy of Your Majesty's finger'; and I gave it back to the king. The king gave it to me again. Considering that the ring was so beautiful and valuable, I said, 'Your Majesty says this in his cups; I would not wish him to regret it and be distressed when he is sober.' I put the ring back in the king's lap. The king took it and threw it into the sea. I exclaimed, 'Oh! what a pity! if I had known for certain that Your Majesty would not put the ring on his finger again and was going to throw it into the sea, well—I would have accepted it, for I had never seen such a ruby.' The king said, 'I offered it to you several times; when I saw your eyes fixed on it, I took it off my finger and presented it to you; although I regarded it as a beautiful ring, if you yourself had not been more precious in my sight, I would not have given it to you; it was your fault for not accepting it; now that I have thrown it in the sea you are sorry. However, perhaps I can contrive to get it back for you.' He said to a page, 'Get into a small boat and go back to the shore; when you land take a horse and gallop back to the palace; tell the treasurer that you want a certain silver casket; take it and bring it here with haste.' Before sending the page he told the

boatman to drop anchor and keep the boat in the same place until he had further instructions; he did so. Meanwhile we carried on drinking until the page arrived with the casket and laid it in front of the king. The king opened a purse which he kept on his waist and took out a silver key; he undid the lock of the casket, and putting his hand inside he removed a golden fish and threw it into the sea. The fish went under the water and dived to the bottom of the sea, disappearing from sight. After some time it came to the surface, holding the ring in its mouth. At the king's command a boatman hurried to the spot with a small boat, picked up the fish with the ring and brought it like that to the king. The king took the ring from the fish's mouth and tossed it into my lap. I bowed to him, picked up the ring and put it on my finger, while the king put the fish back into the casket, locked it up and replaced the key in his purse.

41. Ja'far was wearing the ring [as he spoke]; he took it off his finger and laid it in front of Sulaiman, saying, 'This is the ring, O Master.' Sulaiman picked it up and looked at it; then he gave it back to him and said, 'You should not lose the souvenir of such a [remarkable] man.'

42. The purpose of this book was not to tell stories such as this; however when a particular story seemed out of the ordinary and at the same time fitting, it was related.

43. My object in this chapter was to point out that when the good age arrives and the sick time changes, the sign of it is this, that a just king appears and does away with evil-doers; right counsels prevail; ministers and officers are men of virtue and nobility; every task is allotted to the proper workman; two posts are not given to one man; soldiery and peasantry fear the king; boys[1] are not promoted [to high office]; advice is sought from men of mature wisdom and intelligence; and all things are restored to their proper order with the result that affairs religious and worldly are well arranged and every man has work according to his capability; nothing contrary to this is permitted and all things great and small are regulated by the balance of justice and the sword of governance.

[1] No doubt Nizam al Mulk is referring to Malikshah's small son Mahmud, whom Turkan Khatun wished to be heir, against the advice of Nizam al Mulk; see Browne, *Literary History*, II. 185, and *Rahat as Sudur*, 134. 4.

# CHAPTER FORTY-TWO

*On the subject of those who wear the veil,*
*and keeping underlings in their place*

1. The king's underlings must not be allowed to assume power, for this causes the utmost harm and destroys the king's splendour and majesty. This particularly applies to women, for they are wearers of the veil and have not complete intelligence. Their purpose is the continuation of the lineage of the race, so the more noble their blood the better, and the more chaste their bearing the more admirable and acceptable they are. But when the king's wives begin to assume the part of rulers, they base their orders on what interested parties tell them, because they are not able to see things with their own eyes in the way that men constantly look at the affairs of the outside world. They give orders following what they are told by those who work amongst them such as chamberlains and servants. Naturally their commands are the opposite of what is right, and mischief ensues; the king's dignity suffers and the people are afflicted with trouble; ruin comes to the state and the religion; men's wealth is dissipated and the ruling class are put to vexation. In all ages nothing but disgrace, infamy, discord and corruption have resulted when kings have been dominated by their wives. Let us discuss a little of this subject in the hope that much will be made clear.

2. The first man who suffered loss and underwent pain and trouble for obeying a woman was Adam (upon him be peace) who did the bidding of Eve and ate the wheat,[1] with the result that he was expelled from paradise, and wept for two hundred years until God had mercy on him and accepted his repentance.

*The story of Saudaba, wife of Kai Kavus and her domination over him*

3. When Kai Kavus sent messengers to Rustam asking for the return of Siyavush because he longed to see him,—Siyavush was his son and Rustam had fostered him until he reached the age of

---

[1] It is wheat in Islamic tradition rather than an apple.

manhood—Rustam sent Siyavush to him. Now Siyavush was exceedingly handsome. Saudaba saw him from behind the curtain and was enamoured of him. She said to Kai Kavus, 'Tell Siyavush to come into the women's apartments so that his sisters may see him.' Kai Kavus said to Siyavush, 'Go into the women's apartments for your sisters to see you.' Siyavush said, 'It is my lord's command, nevertheless it were better that they be in their apartments and I in the hall.' When he went into the night-quarters, Saudaba assaulted him and drew him to herself with mischievous intent. Siyavush became angry and wresting himself from her embrace, he left the women's apartments and went to his own house. Saudaba was afraid of what he might say to his father. She said to herself, 'It is better that I anticipate him.' So she went to Kai Kavus and said, 'Siyavush assaulted me and clung to me, and I escaped from him.' Kai Kavus was vexed with Siyavush and there was much fierce and angry talk, until at last it was suggested to Siyavush that he should undergo ordeal by fire. Siyavush said, 'It is for the king to command; whatever he says, I am ready.' So they collected enough firewood to cover half a farsang square, and set fire to it.

4. When the fire had gained strength and reached the height of a mountain, they said to Siyavush, 'Now! Go in!' Siyavush was riding Shabrang. He uttered the name of God, made his horse leap into the flames, and disappeared. After some time he emerged from the far side of the fire in safety with not a hair singed either on himself or on his horse, by God's command. All the people were amazed. The priests took some of that fire and carried it to the fire-temple; and it is still alive—the fire which gave judgment correctly.

5. After this judgment Kai Kavus appointed Siyavush to be amir of Balkh and sent him there. But Siyavush had been offended by his father on account of Saudaba, and he lived unhappily there. He was minded not to stay in the land of Iran. He thought of going to Hindustan, or else to China and Machin [Indo-China]. Piran Wisa, who was Afrasiyab's army-commander, came to know Siyavush's secret intent. He presented himself to Siyavush and paid him compliments on behalf of Afrasiyab. Siyavush welcomed him and entered into a covenant with him. Piran Wisa said that their house was one, and their two families were one; Afrasiyab would hold

him dearer than all his own sons; and if he ever wished to be recon-
ciled with his father and return to Iran, Afrasiyab would intercede
for him, and make a firm treaty with Kai Kavus, and then send
him to his father with all honour and respect. So Siyavush went
from Balkh to Turkistan. Afrasiyab gave him his daughter in
marriage and treated him kindly. However, Garsivaz, Afrasiyab's
brother, became jealous of him, and blackened him in front of
Afrasiyab. Siyavush was innocent but he was slain in Turkistan.
Wailing arose in Iran and her warriors were aroused. Rustam came
from Sistan to the capital. Without permission he entered the
women's apartments of Kai Kavus and seized Saudaba by the hair;
he dragged her outside and cut her to pieces with his sword. No
man dared to tell him, 'You did well,' or 'You did ill.' Then they
girded themselves for war, and went to Turkistan to take vengeance
for the murder of Siyavush. The war went on for many years, and
on both sides many thousand men were slaughtered. And the cause
of all this was Saudaba and her domination over King Kai Kavus.

6. Kings and men of strong judgment have always ordered their
lives in such a way, and followed such a path that they never let their
wives know their secrets; so they remained free from the yoke of their
desires and commands and did not succumb to them; one such was
Alexander.

7. History relates that when Alexander came from Rum and
defeated Darius son of Darius, who was King of Persia, Darius was
killed in flight by one of his own servants. Now Darius had a
daughter perfect in beauty and charm, and she had a sister just as
fair; and in his palace there were other girls of his family—all of
them beautiful. People said to Alexander, 'It befits you to pass by
Darius's night-quarters and see those moon-faced ones, especially his
daughter, for in beauty she has no peer.' Those who said this intended that Alexander should see Darius's daughter, and having
seen her with all her comeliness, marry her. Alexander replied, 'We
vanquished their men; let us not be conquered by their women.' He
heeded them not, and went not into Darius's night-quarters.

8. Another well-known story is that of Khusrau and Shirin and
Farhad. Since Khusrau so loved Shirin that he put the reins into her

hands and did everything that she said, then inevitably she grew bold, and though she was queen to such a great king, she began to prefer Farhad.

9. Buzurjmihr was asked, 'Why was it that the empire of the house of Sasan fell to ruin while you were their counsellor, for today you have no equal in the world?' He said, 'There were two reasons: firstly that the Sasanians entrusted weighty affairs to petty and ignorant officers, and secondly that instead of seeking out men of learning and wisdom, they left matters to women and boys. This is the very opposite of prudence and wisdom, for be assured that whenever a king leaves affairs to women and boys, the kingship will surely depart from his house.'

10. There is a tradition that The Prophet (upon him be peace) commanded, 'Consult women, but whatever they say, do the opposite, and that will be right.' The words of the tradition are [in Arabic], 'Consult them and oppose them.' Had women possessed complete intelligence, The Prophet (upon him be peace) would not have said this.

11. It is reported in another tradition that when The Prophet's illness became severe, he was so weak that when the time came for obligatory prayer, The Companions were all waiting for him to begin the service; 'Ayisha and Hafsa (may Allah be pleased with them both) were sitting at his bedside; 'Ayisha said to The Prophet, 'O Prophet of Allah, it is time for prayer, and you are not strong enough to go to the mosque. Whom will you command to lead the prayer?' The Prophet (upon him be peace) said, 'Tell Abu Bakr to read the prayers.' 'Ayisha said, 'O Prophet of Allah, Abu Bakr is a man of feeble spirit, who cannot possibly stand in your place.' The Prophet said, 'Tell Abu Bakr to say the prayers.' 'Ayisha again said, 'He is a weak man and feeble-spirited.' The Prophet repeated, 'Tell Abu Bakr to say the prayers.' 'Ayisha then said to Hafsa, 'You speak to him, as I have said several times that Abu Bakr is soft-hearted and loves him more than all other Companions do; if he should stand up to pray and see The Prophet's place empty, he would be overcome with weeping and that would spoil his own and all the others' prayers. 'Umar ibn al Khattab is strong and stout of heart; if he be told to do it, nothing will go amiss.' So Hafsa spoke

in this wise to The Prophet; his face flushed with anger and he said, 'You are like Yusuf and Kirsuf in the story; I shall not do what you want; I shall do what is good for the Muslims; go and tell Abu Bakr to lead the congregation.'

12. These are the words of the tradition; and in spite of all the nobility, the learning, the devotion and the piety of 'Ayisha (may Allah be pleased with her), The Prophet (upon him be peace) did the opposite of what she wanted. So imagine what the opinions of other women are worth.

### The story of Yusuf and Kirsu,

13. They say that in the time of The Sons of Israel it was the rule that if for forty years a man had preserved himself from great sins, had fasted and prayed at the proper times and harmed no one, then God would grant him three wishes. Now there was in those days one of The Sons of Israel called Yusuf, a good and pious man, and he had a wife called Kirsuf, as devout and chaste as he. He accomplished this devotional exercise and worshipped God for forty years without default. He thought to himself, 'Now what thing shall I ask from God (be He exalted)? I wish I had a friend to advise me what to ask for—something beneficial.' However much he pondered he could not think of anyone suitable. As he entered his house he caught sight of his wife. With remorse he said, 'In all the world I hold none dearer than this my wife; she is my mate and the mother of my children. My good is her good, and she more than all people desires my good. The right thing is to consult her in this matter.'

14. So he said to his wife, 'Know that I have now completed forty years of devotion, and three wishes will be granted to me. No one in all the world desires my good more than you. Tell me what to ask from God.' His wife said, 'You know that I have only you in all the world; my eye rejoices in you; and you know that the wife is a man's comfort; I am your comfort; your heart is always happy at the sight of me, and your life is sweet with me as companion. Ask God to give me beauty such as he has given to no other woman, and then whenever you come in at the door and see me so fair and charming, your heart will be glad; as long as we are vouchsafed to remain

in this world, we will live in joy and happiness.' The man was pleased at his wife's words. He prayed saying, 'O Lord, give this woman grace and beauty such as Thou hast given to no other woman.' God heard and answered Yusuf's prayer. Next day when his wife got up from sleep, she was not the woman who had gone to bed the night before; she had changed into a form of such comeliness as mortals had never seen.

15. When Yusuf saw her so beautiful he was astonished and he nearly jumped out of his skin for joy. Every day his wife's beauty and excellence grew until it reached a point where the beholder could not bear to look upon her. The report of her beauty spread throughout the world, and multitudes came to catch sight of her. Then one day she looked in the mirror and saw her beauty; her heart was filled with wonder and pride. She said, 'Who is like me in all the world today? who has such grace and beauty as I have? what have I got to do with this pauper who eats barley bread and passes a miserable existence without any of the good things of this world? I am fit for the greatest kings and Chosroes of the world, and if they find me they will adorn me with gold, jewels and brocade.' Vain desires and ambitions of this sort entered the woman's head. She began to be bad-tempered and quarrelsome with her husband, and often said to him, 'You are not fit for me; you have not even got enough bread to eat.' She had three or four children by Yusuf; she ceased to look after them and became so unmanageable that Yusuf was at his wit's end and did not know what to do. He looked up to heaven and said, 'O Lord, turn this woman into a bear.' Immediately the woman turned into a bear and became a scourge, constantly prowling about the walls and roof of his house; it never went away from the house, and all day water ran from its eyes. Yusuf was at a loss to know how to look after his children; he was unable to perform his divine worship, and he constantly missed the time for prayer. Once more he was in distress; he reached such dire straits that he looked up to heaven and said, 'O God, turn this bear back into a woman just as she was before; give her a contented mind, so that she will watch over her children and care for them; then I, Thy servant, will devote myself to worshipping Thee.' Straight away the woman resumed her original form, and proceeded to attend to her

children. She never remembered what had happened, and only thought that she had been dreaming. So the forty years' devotion of Yusuf was [as the Quran 25. 25 says] 'blown dust'—all because of the schemes and desires of a woman.

Thereafter this story became a proverbial warning against doing what women say.

16. The caliph al Ma'mun one day spoke as follows: 'May there never be a king who allows the people of the veil to speak to him about the state, the army, the treasury and the government or to interfere in such matters, or to patronize particular persons; for if they are heeded, at their behest the king may promote one and punish another, or appoint one and dismiss another; [and if this happens] inevitably people will resort to the women's court and present their needs to them since they can be more easily won over. The women, finding themselves the object of attention and seeing their doors thronged with soldiers and peasants, will give way to all sorts of vain desires and initiate all kinds of corrupt practices. Soon heretics will gain access to them. Then it will not be long before the king's majesty vanishes, and the dignity and splendour of the court and the government depart; the king will lose the respect of all, and reproaches will come in from surrounding countries; the country will lapse into confusion, the troops will become disaffected, and the wazir will be powerless to prevent it.'

17. The best procedure is for the king to follow the established custom which great and prudent kings have practised and which God (to Him be power and glory) himself has commanded [Quran 4. 38]: 'Men are rulers over women.' (He says: We appointed men over women to keep them under control.) If women had been able to control themselves, He would not have set men over their heads. So if anyone places women over men, whatever mistakes and mischiefs occur are his fault, for permitting such a thing and changing the custom.

18. It was a dictum of Kai Khusrau that any king who wants his house to endure, his country not to be destroyed and his own pomp and dignity not to fall to the ground, must never permit people of the veil to have any say except in matters concerning their own underlings and servants. In this way they will preserve the ancient custom and keep themselves free from all anxieties.

19. 'Umar ibn al Khattab (may Allah be pleased with him) said, 'The words of people of the veil are, like their persons, indecent. Just as it is wrong to display their persons in public, so also it is unseemly to repeat their words.'

20. May that which has been mentioned on this subject be acceptable, and let it be known that these words are full of benefit.

## Concerning underlings

21. God (be He exalted) has created the king to be the superior of all mankind and the inhabitants of the world are his inferiors; they derive their subsistence and rank from him. He must then keep them in such a position that they always know their places and do not put off the ring of service from their ears nor loose the belt of obedience from their waists. At all times he must let them know how they stand whether in merit or demerit, so that they do not forget themselves nor do whatever they like. He should know the measure and rank of every one, and be constantly enquiring into their circumstances lest they deviate from the letter of his commands or overstep the limits which are set for them.

22. One day Buzurjmihr said to Nushirwan The Just, 'The country belongs to the king, and the king has given the country but not the people of the country, to the army. If the army are not interested in the king's country, and lack kindness and mercy towards the people, and try only to fill their own purses, they will not care whether the country is deserted or the peasantry impoverished. When the army has power over the country to strike, to fetter, to imprison, to chastise, to betray, to appoint and to dismiss, then what difference is there between the king and them? for these things have ever been the king's prerogative, not the business of the army; armies have never been allowed to exercise such power and authority. In all ages the crown, the golden stirrup, the gilt cup, the throne and the coinage have belonged by right to the king alone.' And he went on, 'If the king wishes to have glory and virtue above all other kings, then let him refine and polish his morals.' The king said, 'How shall I do that.' He said, 'Banish the bad qualities from yourself, and take hold of the good qualities and exercise them. The good

qualities are these: modesty, good temper, clemency, forgiveness, humility, generosity, truthfulness, patience, gratitude, mercy, knowledge, intelligence and justice. And the bad qualities are these: hatred, envy, pride, anger, lust, greed, desire, spite, mendacity, avarice, ill temper, cruelty, selfishness, hastiness, ingratitude and frivolity.'

23. He who is cognizant of these qualities knows how to regulate all things and in the management of subordinates and the direction of affairs of state will need no guide.


## CHAPTER FORTY-THREE

*Exposing the facts about heretics who are enemies of the state and of Islam*

1. Your humble servant wanted to compose a few chapters on the risings of various rebels, so that all the world might know how great has been my concern for this kingdom, and how sincere my loyalty and devotion to the empire of the Saljuqs, especially to The Master of the World (may Allah perpetuate his reign) and to his children and family (may the evil eye be averted from this epoch).

2. Seceders have existed in all ages, and from the time of Adam (upon him be peace) until now in every country in the world they have risen up in revolt against kings and prophets. Never has there been a more vile, more perverted or more irreligious crowd than these people, who behind walls are plotting harm to this country and seeking to destroy the religion. Their ears are alert for the sounds of sedition and their eyes are open for signs of the evil eye. If in any way (we take refuge with Allah!) through some celestial accident any misfortune should befall this victorious empire (may Allah The Mighty strengthen it) these dogs will emerge from their hiding places, and will revolt against this empire and support the claims of the Shi'a. The greatest reinforcement of their strength comes from the Rafidis and Khurramdins, and as far as they can they will leave

nothing undone in the pursuit of mischief, murder and heresy. In their speech they claim to be Muslims, but in reality they act like unbelievers; their inward purposes are at variance with their outward appearances; their words are the opposite of their deeds. The religion of Muhammad The Elect (may Allah pray for him and bless him) has no more vile enemy than them, and the kingdom of The Master of the World has no worse opponent.

3. There are certain persons who on this very day hold privileged positions in this empire and who have raised their heads from the collar of the Shi'a, and as members of this faction they secretly do its business, assist its policies and preach its doctrines. They try to persuade The Master of the World to overthrow the house of the 'Abbasids, and if I were to lift the lid from the top of that pot—oh! the disgraceful things that would be revealed! But—worse than that —as a result of their representations The Master of the World has become weary of his humble servant, and is not prepared to take any action in the matter, because of the economies which these people recommend, thereby making The Master of the World greedy for money. They make out that I am interested in my private advantage and so my humble advice finds no acceptance. One day The Master will realize their iniquity and treachery and criminal deeds—when I have disappeared. Then will he know the measure of my devotion and loyalty to this victorious empire; for I have not been ignorant of their characters or their plottings and I have at every opportunity made them known to The Sublime Intellect (may Allah exalt it) and not concealed them. But when your humble servant saw that his words on this subject were not believed, he did not repeat them.

4. However I have introduced into this book of Rules [for Kings] a section dealing with the revolts of these [heretics], in order to explain as concisely as possible who they are, what sort of beliefs they hold, whence they first originated, how many times they have emerged, and in each case who was responsible for putting them down—so that after my death this book may be a reminder for The Master of the Kingdom and the Faith. For this same accursed faction has broken out and perpetrated massacres even in the lands of Syria, Yemen and Spain. I will only relate, in the manner of an epitome, what they have done in Persia. Whoever wishes to learn all the

facts about them and all the disasters which they have caused to the kingdom and the faith should study the histories, especially the History of Isfahan.

Now I will proceed to describe about one hundredth of what they have done in the land of Persia—for that is the principal part of the kingdom of The Master of the World—so that their story from beginning to end may be known to The Sublime Intellect (may Allah The Mighty exalt it).

## CHAPTER FORTY-FOUR

*On the revolt of Mazdak, the doctrines of his sect, and the circumstances of his death at the hands of Nushirwan The Just*

1. The first person in the world to introduce atheistic doctrines was a man who appeared in the land of Persia; he was a Zoroastrian high priest[1] in the time of King Qubad ibn Firuz the father of Nushirwan The Just; and his name was Mazdak Bamdadan. He plotted to corrupt the Zoroastrian faith to the disadvantage of its adherents, and spread evil ways in the world. Now it so happened that Mazdak was well versed in astrology, and from the motions of the stars he foretold that in that age a man was to appear who would introduce a religion to cancel the Zoroastrian, Jewish, Christian and idolatrous faiths; this new religion he would impose upon the necks of mankind by miracles and by force, and it would last until the resurrection. Mazdak conceived the vain fancy that he would be this person, and he began to ponder how he should convert the people and propagate the heresy. He knew that in the king's council he enjoyed the utmost respect and the highest estate, while his word was supreme among all the nobles; never had he been heard to utter a vain word—until he laid claim to prophethood. What he did was to tell his minions to make a tunnel in a certain place; they gradually bored a hole so that the end of it came up in

[1] Persian *mūbad-mūbadān*: cf. page 44, line 28.

the fire-temple, just at the spot where the fire was made; it was only a small opening. Then he began to state his claim to be a prophet, and said, 'I have been sent to renew the faith of Zoroaster because people have forgotten the meaning of the Avesta and Zend, and have ceased to obey the commands of The Good One as Zoroaster laid down; just as in the case of The Sons of Israel when they were disobedient and failed to perform the laws of Moses (upon him be peace) which he received from God in the Torah, He sent a prophet, as promised in the Torah itself, to cast out the disobedience from The Sons of Israel, to restore the authority of the Torah and bring the people back to the right way.' These words reached the ears of King Qubad.

2. The next day he called his nobles and priests and held court for the redress of wrongs. He summoned Mazdak and said to him publicly, 'Do you claim to be a prophet?' He said, 'Yes. I have come because our enemies have corrupted the faith which Zoroaster instituted, and cast it into doubt; I will restore it to health. For the most part the people are wrong in their interpretation of the Avesta and Zend; I will shew them the true meaning.' Qubad said, 'What is your [proof or] miracle?' He said, 'My miracle is this, that I will make the fire speak—the fire which you regard as your *qibla*[1] and sanctuary; and I will ask God (to Him be power and glory) to command the fire to bear witness to my prophethood, so that the king and everyone with him may hear.' The king said, 'O nobles and priests, what do you say to these words which Mazdak speaks?' The priests said, 'The first thing is this, that he is calling us to our own faith and book, and he is not disobeying Zoroaster. It is true that there are passages in the Avesta and Zend which can bear ten different meanings, and every priest and doctor explains and interprets them differently. It is possible that he may give a better interpretation and more fitting meaning to those passages. But as for his saying that he will give voice to this fire which is the object of our worship—this is a marvel which is not within the power of a man. More than this the king knows best.' Then Qubad said to Mazdak, 'If you make the fire speak I will bear witness that you are a prophet.' Mazdak said, 'Let the king appoint a time when he will

---

[1] The direction in which to face at prayer.

come to the fire-temple with his priests and nobles, and at my bidding God (to Him be power and glory) will make the fire speak. If he wills, let it be this very day or this very hour.' Qubad said, 'We propose to come to the fire-temple tomorrow.' The next day Mazdak sent one of his minions into that hole and said, 'Each time that I call upon The Good One with a loud voice, you get beneath the hole and say: Let all worshippers of The Good One adopt and practise the words of Mazdak; thus they will find prosperity and good fortune in both worlds.'

3. So Qubad and the nobles and priests went to the fire-temple. Mazdak was called; he came and stood beside the fire, and called upon The Good One with a loud voice and blessed Zoroaster, and was silent. From out of the fire there came a voice after the manner we have related so that the king and all the nobles heard it and were amazed; Qubad made up his mind to believe in Mazdak, and they returned from the fire-temple. Thereafter Qubad drew Mazdak daily nearer to himself, until at last he believed in him. He gave him a golden throne inlaid with jewels, and ordered it to be placed on the dais in the audience-hall. At the time of audience Qubad would sit on the dais, and he would seat Mazdak on the throne, and Mazdak would be much higher than Qubad. Then people began to join Mazdak's religion, partly out of liking and sympathy, and partly for the sake of agreeing with the king. From various provinces and districts they came to the capital, and either openly or secretly entered Mazdak's religion. The military for the most part had no zeal for it, but out of respect for the king they dared not say anything; of the priests not one went over to Mazdak's religion; they said, 'Let us see what [proof] he adduces from the Avesta and Zend.'

4. When Mazdak saw that the king had embraced his religion and that people from far and near were accepting his invitation, he introduced the subject of property, and said, 'Wealth must be divided among the people, for all are God's slaves and children of Adam. Whatsoever people may need, the expense must be met from the communal funds, so that no man suffers neediness and privation in any respect.' After he had convinced Qubad and his other adherents on this point and they had agreed to the sharing of wealth, then he said, 'Your wives are like your other possessions; they too

should be regarded as common property. If any man feels desire for a woman let him come together with her. There is no jealousy or anger in our religion and nobody is deprived of the pleasures and lusts of the world. The doors of desire and satisfaction are open for everybody.' Then by reason of the community of property and the sharing of women, people were all the more eager to adopt his religion, especially the common people. And he laid down the custom that if someone invited twenty men to his house not only would he provide bread and meat and wine and minstrels, but all the guests would get up one by one and make use of his wife; and they thought it no wrong. Their custom was that whenever a man went into a room to have commerce with a woman, he put his hat on the door and then went inside. If another person was seized with the same desire, on seeing the hat hanging on the door he turned back, knowing that somebody was already engaged in that business within.

5. Then Nushirwan sent someone secretly to the priests and said, 'Why do you stay thus silent and helpless? Why do you not say something about Mazdak and give some advice to my father? What is this vain attitude you have adopted? Have you been taken in by the deceit of this impostor? Why, has this dog not ruined people's property, ripped the veils from their womenfolk, and made the common people masters of all? Very well, then ask him on what authority, at whose bidding he is doing all this. For if you remain silent, your property and your wives will be lost; and dominion and power will depart from our family. Arise and go before my father, and acquaint him of this matter and give him counsel. Then hold argument with Mazdak and see what proof he can produce.' And to the nobles he sent messages saying, 'My father has been overcome by a vicious melancholy, and his wit has been impaired so that he cannot distinguish between good and evil. Please consider how he may be cured lest he should listen to Mazdak and act upon his words; and you too should beware of being deceived like my father; for this is a vain thing, and vanity does not endure, nor will it profit you in the future.'

6. The nobles were frightened at Nushirwan's words and threats, and although some of them had intended to go over to Mazdak's

religion, on account of Nushirwan they withdrew, saying, 'Let us see where Mazdak's affairs lead and what are the grounds for Nushirwan's assertion.' Nushirwan at this time was eighteen years old.

7. Then the priests agreed amongst themselves, and went to Qubad and said, 'From the time of Adam (upon him be peace) until the present we have never read in any history of such statements being made and such orders being given as these of Mazdak, nor have we heard of such things from any of the various prophets which have been in Syria. To us it appears as an abomination.' Qubad said, 'Speak to Mazdak and see what he says.' They called Mazdak and said, 'What justification have you for these injunctions of yours?' Mazdak said, 'Zoroaster commanded so, and thus it is written in the Avesta and Zend, but men have not known the interpretation thereof. If you do not believe me, ask the fire.' Again they went to the fire-temple and put their question to the fire. From the midst of the fire a voice came out, 'It is indeed as Mazdak says and not as you say.' Once more the priests returned abashed. The next day they saw Nushirwan and reported the matter. Nushirwan said, 'This Mazdak is succeeding because his religion is the same as the religion of the fire-worshippers in all but two respects.'

8. After a period had passed over these events, one day Qubad and Mazdak were talking; Qubad chanced to say, 'Have people been eager to come over to our religion?' Mazdak said, 'They would have come over one and all if Nushirwan had allowed them; but he has been obstinate and has not accepted the religion.' Qubad said, 'Do you mean that he is not of our faith?' He said, 'No.' Qubad said, 'Call Nushirwan.' Nushirwan was brought. Qubad said, 'Are you not a believer in Mazdak's religion?' He said, 'No, praise be to Allah.' He said, 'Why?' He said, 'Because he is an impostor and a cheat.' He said, 'Wherefore cheat? Did he not make the fire speak?' Nushirwan said, 'Four things are opposites of one another, and have no colour—water, fire, earth and wind. Let him make water, wind and earth speak as he did the fire, and then I will believe in him.' Qubad said, 'But all that he says comes from interpretation of the Avesta and Zend.' Nushirwan said, 'He who composed the Avesta and Zend did not say that wealth and wives were free to be shared,

and in all these years no scholar has produced such an interpretation. Religion exists for the protection of wealth and wives; if these two become free, then what will be the difference between beasts and men, for it is of animals to be equal in feeding and coupling, not intelligent human beings.' Qubad said, 'That may be, but why have you opposed me, your father?' He said, 'I have learnt that from you, although it was never the custom before. When I saw you opposing your own father, I too opposed you. If you renounce that, then I will turn back from this.' Qubad and Mazdak in their conversation with Nushirwan eventually reached a point where they said plainly, 'Either you produce evidence to disprove this religion of Mazdak and to refute his arguments, or bring someone whose arguments are stronger than Mazdak's; otherwise we shall punish you as a warning to others.' Nushirwan said, 'Give me forty days grace and either I will bring you evidence, or I will bring someone to answer Mazdak.' They said, 'Very well,' and thereupon they all parted.

9. Having returned from his father's presence, Nushirwan the very same day sent a messenger with a letter to Pars, to the city of Gul,[1] to a certain aged and wise priest who dwelt there, saying, 'Please come with all speed, for such-and-such has happened between myself, my father and Mazdak.'

10. When the forty days were up Qubad gave audience. He took his seat upon the dais; then Mazdak came and mounted the dais, and sat upon the throne. Qubad ordered Nushirwan to be brought in. Mazdak said to Qubad, 'Ask him what he has found to answer us.' Qubad said, 'Come, what have you found?' Nushirwan said, 'I am making my arrangements.' Mazdak said, 'The time for arrangements has passed; have him punished.' Qubad was silent. Mazdak gave a sign for attendants to seize Nushirwan. When they moved towards him, he laid his hand on the balustrade of the hall, and said to his father, 'Why are you in such haste to ruin your own house? The term has not yet expired.' They said, 'How so?' He said, 'I asked for forty days entire, and today is included in the forty until it is over. After that you know best; do whatever you will.' The

---

[1] This is evidently an earlier form of the name Gūr or Jūr (later Fīrūzābād): see Le Strange, *Lands*, 255–6.

commanders and priests shouted their assent and said, 'He speaks true; the term was forty days, not forty less one.' Qubad said, 'Let him go for today,' and they released him.

11. Qubad then rose and left the audience-hall and the people dispersed; Mazdak returned to his house and likewise Nushirwan. Just then the priest whom Nushirwan had summoned from Pars arrived, mounted on a fast camel. By constant enquiry he reached Nushirwan's palace and dismounted and went inside. Softly he said to a servant, 'Go and tell Nushirwan that the priest from Pars has arrived and wishes to see him.' The servant quickly went into the room and told Nushirwan. Nushirwan came out of the room and embraced the priest for joy, and said, 'O priest, know that this day I have escaped from the other world'; and he told him of all the circumstances. The priest said, 'Do not be anxious, for everything is as you have said, and you are right and Mazdak is wrong. I will give answer to Mazdak as your representative, and I will make Qubad regret what he has done, and bring him back to the [right] road. But now please contrive for me to see Qubad, before Mazdak comes to know that I am here.' He said, 'That is easy; I will arrange for you to see the king tonight in private.' At the time of afternoon prayer Nushirwan went to his father's palace and requested an audience. When he saw his father, he pronounced his eulogy and then said, 'There has arrived from Pars a priest who will give answer to Mazdak, but he has besought me that tonight the king should hear what he has to say in private, and see his proof; thereafter let the king order whatever is appropriate.' Qubad said, 'Very well; bring him.'

12. Nushirwan returned, and when it was dark took the priest to his father. The priest blessed Qubad, and praised his forefathers; then he said to the king, 'This Mazdak has fallen into error; this task was not destined for him.' The king said, 'Why?' He said, 'I know him well, and I know the extent of his learning. He knows something about the science of the stars, but about their decrees he is mistaken. It is foretold that at the coming conjunction a man will appear who will lay claim to prophethood; he will produce a new book, and perform wonderful miracles, and cut the moon into two halves[1] in the sky; he will call the people to The Good One, and

---

[1] See *The Quran*, Sura 54, 'The Moon', verse 1.

found a holy religion to abolish the Magian religion and all other religions; he will promise paradise and threaten purgatory; he will protect people's property and wives by divine ordinances; he will shun the devil and consort with the angel [Gabriel]; he will destroy fire-temples and idol-temples, and his religion will spread through all the world and will last until the resurrection; heaven and earth will bear testimony to his prophethood. Now this Mazdak has conceived the fancy that he should be this person. But firstly this person will not be a Persian: and Mazdak is a Persian. He will prohibit the people from fire-worshipping, and deny Zoroaster: while Mazdak actually follows Zoroaster and prescribes fire-worshipping. He will not allow a man to look at another's wife, nor to take a grain of another's property; for a single unlawful diram he will order hands to be cut off: but Mazdak has made wealth and wives common property. He will receive his orders from heaven, and speak from angelic inspiration: but this man follows the fire. No, Mazdak's religion has no foundation. Tomorrow I will disgrace him in front of Your Majesty, for he is in error and is only intent on taking the kingship away from your house and wasting your treasure, and making you the equal of every mean fellow.' His words were pleasing and acceptable to Qubad.

13. The next day Qubad came to the audience-hall, and Mazdak sat upon the throne and Nushirwan stood in front of the dais, and the priests and nobles presented themselves. Then the priest from Pars said to Mazdak, 'Will you ask the first question or shall I?' Mazdak said, 'I will.' The priest said, 'If you want yourself to be the questioner and me to answer, then come here where I am and I will go where you are.' Mazdak was ashamed, and said, 'The king himself seated me here; you ask and I will answer.' The priest said, 'You have instituted community of property; is it not so that those who build inns, bridges and mosques do so for the sake of reward in the next world?' He said, 'Yes.' He said, 'If wealth is to be shared with everyone else, when people do good works, who will get the reward?' Mazdak was unable to answer. Again he said, 'You make wives common property; suppose twenty men lie with one woman, and the woman becomes pregnant; when she gives birth, whose will the child be?' Mazdak failed to reply. Then he said, 'Your purpose

is to ruin utterly the pedigrees and possessions of the people. Consider the king who sits upon this throne and is our ruler; he is the son of King Firuz and he inherited the throne from his father, just as King Firuz inherited it from his father. If ten different persons lie with the king's wife, then when a child is born, how shall they say whose child it is? Will the line of descent not be broken? When that happens the kingship surely leaves the family. High and low rank depend upon riches or poverty; if a man is poor he is out of necessity compelled to enter the service and hire of a rich man; thus high and low rank are manifested. When all property is shared, differences of rank will disappear from the world. The meanest wretch will be equal to the king; in fact kingship will be nullified. You have come to annihilate the wealth and sovereignty of the royal family of Persia.' Mazdak could not say anything; he remained silent. Qubad said, 'Answer him.' He said, 'The answer is that you should instantly order his head to be cut off.' Qubad said, 'A man's head cannot be cut off without proof.' He said, 'I will ask the fire what it commands, for what I say is not from myself.' People had been much distressed for Nushirwan's sake; now they rejoiced that he had escaped death. Mazdak was angry with Qubad, because he had told him to kill the priest and kill Nushirwan, but he had not done so. Mazdak said to himself, 'My followers are now many amongst the peasantry and the army. I must arrange to remove Qubad from the scene; then I will kill Nushirwan and my other enemies.' So they settled that on the following day they would go to the fire-temple and see what the fire ordered; and they dispersed.

14. When night came on, Mazdak called two of his minions and co-religionists and gave them gifts of money; and he promised to make them both generals. Then he made them swear not to say anything of this to anybody, and he gave them two swords, and said, 'Tomorrow when Qubad comes to the fire-temple with the priests and nobles, if the fire orders Qubad to be killed, you both straightaway draw your swords and kill him. Nobody else of course will come into the fire-temple armed.' They said, 'We obey.' The next day the nobles and priests went to the fire-temple, and Qubad likewise. Now the priest [of Pars] had told Nushirwan, 'Tell ten of your retainers to conceal swords beneath their clothes when they go

with you to the fire-temple, in case Mazdak attempts some treachery.' Nushirwan did so, and went to the fire-temple. Whenever Mazdak intended to go to the fire-temple, he instructed his minion beforehand what to say from under the hole. So having told the minion what to say, he himself went to the temple. He said to the priest, 'You ask the fire to speak to you.' The priest put some questions to the fire, but he got no reply. Then Mazdak said to the fire, 'Judge between us, and bear witness that I am right.' From the midst of the fire the voice came, 'Since yesterday I have become weak; strengthen me with the heart and liver of Qubad, so that I may tell you what to do. Mazdak is your guide to everlasting happiness.' Then Mazdak said, 'Strengthen the fire!' Those two men drew their swords and assaulted Qubad. The priest said to Nushirwan, 'Rescue Qubad!' Nushirwan and his ten men drew their swords and intercepted those two persons and prevented them from striking Qubad; Mazdak was all the time saying, 'The fire speaks at the bidding of The Good One.' The people then split into two parties; one party said, 'Let us throw Qubad dead or alive into the fire'; others said, 'Let us hesitate in this until we can see more clearly.' At the close of the day they went back and Qubad was saying, 'Perhaps I have been guilty of some sin for which the fire wishes to use me as food; anyway I would rather be consumed in the fire of this world than in the fire of the next world.'

15. The next time that the priest was alone with Qubad he spoke about bygone priests and kings, and citing these and others as proof, he argued that Mazdak was not a prophet, but the enemy of the royal family; the proof of this was that first he had tried to kill Nushirwan; when he was unsuccessful, he attempted to kill him, Qubad; why did he fancy that the fire had spoken; the fire had never yet uttered a word, so why should it do so then; he would contrive to expose this fraud and shew the king whether it was the fire that spoke or someone else. He so affected the king that he repented of his deeds; then he added, 'Do not treat Nushirwan as a child, because in fact he is in command of the whole world; whatever course he decides upon, do not swerve from it, if you want the throne to remain in your house; and do not reveal your secrets to Mazdak.'

16. Then the priest said to Nushirwan, 'I want you to try to

allure one of Mazdak's servants, and tempt him with money to tell us the truth about the fire, so that I may remove all doubts from your father's mind.' Nushirwan induced someone to strike up a friendship with one of Mazdak's minions and by some device to bring the man to him; Nushirwan seated the man in a private place and laid a thousand dinars in front of him, and said, 'I am going to ask you something; if you speak the truth, I will give you these thousand dinars; and I will make you one of my intimates and promote you to high rank; if you lie, I will even now remove the head from your body.' The man was afraid and said, 'If I speak the truth, will you keep the promises you have made?' He said, 'Yes, and more.' He said, 'I will tell you.' Nushirwan said, 'Tell me what trick Mazdak has played to make the fire speak to him.' The man said, 'If I tell you this truly, can you protect me and my secret from Mazdak?' He said, 'I can.' He said, 'Know that near the fire-temple there is a piece of ground; Mazdak has bought this and surrounded it on all four sides by a high wall; from there to a point beneath the fire-temple he has driven a tunnel, ending in a small hole which opens into the middle of the fire. He always sends one of his minions into the tunnel, and instructs him to go underneath the fire, put his mouth to the hole and say such-and-such, so that whoever hears will think that it is the fire speaking.' When Nushirwan heard this he knew that the man was speaking the truth. He was glad and gave the man the thousand dinars.

17. When night came on, he took this man to his father, and made him repeat his words in front of his father. Qubad was amazed at the cunning and audacity of Mazdak; all doubts were completely removed from his mind. Straightaway the priest was brought in, and Qubad praised him and explained everything to him. The priest said, 'I told Your Majesty that he was a fraud.' Qubad said, 'Now we have found out. What is the best way to destroy him?' The priest said, 'He certainly must not get to know that you are aware of his deception and have recanted. It is better that you should hold another meeting, and I will dispute with him in front of everybody. In the end I will abandon the contest and confess defeat, and return to Pars. Thereafter you should do whatever Nushirwan sees fit so that this matter may be settled.' After a few days King Qubad

commanded the priests and nobles to present themselves, and taking the side of the priest of Pars to dispute with Mazdak and look more closely into his claims.

18. The next day the meeting was held, with Qubad sitting upon the dais, and Mazdak on his throne. The priests all spoke in turn, and the priest of Pars said, 'What amazes me is the fire speaking.' Mazdak said, 'There should not be amazement at the mighty works of God. Do you not remember how Moses (upon him be peace) made a serpent out of a piece of wood, and caused twelve springs of water to flow from one piece of stone; how he parted the waters of the sea, and said, "O Lord, drown Pharaoh with all his host", and God drowned him? God also made the earth obey Moses, so when Moses said, "O earth, swallow up Qarun", it swallowed him up; and Jesus (upon him be peace) made the dead alive. All these things are not within the power of man; but they are in the power of God. I too am His apostle and He has made the fire obey me. If you do what I say and what the fire says, you will achieve salvation in both worlds; if you do not obey, God will torment you and destroy you all.' The priest of Pars rose to his feet and said, 'I have no answer for a man whose words are from God and from the fire, and whose command the fire obeys. I retire from the contest in the face of one who can do something which I cannot. I am going; I cannot continue my presumption any longer.' So he departed, and took the road to Pars. Qubad left the audience-hall, and Mazdak went to the fire-temple to do seven days homage to the fire. The other people returned home, and those persons who had been converted to Mazdak's religion believed in him all the more firmly, and they were delighted.

19. When it was night, Qubad called Nushirwan and said, 'The priest has gone, and he has left me in your hands, because you are capable of putting an end to this religion. Now what are your plans?' Nushirwan said, 'If your Majesty will leave this task to me and say nothing to anybody, I will undertake to remove all trace of Mazdak and the Mazdakites from the world.' Qubad said, 'I shall not speak of this matter with anyone but you; the secret will remain with us alone.' Then Nushirwan said, 'Know that the priest of Pars has ostensibly confessed his defeat, and left for Pars, while Mazdak and

the Mazdakites are encouraged and emboldened: so we have them in our net [lit: sack]. Hereafter whatever we decide to do with them, it will be admissible. It is easy to kill Mazdak, but his followers are many. If we killed Mazdak, the Mazdakites would flee and disperse throughout the world; they would try to convert the people, and they would occupy mountain strongholds, and give trouble to us and our country. We must arrange matters so that all are destroyed and not one of them escapes from our swords.' Qubad said, 'What do you think is the best method?' Nushirwan said, 'What we should do is this: when Mazdak leaves the fire-temple and comes to see you, you should increase his rank and treat him with greater respect than you used to do; then one day when you are talking to him in private, tell him that since the priest of Pars withdrew and confessed defeat, I have become more tractable; I am repentant and disposed to believe in him.'

20. At the end of the week, when Mazdak came to Qubad, Qubad treated him respectfully and humbled himself, and he spoke about Nushirwan in the terms they had agreed. Mazdak said, 'The majority of people look to Nushirwan and hang on his words and deeds. If he comes into this religion, all the world will accept it. I hereby ask the fire to be my intercessor, and I pray The Good One to make this religion a livelihood for Nushirwan.' Qubad said, 'Yes indeed, for he is my heir, and the army and the peasantry love him.' Mazdak said, 'When he comes into my religion, the rest of the world will have no excuse.' Qubad said, 'As soon as Nushirwan comes into our religion, I swear by The Good One that just as Gushtasp built a golden kiosk in honour of Zoroaster on top of the cypress [called] Kishmar, so in your honour I will erect a stone tower in the middle of the Tigris, and place a golden kiosk on top of it, brighter than the sun.' Mazdak said, 'You give him counsel, while I pray; I am confident that The Good One will answer my prayers.'

21. When night came on, Qubad told Nushirwan all that had passed. Nushirwan said, 'After a week let my lord call Mazdak and say: Last night Nushirwan had a dream and he was afraid; in the early morning he came to me and said he had dreamed that a great fire was attacking him and that he was seeking refuge; a handsome person appeared before him and he asked him what the fire wanted

from him. He said the fire was angry with him because he had called it a liar. He asked him how he knew. He said that the angel was aware of all things. Then he woke up. Now he is going to the fire-temple, and is taking much ambergris and aloes-wood to throw on the fire. For three days he is going to do service to the fire and homage to The Good One.' Qubad and Nushirwan said and did these things respectively; Mazdak was very happy.

22. One week after this event, Nushirwan told his father to tell Mazdak that Nushirwan had said to him, 'I am sure now that this religion is right, and that Mazdak is an apostle of The Good One. I would like to follow him, but I am afraid to so so because most of the people are opposed to his religion; we must not let them revolt and seize the country from us by force. I wish I knew how many people had embraced this holy religion and who they were. If they are many in number and powerful, of course that is good; but if not, I will wait until they gain strength and grow in number, and I will assist them with grants of arms and provisions. Then when we have complete power we will proclaim our religion and force the people to accept it.' Nushirwan went on [to Qubad], 'If Mazdak says that his followers are many, tell him to make a register and write all their names in it, with the object of shewing it to me for my encouragement so that I may have no excuse for remaining aloof. By this means we shall come to know the number of the Mazdakites and who they are.' Qubad said the prescribed words to Mazdak. Mazdak was happy and said, 'A great many people have embraced this religion.' He said, 'Make a register and follow my instructions so that Nushirwan will have no further excuse.' Mazdak did so, and brought the register to Qubad. They counted the names; they came to 12,000, comprising townspeople, villagers and soldiers. Qubad said, 'Tonight I will call Nushirwan and present this register to him; if he comes over to our religion, I will instantly cause trumpets and drums to be sounded as a signal, and I will broadcast such a din that when you are in your palace and hear the sound of trumpets and drums, you will know that Nushirwan has accepted our religion.'

23. When Mazdak had gone away and night had come on, Qubad called Nushirwan and shewed him the register, and told him of the signal he had arranged with Mazdak. Nushirwan said,

'Excellent; now have them sound the trumpets and drums, and tomorrow when you see Mazdak tell him that Nushirwan responded favourably and came over to our religion by virtue of his seeing the register and the number of people; tell him also that I said that had there been only 5,000 it would have been enough; since there are 12,000 men, even if the rest of the world were against us, there would be nothing to fear; hereafter whatever plans we make, Your Majesty, Mazdak and myself will all consult together.'

24. When one watch of the night had passed Mazdak heard the sound of trumpets and drums. He rejoiced and said, 'Nushirwan has come over to our religion.' The next day Mazdak went to the audience-hall; Qubad sat on the dais and told Mazdak all that Nushirwan had said; Mazdak was glad. When they left the audience-hall, Qubad and Mazdak sat down in private together, and they sent someone to fetch Nushirwan. Nushirwan arrived and laid a multitude of gold and choice gifts before Mazdak, and scattered pearls as largesse. He apologized for past mistakes, and then they discussed all manner of things. Eventually Nushirwan spoke to his father as follows and they agreed on it; 'You are the lord of the world, and Mazdak is the apostle of The Good One. Grant me the command of our people's army, and I will see to it that in all the world there remains nobody who is not in obedience to us and our religion; all will willingly and eagerly accept it.' Qubad and Mazdak said, 'Your wish is granted.' Nushirwan said, 'Then the best course of action is for Mazdak to write letters and send messengers to all districts to his adherents and tell them that three months hence on a certain day in such-and-such a week everyone from far and near must be present at our palace. From this day until that we shall be making preparations of all kinds for them, but nobody shall know what our business is. On the appointed day we shall spread a feast with enough places for them all to sit down and room for more besides. Having eaten the food they will remove to another hall and there engage in a drinking party in which each person will drink seven cups of wine. Then twenty or thirty at a time we will invest them with robes of honour until all are invested; and if any man is not completely armed we will tell him to take what he needs from the armoury, and gird it on. That same night we shall go forth and proclaim the religion. Those

who accept it will be safe; if anybody refuses we shall kill him.'
Qubad and Mazdak said, 'There is nothing to add to this.' Having
agreed on this they rose. Mazdak sent letters everywhere and warned
all people far and near that on such-and-such a day of such-and-such
a month they should be present at the court, fully armed and
equipped; he told them to be confident, for everything was as they
desired.

25. On the appointed day all the 12,000 men arrived at the king's
palace. There they saw such a feast prepared as they had never seen
before. Qubad sat on the dais, and Mazdak on the throne, while
Nushirwan stood with loins girt as if to shew that he was the host.
Mazdak could not contain himself for joy. Then Nushirwan seated
everyone at the table in order of rank until all were sitting down.
When they had finished the food, they moved from this hall to
another; there they saw an assembly-room such as their eyes had
never beheld before. Qubad and Mazdak were there sitting on the
dais and all the guests were made to sit in order as before. Minstrels
began to sing and cup-bearers took round the wine. After several
rounds about two hundred pages and servants with silken covers and
linen wrappings on their arms came in and stood on the edge of the
throng. After a time Nushirwan announced, 'Let them take the
robes into the other hall, for it is crowded here; the guests will enter
by twenties and thirties and put on their robes; then they will pass
from that hall to the polo-field, and wait there until all are robed.
When all have been invested, the king and Mazdak will come on
to the polo-field and cast an eye upon them and inspect them.
Meanwhile I will have the armoury opened and weapons brought.'
Now previous to this Nushirwan had sent someone out into the
villages and summoned about three hundred casual labourers each
with a spade, for the ostensible purpose of clearing the palace and
grounds of dirt and rubbish. When the men came from the villages
he mustered them all on the polo-field and shut the gate tight. Then
he said to them, 'During today and tonight I want you to dig 12,000
pits in this field, each one a yard and a half deep, and keep the spoil
at the side of the pits.' He ordered the watchmen to detain them all
when they had finished digging the pits and prevent any of them from
going out. On the night [of the feast] he concealed four hundred

armed men in the [robing-]hall and instructed them as follows,
'Take each party of twenty or thirty men as I send them from the
assembly-room to the [robing-]hall, and lead them on to the field;
strip them all naked and put them head first into the pits up to the
navel with their legs in the air; shovel back the earth all around them
and tread it down so that they are firmly planted in the pits.'

26. After the clothes and robes had been taken from the assembly
into the [robing-]hall, they brought in two hundred horses with
gold and silver trappings, as well as gilt shields, belts and swords.
Nushirwan had them taken into the [robing-]hall. Then he picked
the people in twenties and thirties, and sent them into the hall.
From there they were taken on to the polo-field and put head downwards into the pits, which were then filled with earth. Thus they
destroyed them all. Then Nushirwan said to his father and Mazdak,
'They have all put on their robes and are standing ready on the polo-
field. Come and see them.' Qubad and Mazdak arose and went on
to the field. As far as he could see from end to end of the field Mazdak
saw nothing but legs sticking up in the air. Nushirwan turned to
Mazdak and said, 'For an army of which you are the commander
what better kind of investiture could there be than this? You came
only to despoil the people's property and wives, and take the kingship from our family.' They had made a high mound on one side
of the field and dug a pit in it. At Nushirwan's command they took
Mazdak and placed him up to his chest in that pit. Then they filled
it all round with plaster so that only his neck and head shewed
above. Nushirwan said, 'Now look upon your believers!' and to his
father he said, 'Behold the wisdom of the wise! The best thing for you
now is to remain awhile indoors until the people and the army calm
down, for this trouble arose through your weak-mindedness.' So he
kept his father indoors. On his orders the villagers who had been
brought for digging the pits were released, and the gates of the polo-
field opened for the people to see the sight, and they plucked Mazdak's
beard and moustaches until he died. Then Nushirwan held his
father in captivity, and having summoned all the nobility, he
ascended the throne as undisputed sovereign, and began that reign
which was devoted to justice and generosity. This story has come
down as a memorial of him.

# CHAPTER FORTY-FIVE

*On the revolt of Sinbad the Magian and the rising
of the Khurramdins [Khurramiya]*

1. From this [Nushirwan's] time until the days of Harun ar
Rashid no one of this sect appeared in the world. Now it so happened that Mazdak's wife, Khurrama bint Fada, had fled from
Mada'in with two persons, and she arrived at the village of Rayy,
and began to call people to her husband's religion, with the result
that a certain number of Zoroastrians adopted it. People gave them
the name of the Khurramdins. However they concealed the religion
while constantly looking for an excuse to emerge and reveal it. In
the year 137 after the flight of The Prophet (upon him be peace)
when Abu Ja'far al Mansur (Dawaniqi) slew Abu Muslim Sahib
ad Daula [The Master of the Empire] at Baghdad, there was in the
city of Nishapur a Zoroastrian mayor called Sinbad.[1] This man
had enjoyed long-standing friendship with Abu Muslim, and the
latter had promoted him and made him an army-commander. After
the killing of Abu Muslim he emerged in revolt and came from
Nishapur to Rayy, and he stirred up the Zoroastrians of Rayy and
Tabaristan, knowing that the people of Kuhistan and 'Iraq were
mostly Rafidis and Mazdakites. Pursuing his intention of preaching
the religion openly, first of all he killed Ba 'Ubaida the Hanafi, who
was the governor of Rayy on behalf of al Mansur, and seized the
hoards which Abu Muslim had laid up at Rayy. Having thus
acquired some strength he sought to avenge Abu Muslim's blood;
he claimed that he was Abu Muslim's apostle, and told the people
of 'Iraq and Khurasan that Abu Muslim had not been killed, but
that when al Mansur tried to kill him, he recited the greatest name of
God, and turned into a white dove, and escaped from his hands;
he was now in a brazen fortress where he dwelt with the Mahdi
and Mazdak; soon all three would appear and their chief would be
Abu Muslim with Mazdak as his wazir. He professed to have letters
from Abu Muslim.

[1] See Browne, *Literary History*, I. 313–14.

2. When the Rafidis heard mention of the Mahdi, and the Maz-dakites the name of Mazdak, a great multitude gathered at Rayy, and Sinbad's affair grew in magnitude until eventually 100,000 people joined him. Whenever he was alone with Zoroastrians, he would say, 'According to one of the books of the Sasanians which I have found, the Arab empire is finished. I shall not turn back until I have destroyed the Ka'ba, for this has been [wrongly] substituted for the sun; we shall make the sun our *qibla* as it was in olden time.' And to the Khurramdins he would say, 'Mazdak was a Shi'ite and his command is that you make common cause with the Shi'a.' Thus he kept all three groups satisfied. He defeated al Mansur's forces on several occasions and killed some of his generals; so after seven years al Mansur appointed Jahwar 'Ijli to fight him. Jahwar summoned the troops of Khuzistan and Pars, and went to Isfahan; he collected auxiliaries from Isfahan and Qum and also took the 'Ijlis with him. Then he moved to Rayy and there fought a fierce battle for three days with Sinbad. On the fourth day Sinbad was slain at the hand of Jahwar and all his company were routed, and dispersed to their homes. Then the Khurramdini and Zoroastrian religions became amalgamated, and they held conversations in secret, and gradually grew more organized until they reached the stage where the Muslims began to call the sect Khurramdin. After Jahwar had killed Sinbad, he entered Rayy and slaughtered all the Zoroastrians, plundering their houses and carrying off their women and children into captivity.

# CHAPTER FORTY-SIX

### *On the risings of the Qarmatis [Carmathians] and Batinis in Kuhistan, 'Iraq and Khurasan*

1. The origin of the Qarmati religion was as follows. Ja'far as Sadiq had a son whose name was Isma'il; he died before his father leaving a son named Muhammad; and this Muhammad lived until

the time of Harun ar Rashid. Now one of the Zubairis suggested to
Harun ar Rashid that Muhammad was plotting a revolt and preaching in secret with the intention of seizing the caliphate. Harun ar
Rashid brought Muhammad from Medina to Baghdad and put him
in prison, and during this confinement he died, and was buried in
the cemetery of the Quraish. Muhammad had a certain Hijazi page
called Mubarak, and he was a calligrapher in the fine script known
as *muqarmaṭ*; for this reason he used to be called Qarmatwaih. This
Mubarak had a friend in the city of Ahwaz whose name was ʿAbd
Allah ibn Maimun al Qaddah. The latter was one day sitting with
him in private and said, 'Your master Muhammad ibn Ismaʿil was
my friend and he used to tell me his secrets.' Mubarak was deceived
and impatient to know what they were. Then ʿAbd Allah ibn
Maimun made Mubarak swear not to disclose what he was going to
tell him except to persons fit to hear it. He then made several
statements, introducing obscure words from the language of the
imams, mixed up with sayings of the naturalists and utterances of
the philosophers, and consisting largely of mention of The Prophet
and the angels, the tablet and pen, and heaven and the throne. After
that they parted; Mubarak went towards Kufa, and ʿAbd Allah to
Kuhistan and ʿIraq; and they sought to win over the people of the
Shiʿa.

2. This was at the time when Musa ibn Jaʿfar was in prison.
Mubarak carried on his activities in secret, and disseminated his
propaganda in the district around Kufa. Of the people who accepted
his teaching, the Sunnis called some of them Mubarakis and others
Qarmatis. Meanwhile ʿAbd Allah ibn Maimun preached this
religion in Kuhistan. Incidentally he was a very clever conjuror,
and Muhammad ibn Zakariyya [Razi][1] has mentioned his name in
his book *Makhāriq al Anbiyā* [Frauds of the Prophets]. He then
appointed a man called Khalaf to succeed him and said to him, 'Go
in the direction of Rayy, for thereabouts in Rayy, Qum and Kashan
the people are all Rafidis, professing Shiʿa beliefs; so they will accept
your teaching.' ʿAbd Allah himself departed in fear towards Basra.

So Khalaf went to Rayy. In the district of Fashabuya there is a
village which they call Kilin. There he stayed and practised

---

[1] See *Chahar Maqala*, Translation, 148 (note XXVII).

embroidery at which craft he was expert. He remained there some time without being able to reveal his secrets to anybody, till at last by dint of great efforts he managed to find a suitable person, and instructed him in the religion. He made out that the religion was that of the house [of the Prophet] and had been kept hidden; and said, 'When the Qayim [Mahdi] appears the religion will be revealed, and the time of his coming is near. It behoves you to learn now, so that when you see him you will not be ignorant of the religion.' So he began secretly to instruct the people of this village in the religion. One day the headman of Kilin was passing outside the village when he heard a voice coming from a ruined mosque. He approached the mosque and listened. This Khalaf was expounding his religion to some of the people. On returning to the village he said, 'O people, thwart this man's business. Do not go near him. Judging by what I have heard him say, I am afraid that our village may suffer through his activities.' Incidentally Khalaf's speech was imperfect and he could not pronounce the letters *ṭā* and *ḥā*. When he knew that he had been discovered, he fled from that village and went to Rayy where he died. He had converted a few of the inhabitants of Kilin, and his son Ahmad ibn Khalaf took his place and continued to foster his father's religion. Ahmad ibn Khalaf found a man named Ghiyath who was well versed in literature and grammar. He made him his successor as propagandist.

3. This Ghiyath then embellished the elements of their religion with verses from the Quran, traditions of The Prophet (upon him be peace), Arab proverbs, and various verses and stories. He composed a book entitled *Kitāb al Bayān* [The Book of Explanation] and in it he described in the manner of a lexicon the meaning of such terms as 'prayer', 'fasting' and other religious precepts. Then he held argument with people of the Sunna, and news spread to Qum and Kashan that a man called Ghiyath had come forth from the village of Kilin as a missionary, and was giving glad tidings and teaching religion. The people of these cities flocked to Ghiyath and began to learn the new religion. Eventually the jurist 'Abd Allah Za'farani was informed of this, and he knew that the religion was a heresy. So he urged the people of Rayy to attack the heretics; some of the latter were known by the people of the Sunna as Khalafis, and others

as Batinis. By the year 200 (from the hijra) the religion was wide-spread. This was the year in which a man called Sahib al Hal [The Master of the Situation] led a revolt in Syria and captured most of that country. Ghiyath had been forced to flee from Rayy and he went to Khurasan, and stayed at Marv-ar-Rud, where he proselytized the amir Husain ibn 'Ali. Husain was converted; his command extended over Khurasan, especially Taliqan, Maimana, Paryab, Gharchistan and Ghur. After adopting the new religion he converted a number of people in these districts.

4. Ghiyath then nominated a successor at Marv-ar-Rud to maintain the converts in the religion and to extend their numbers, while he himself returned to Rayy and began to preach again there. Then he left someone else to carry on the propaganda—a man from the district of Fashabuya called Abu Hatim, who was well versed in Arab poetry and strange tales. Even before he went to Khurasan he had already promised that before long in such-and-such a year the Qayim (whom they call the Mahdi) would appear, and the Qarmatis had trusted in this promise. The people of the Sunna found out that Ghiyath had returned and was once more calling the people to the religion of the Batinis (Allah curse them); and now he continued to promise that at a certain time, the Mahdi would appear, and he kept up this deceit in his preaching for some time. However it chanced that the promised time for the coming of the Mahdi arrived, and he was proved false. The Shi'ites then turned against him, and reviled and renounced him; the Sunnis sought to kill him; but he fled and nobody could find him.

5. After that, a group of persons in the city of Rayy came to an agreement with one of the grandsons of Khalaf, and they combined under his leadership. When he was about to die he named his son as successor, a man named Abu Ja'far The Elder; but he was overcome by melancholia, so he appointed a certain Abu Hatim to deputize for him. By the time Abu Ja'far got better, Abu Hatim had consolidated his position, and holding Abu Ja'far of no account, had taken over the leadership. So the leadership passed from Khalaf's family. This Abu Hatim sent missionaries abroad into the districts on all sides of Rayy, such as Tabaristan, Gurgan, Isfahan and Adharbaygan, and proceeded to convert the people. The amir of

Rayy, Ahmad ibn 'Ali, accepted his invitation and became a Batini.

6. Then it happened that the Dailamites revolted against the 'Alawids of Tabaristan, saying, 'You say that yours is [the true] religion, but Muslims keep writing to us from surrounding places telling us not to listen to your words because they are heresy. Your argument is that true knowledge has gone from our tribe. But knowledge is common property; it does not go away. If you learn, you know; whoever learns, knows. Knowledge is not inherited. God (to Him be power and glory) sent The Prophet (upon him be peace) to all mankind alike; He did not distinguish some people as noble, and others as common, for them to say that His commands are this for the nobility, or that for the commons. So it is clear to us that you are liars.' The amir of Tabaristan was a Shi'ite, and he supported the 'Alawids; the Dailamites defied him too and said, 'Decrees and documents have been brought from Baghdad, Isfahan and Khurasan to the effect that your religion is not the pure Muslim faith. If you do and say nothing but what God and The Prophet have commanded, we will accept you and embrace your religion. Otherwise the sword is betwixt us and you. We are mountain people and craftsmen; we understand but little of the religious law.' By chance Abu Hatim went at this time from Rayy to Tabaristan, and he visited the Dailamites, whose chief was Shiruy ibn Wirdadavandi. He went to him and made an alliance with him, vilifying the 'Alawids; he set about defaming them and declared that they were infidels and heretics. He said, 'Soon an imam will come forth from the Dailamites, and I know what his doctrine and discourse will be.' The men of Dailaman and Gilan accepted his teaching with alacrity, and his dealings with them prospered. This was in the days of Mardavij. 'They fled from the rain and fell into the gutter': they sought the path of orthodoxy but they fell into the snare of heresy. For some time they continued their association with him.

7. When they saw that the period had elapsed in which he had promised that the imam would appear, they said, 'This religion is baseless; it seems to be the scheme of a petty impostor.' They renounced him altogether, and renewed their devotion to the members of The Prophet's family (Allah pray for him and give him peace).

They attacked Abu Hatim with intent to kill him, but he fled, and in that flight he died. Whereupon the affairs of the sect of the Shi'ites degenerated into disorder and decay. Many of its adherents recanted, and went over to the Sunna in repentance. The Shi'ites remained in confusion, but secretly they reorganized themselves and eventually settled down under the leadership of two men—'Abd al Malik Kaukabi and Ishaq; the latter lived at Rayy and the former at Girdkuh.

### On the emergence of the Batinis in Khurasan and Transoxiana

8. The amir of Khurasan was Nasr ibn Ahmad. When Husain ibn 'Ali Marv-ar-Rudi was on the point of death—the man who was converted Batini by Ghiyath—he handed on his mission in Khurasan to Muhammad ibn Ahmad Nakhshabi and made him his successor. This man was of that [brilliant] company of The Philosophers of Khurasan,[1] and he was a theologian. Husain enjoined him in his will to leave a deputy in that place and himself to cross the Oxus and go to Bukhara and Samarqand to convert the people of those cities, paying particular attention to the nobility at the court of the amir of Khurasan, Nasr ibn Ahmad; this would strengthen his position. So when Husain died, Muhammad Nakhshabi succeeded him and proselytized many of the people of Khurasan and they yielded to his invitation. There was a man called the son of Sawada, who had escaped from the hands of the Sunnis at Rayy, and fled to Husain Marv-ar-Rudi in Khurasan; he was one of the leaders of the Batinis. Muhammad Nakhshabi made him his successor at Marv-ar-Rud, and himself crossed the river, and went to Bukhara. He found that the reputation of the sect was low there, and he did not dare to come into the open. So he left there for Nakhshab, where he succeeded in converting Abu Bakr Nakhshabi, who was a boon-companion of the amir of Khurasan and one of his relations. He also converted Ash'ath who was the amir's private secretary and ranked as a boon-companion. Other converts were Abu Mansur Chaghani who was head of the military department

---

[1] See Browne, *Literary History*, I. 365–6.

and had married Ash'ath's sister, and Aitash who was the amir's private chamberlain and the friend of those just named.

9. This group then said to Muhammad Nakhshabi, 'There is no need for you to remain in Nakhshab; arise and go to Bukhara the capital. We will see to it that we exalt your cause to the skies, and bring persons of reputation into this religion.' So he arose and went from Nakhshab to Bukhara where he consorted with the same class of notables and disseminated his propaganda amongst them. He made his converts swear not to say anything to anyone until he told them and made the word public. At first he was preaching the Shi'a religion; later he gradually shifted to Batini doctrines, and it was into this sect that he brought the mayor of Bukhara, the revenue officer and the leading merchants; also he converted Hasan Malik who was governor of Ilaq and one of the king's courtiers, and 'Ali Zarrad who was the private steward. Most of these whom we have mentioned were relations or confidants of the king. When his following had increased, he had designs upon the king himself. He persuaded the courtiers constantly to speak favourably of him in front of Nasr ibn Ahmad in drunkenness and sobriety. They did this and took his part so well that Nasr ibn Ahmad became eager to see him. So they took Muhammad Nakhshabi before the amir of Khurasan, and extolled his learning; the amir received him gladly and treated him kindly. At every opportunity Muhammad brought a part of his teaching to the amir's attention, and whatever he said, the amir's companions added their approval and applause saying, 'It is so.' Nasr ibn Ahmad treated him with increasing favour and at last accepted his solicitation; Muhammad Nakhshabi then became so influential that the king did whatever he said.

10. When Muhammad Nakhshabi's affairs reached the point where his propaganda was made public and the king himself supported the Shi'ites, the Turks and officers of the army were displeased that the king had become a Qarmati. Then a number of learned men got together and approached the commander-in-chief of the army and said, 'Come to the rescue, for Islam has been corrupted in Transoxiana, and this wretched Nakhshabi has led the king astray and made him a Qarmati; now he is preaching openly and misleading the people.' The commander said, 'I will keep watch; you

go back and keep quiet; I hope that God will put matters right.'
The next day he mentioned this subject to Nasr ibn Ahmad; but it
did no good. Murmurs then arose amongst the troops and they said,
'We totally disagree with the course which the king has adopted;'
and the army officers began to communicate with one another to see
what to do about the matter. As they got to know one another's
feelings it became clear that the troops and their leaders refused to
acquiesce in the king's conduct, except one or two of the Turkish
chiefs who had themselves been converted. In the end the army chiefs
agreed that they did not want an infidel king and would not tolerate
such; they would kill him and set up the army-commander in his
place; they would swear not to go back on this decision. Both from
religious principles and from personal ambition the commander-in-
chief consented to this and said, 'First we must arrange that we chiefs
meet together in a suitable place to form an alliance, take oaths, and
discuss how best we should deal with this matter without the king
knowing.'

11. One of the army chiefs was an old man called Talan Auka;
he said, 'The best plan is for you as commander-in-chief to submit
to the king that the officers want you to give them a feast. Of course
he will not say no. He will say, "If you have the wherewithal and
can do it, proceed." Then you say that you lack nothing in the way
of food and drink, but as regards mattresses, floor coverings and other
furnishings and decorations such as are of gold and silver, you do not
possess enough. The king will say, "Take whatever you need from
my treasury, my furniture store and my cellar." Then you say that
you are giving this feast to the army on condition that when it is
over they will gird their loins for war against infidels, and go with
you to Balasaghun, because the infidel Turk has seized the province
and the cries of the suffering people have exceeded all bounds; they
must not have cause to think ill of the king. Then make preparations
for the feast and invite the army to come on such-and-such a day;
and borrow all the gold, silver, carpets, brocade and choice things
which you can find in the king's treasury, cellars and furniture store,
and take them to your house. On the appointed day when all the
army has arrived at your house, close the house door on the excuse
that it is getting crowded; then take the officers into one of the rooms

to drink sherbet, and lay this matter before them. Those who are at the root of the movement—that is we—will of course be with you; those that are the branches will agree with us unanimously as soon as they hear our argument. We shall administer the oath and covenant to them all, and swear allegiance to you as king. Then we will come out of the room and proceed to the trays to eat. Having eaten the food we will go across to the drinking-hall where each one of us will drink three goblets of wine. All the gold and silver articles in that hall we will present to the officers. Then straightaway we will leave and go to the king's palace, seize the king and kill him. We will not spare a single one of his companions and co-religionists, and we will loot all the contents of his palace and treasury. Then we will set you upon the throne; and we will tell the army to draw their swords, and fall upon towns and villages, and slaughter all the Qarmatis they can find, and burn [their bodies] and plunder their houses.' The commander-in-chief said, 'This is a good plan.'

12. The next day he said to Nasr ibn Ahmad, 'The officers want me to give them a feast, and every day they are requesting me.' Nasr ibn Ahmad said, 'If you have the wherewithal to entertain them, do not fail to do so.' He said, 'Your slave has no shortage of food and drink, but carpets and furnishings and festive decorations, such as gold and silver are lacking. Those who entertain should do it well or not at all.' Nasr said, 'You may take whatever you need of these things from my treasury, my cellars, and my furniture store.' The commander bowed and came out. The next day he invited all the army to come to his house on such-and-such a day. Then he took the gold and silver and carpets and other things—all that was to be found in the king's treasury, cellar and stores; and he gave a feast the like of which none had seen in those days. He received all the officers with their troops and retinues at his house, and according to plan he had the house door shut and took the nobles and officers into one of the rooms, and made them all swear oaths of allegiance.

13. When they came out of the room and went to the trays to eat, one of them got out of the house by way of the roof and straightaway informed Nuh ibn Nasr what the officers had just done. Nuh mounted immediately and rode at the gallop to his father's palace, and said, 'Why are you sitting there, when the officers of your army

have this very hour sworn oaths and entered into a conspiracy with the commander-in-chief; as soon as they have finished eating they will go to the drinking-hall, and when each one has drunk three goblets of wine they are going to steal all the gold and silver brought from your treasury; then they will come out and rush headlong at our palace and kill you and me and everyone they can find. The purpose of this feast is to destroy us.' Nasr said to Nuh, 'Now what shall we do?' Nuh said, 'The best thing you can do is now, before they get up from eating and go to the drinking-hall, to send two private servants to whisper in the commander-in-chief's ear that the king says, "I hear that you have spared no pains and prepared a magnificent feast. Now I have in my possession a set of golden banqueting dishes inlaid with jewels, such as no other king today possesses. They had been put somewhere outside the treasury, and I have just remembered them. Take these too, to provide the finest possible decoration for your feast. They are worth more than two million dinars. Come quickly and I will give them to you before the guests go into the drinking-hall." Undoubtedly in his greed of wealth he will come. As soon as he arrives we will chop off his head. Then I will tell you what to do.'

14. Immediately Nasr sent two private servants to deliver the message. The people were then busy eating. The commander-in-chief told one or two of his confederates why the king was calling him. They said, 'Go, and fetch these things also, for today it suits us to get all we can.' The commander went with all speed to the king's palace; there he was summoned into a room and the king straightaway ordered some pages to cut off his head and put it into a bag. Then Nuh said to his father, 'Mount, and let us go to the commander-in-chief's house taking the bag with us. There in front of all the officers you must abdicate the kingship and make me your successor; only so can I satisfy them and ensure that the kingship remains in our family, for the troops will not put up with you any longer, and anyhow you are bound to die one day.' So they both mounted and rode swiftly to the commander-in-chief's house. The officers looked and saw the king come in at the door with his son. They all rose and went to greet him, and not one of them knew what was happening. They said, 'Perchance the king desired to join in

the feast.' Nasr ibn Ahmad went and sat in his rightful place, with arms-bearers standing behind him; Nuh sat on his father's right hand and said, 'Pray be seated; finish the food and enjoy the feast.'

15. So they ate the food and made general feasting. Then Nasr said, 'Know that I am aware of your conspiracy. When I learned of your intention, I was offended with you. Hereafter you will have no confidence in me, nor I in you. If I have deviated from the path [of orthodoxy], or adopted a heretical doctrine, or committed any other sin which has offended you, surely my son Nuh has no blemish?' They said, 'No.' He said, 'You are no longer fit to be my army and I am not worthy to be your king. So I hereby nominate Nuh as my heir; he is now your king. Whether I was right or wrong, I shall now devote myself to regret and repentance before God. He who misled you in this way has met with his just reward.' Then he told them to produce the commander-in-chief's head from the bag and throw it in front of the company. He himself descended from the throne and knelt on a prayer mat; while Nuh ascended the throne and sat in his father's place. When the officers heard and saw all this they were astonished, and could not find any excuse or objection. They all bowed their heads to the ground, and congratulated Nuh, throwing all the blame on the shoulders of the commander-in-chief and saying, 'We are all slaves under your command.' Nuh said, 'Know that in all respects I am Nuh, not Nasr. What is past is past. I now consider this mistake of yours as rectified. Through me all your desires will be fulfilled. Obey my commands and go and attend to your affairs.' He called for shackles and ordered that his father should be fettered, taken straight to Kuhundiz and incarcerated. Then he said, 'Come, let us go to the drinking-hall.'

16. When they had seated themselves in the drinking-hall and each one had drunk three goblets of wine, he said, 'You had planned that after drinking three goblets of wine you would plunder everything in this hall. So far from allowing plunder, I now make you a present of everything. Take it all and divide it amongst yourselves, to each according to his station so that everyone receives a share.' So they picked up all the things and put them into sacks, which they sealed and handed over to a trusted person. Then Nuh said, 'If the commander-in-chief plotted mischief against us, he met with his

just reward; and if my father deviated from the right path, he is now suffering his punishment. As for you, your scheme was that after enjoying this feast you would go to Balasaghun to wage war against the infidel Turks. But we should be warring against the infidels on our own doorstep. Arise! let us engage in holy war. Go and kill all those in Transoxiana and Khurasan who have become heretics and adopted this religion which my father adopted; and all their goods and riches are yours. I have just made you a present of all my father's property which was in this hall; tomorrow I will let you have what is in the treasury, for the chattels of the Batinis are only fit for plunder. Having finished this important work, we will turn to the infidel Turks. But first I wish you to bring forth Muhammad Nakhshabi and behead him and all my father's confederates; then scour the city and the surrounding districts.'

17. Immediately they galloped off and brought Muhammad Nakhshabi and beheaded him. Also they executed Hasan Malik, Abu Mansur Chaghani and Ash'ath, together with several amirs who had become Batini; then they ranged through the city and slaughtered all they could find of the heretics, and they recognized them because they had been openly discussing their doctrines with the king and preaching in public. On the same day Nuh sent an amir with troops to cross the Oxus and go with speed to Marv-ar-Rud; first he was to capture the son of Sawada and kill him; then they were to brandish their swords, and wherever in all Khurasan they saw, or found, or heard of any of this sect they were to kill them all; and he commanded them to beware lest any Muslim should be slain by mistake, and he swore that if any Muslim were murdered he would kill the murderer and would not listen to any excuse. Then for seven days they ranged through Bukhara and its environs, killing and plundering, until the point was reached where not one of the heretics remained throughout Khurasan and Transoxiana; or if any were left they durst not shew themselves. Thus the sect remained concealed in Khurasan.

### On the appearance of the Batinis in the lands of Syria and the West

18. Now we come to the story of Syria. When 'Abd Allah ibn Maimun went to Basra, where he carried on his teaching secretly

and also where he died, his son Ahmad departed and went to Syria, and from Syria to the West [N. Africa]. There his affairs prospered and his teaching was accepted. Then he returned to Syria and dwelt there in a city called Salami. There a son was born to him, and he called him Muhammad. When Ahmad died his son was only small, so his brother Sa'id ibn al Husain took his place and went towards the West, changing his name and calling himself 'Abd Allah ibn al Husain. He had a friend called Abu 'Abd Allah Muhtasib; he sent him as his lieutenant to the Bani Aghlab and to the districts which they inhabited, to summon the people to this religion. The Bani Aghlab were mostly desert-dwellers and a great number of them accepted the religion. Then he gave the command that thereafter they were to operate with the sword, and kill everyone who was not of their faith. This they did, and a large company of the Bani Aghlab banded together and went into the towns to kill. Eventually they gained the mastery over most of the lands of the West. Now Zikrawaih, the one known as Sahib al Hal [The Master of the Situation], was ruler over some of the towns of the West; he was a Sunni and 'Ali Wahsudan Dailami was his general. He sent 'Ali with the Syrian army to make a surprise attack on Abu 'Abd Allah Muhtasib. The latter fled but the Syrian army pressed home their attack and killed as many as they could of the Bani Aghlab and scattered the rest to the ends of the earth. Abu 'Abd Allah reached one of the towns of the Bani Aghlab where he put on a hood and lived like an ascetic and was well treated by the people. Sahib al Hal constantly sent messengers to them demanding that he should be handed over to him; but they made excuses and did not do so. Abu 'Abd Allah was apprehensive lest the Bani Aghlab should defer to Sahib al Hal and surrender him. So he went and lived on one of the islands belonging to the Bani Aghlab. There he built himself a house, and the Bani Aghlab used to send him alms. When he died his son succeeded him. The state of affairs in that part then remained unchanged for long periods.

## *On the appearance of the Batinis in the district of Herat and Ghur, and their destruction*

19. In the year 295 (from the hijra) Muhammad ibn Harthama, the governor of Herat, informed Isma'il ibn Ahmad the Samanid (called The Just Amir—may Allah have mercy upon him), that in the foot-hills of Ghur and Gharcha a man known as Abu Bilal had appeared and had spread the doctrines of the Qarmatis; people of all classes had gathered about him and he had styled himself Dar al 'Adl [The Abode of Justice]; many people from the country around Herat had gone to join him and were swearing allegiance to him; their numbers exceeded 10,000. He said, 'If Your Majesty neglects to deal with him the number of his followers will be doubled; then it will be a difficult business. They say that this Abu Bilal is the one who was a boon-companion of Ya'qub ibn Laith, and that now he claims to be his successor in the hierarchy of the rebels.' When the amir Isma'il heard this, he said, 'I am given to understand that Abu Bilal's blood has come to the boil!' Then he gave orders to his chamberlain, Zakari, saying, 'Choose five hundred of the cleverest and bravest of all the pages; see that they are paid; make Bighish their leader as he is an intelligent boy and let him be given 10,000 dirams; and let five hundred suits of mail and sets of horse-armour be prepared. Tomorrow take them to Juy-i Muliyan[1] to parade before me for review.' The chamberlain Zakari did this.

20. Then the amir Isma'il ordered a letter to be written to Abu 'Ali Marvazi [at Marv-ar-Rud] saying, 'Give your men their pay, and come outside the city so that you are there before the pages arrive; then go with them to Herat and join forces with Muhammad ibn Harthama.' And to Muhammad ibn Harthama he wrote, 'Have your troops ready and wait outside the city until Bighish and Abu 'Ali reach you.' He promised Bighish that as soon as a report reached him from Muhammad ibn Harthama that he, Bighish, had success-fully accomplished his mission, he would give him a province. And to the rest of the pages he said, 'This is not the campaign against 'Ali ibn Sharwin, or 'Amr ibn Laith, or Muhammad ibn Harun, for in

---

[1] See *Chahar Maqala*, Translation, 121 (note XVI).

those cases we had large and well equipped forces. For this operation I am relying on you. In the foot-hills of Herat some rebels have appeared and have spread the doctrines of the Qarmatis; the majority of them are shepherds and farmers. If you are successful I will give you all robes of honour and presents, and raise your rank.' Then he appointed an experienced secretary to look after their administration.

21. As soon as they reached Marv-ar-Rud, Abu 'Ali joined them with his men. They garrisoned the ends of the roads so that the rebels should not get news of them. When they arrived at Herat, Muhammad ibn Harthama came out with his troops at once and blocked the land routes so that no news reached Abu Bilal. Then they went up into the mountains, and after three days' march up hill and down dale and over difficult passes, they reached the rebels who were unsuspecting. They surrounded them unawares, put them to the sword and killed them all. Abu Bilal, Hamdan, Abu Zaka and ten other of their chiefs were taken prisoner. Within seventy days they returned to Bukhara. Abu Bilal was imprisoned at Kuhundiz and there he died. The other ten were sent to Balkh, Samarqand, Farghana, Khwarazm, Nishapur and Marv where they were hanged. Thus their substance was completely eradicated from Ghur and Gharcha. In this same year the amir Isma'il died and his brother Nasr ibn Ahmad[1] came to the throne—he whose story we have already related.

## On the emergence of the Batinis in Khurasan and Transoxiana [continued]

22. When Nuh fettered and imprisoned his father for life, the officers of the army were vouchsafed a general pardon, and Nuh reigned as king for many years. When Nuh died, his son Mansur succeeded him and followed in his father's footsteps. After fifteen years of his reign had passed, missionaries once more began preaching secretly in Khurasan and Bukhara, and again led the people astray. The majority of those who were converted were persons whose fathers and grandfathers had lost their lives because of this religion. Mansur was known in his time as The Righteous Amir. His wazir

---

[1] The author has confused the Nasr ibn Ahmad who was Isma'il's brother and predecessor on the Samanid throne with the Nasr ibn Ahmad who was his grandson and succeeded him next but one.

was Abu 'Ali Bal'ami; his commander-in-chief of Khurasan was
Alptigin, Sabuktigin's master; Mansur ibn Bayqara was his great
chamberlain; Abu Yahya ibn Ash'ath was governor of Farghana;
Sarhang Husain, governor of Isbijab; Isma'il, governor of Chach;
Abu Mansur 'Abd ar Razzaq, governor of Tus; and Washmgir,
governor of Gurgan. Of the amirs who were resident at the capital
there were Babdah, Nasr Malik, Hasan Malik, Abu Sa'id Malik,
Haidar Chaghani, Abu 'l 'Abbas Jarrah, Baktuzun, Bakinak,
Khamartigin, and the like. In short Mansur ibn Bayqara, Abu
Sa'id Malik, Abu 'l 'Abbas Jarrah, Khamartigin, Bakinak, Abu
'Abd Allah Jaihani and Ja'far secretly joined the Batinis. The
propagandists who converted this group were two: one was Abu
'l Fadl Zangurz Bardiji and the other was a one-eyed man called
'Atiq. All the members of this company were men on whom the
business of the court, audience-hall and divan depended, and in
whose hands was the management of the affairs of the whole country.
Surreptitiously they put their co-religionists into positions of power
and promoted them; and unless their work became too much for
them they did not delegate it to others. Officially and unofficially
they supported and assisted one another. If one of them stumbled
the rest stood by him and assisted him to discharge his obligations.
Thus their power increased daily, and all over Khurasan and
Transoxiana, wherever they were to be found, they joined together,
and with their help the Batini propaganda was published and their
doctrines were spread abroad. People in far off places began to think
that the whole court had become Batini. Then Abu Mansur 'Abd
ar Razzaq also joined the Batinis. The Batinis at the court wrote to
The Wearers of White[1] at Farghana, Khujand and Kasan urging
them to revolt, saying, 'Our arguments and yours are in origin the
same. We too are going to revolt, and our plan is first to capture the
king. Then we will join forces and conquer all the provinces on this
[north] side of the Oxus. Later we will attack Khurasan.'

23. The Batinis then united and with the co-operation of [Mansur]
ibn Bayqara they proceeded to vilify Abu 'Ali Bal'ami the wazir
and the amir Baktuzun in front of the king. Both these men were

---

[1] Persian *sapīd-jāmagān*: see Minorsky, *Hudud al 'Alam*, 117, 356, and Browne,
*Literary History*, I. 318.

[orthodox] Muslims, and all the pages were under the control of Baktuzun. Mansur ordered them both to be imprisoned in Kuhundiz and fettered. This caused serious confusion in the affairs of the country. When Alptigin saw that most of the nobles and courtiers had adopted the religion of the Batinis and that these two men, who were good Muslims and loyal to the king, had at their instigation been imprisoned, he set out from Nishapur to go to Bukhara and inform the king of the activities of the Batinis, and take measures to deal with them. Abu Mansur 'Abd ar Razzaq came to know of this; he was the amir of Tus and he was well provided with troops and equipment. He blocked Alptigin's path so that he could not reach the capital without a battle. Alptigin got news of this; he changed his route, and went by way of Sabzvar, until he reached the bank of the Oxus and halted at Amuy [Amul]. Abu Mansur 'Abd ar Razzaq turned back and despatched a letter to Mansur ibn Bayqara and the rest of that group, saying that Alptigin had come to spoil their position. After consulting together they represented to the king that Alptigin was in rebellion against him, saying, 'He has never come to the court before although you have called him so many times. Now in defiance of you he has suddenly arrived at the bank of the Oxus and intends to cross without your summoning him.' The king sent Bik Arslan Hamidi and Hasan Malik with a force of men to the Oxus, and they took all the boats from the other side so that Alptigin could not cross.

24. When Alptigin saw that they would not let him cross, he wrote a letter submitting the reason for his coming, and saying, 'Most of your nobles, courtiers and officials have adopted the religion of the Qarmatis: both great and small have joined in it, and they are planning to revolt; while on their word you have imprisoned the two men who in all the country are your most orthodox and loyal subjects. I had come to take measures against them. If you listen to the Qarmatis rather than to me, you may take the consequences. I, your slave, have informed Your Majesty. Now I am going to Balkh.' He sent a similar letter to the judge of Bukhara and the religious leaders saying, 'The Qarmatis have become powerful; at any time they may revolt; and the king is heedless; give him due counsel so that the faith and the kingdom may be saved.' And he went

to Balkh. The letters arrived. The judge Abu Ahmad and the religious leaders of Bukhara were aware of the situation but dared not say anything about it because the majority of the Qarmati company were of the king's select courtiers. They said, 'Maybe the king will not hear our word against them. Each one of them has a province and an army. They are rich and powerful; besides, they would become our enemies.'

25. One afternoon Abu Ahmad the chief judge went to the king's palace and requested a private audience; the king called him in and sat alone with him. Abu Ahmad said, 'Doctors of religion are always ready to give advice and counsel. Your father Nuh (The Praised Amir—the mercy of Allah upon him) used to meet religious teachers every day and he never used to do anything without consulting them. Consequently all crooked things were by him made straight. Because you seldom sit with men of virtue and learning, all that your father made straight has in your time become crooked.' He then shewed Alptigin's letter to the king; and he also shewed him another letter written by the religious leaders, so that the king should know that what he said was not from himself alone. Then he personally warned the king and talked to him so as to awaken him to the situation.

26. As it happened it was reported the next day that The Wearers of White had revolted in Farghana and were killing all the Muslims they could find. The day after that news also came from the Khurasan side that the Qarmatis were openly proclaiming the Shi'a religion in Taliqan and the foothills, and were committing murders and other crimes. So Mansur (The Righteous Amir) offered the wazir-ship to Abu Ahmad; he declined to accept, saying, 'If I take the office of wazir, who else is there now to give the king impartial information and advice? Besides interested parties will say that the judge has done all this for the sake of the wazirship, not for the sake of the faith.' The king was pleased with his words, and said, 'Then what is the best thing to do about the wazirship?' He said, 'You have a wazir, who is not only capable and worthy, but is a good Muslim and the son of a wazir as well.' He said, 'Where?' He said, 'He is a prisoner in Kuhundiz.' Mansur gave the command and Abu 'Ali Bal'ami and Baktuzun were released from Kuhundiz; and on the

same day they were fêted and reinstated in their posts with the utmost dignity and ceremony. The next day the king, the wazir, the judge and Baktuzun had a private meeting, and the king was made aware of the state of affairs far and near. They decided that first they would deal with the Qarmatis of Farghana and Sughd, known as The Wearers of White, and with the Qarmatis of Taliqan; then they would attend to Abu Mansur 'Abd ar Razzaq, and after that to the nobles and courtiers.

27. The next day scholars and teachers came in from every city to the wazir's court to complain to him and request him to inform the king about the revolt of the Qarmatis. Now Abu 'Ali deliberately delayed taking action with the result that the scholars said, 'He would not have hesitated if it were not for the fact that he is in league with them.' Then Abu 'Ali having openly suggested it to the king, ordered that a meeting should be held, attended by the Qarmatis on the one hand, and the scholars on the other; after debating the matter, they would abide by what they agreed to be in accordance with the precepts of the religious law of Islam. So the next day Abu 'Ali Bal'ami convened a meeting in the king's palace, and brought together Abu Ahmad Marghazi, the chief judge at the court, and all the religious leaders; and he summoned the Qarmati missionaries and leaders, and sent persons out to fetch as many of their spokesmen as could be recognized, in order that they might hold a religious discussion. So they debated and the Qarmatis were defeated. 'Atiq the one-eyed was beaten a hundred lashes and sent to Khwarazm where he died in prison; Abu 'l Fadl Zangurz was also given a hundred lashes and banished with his wife and children to Marv, and he died there. Then Baktuzun and Abu 'l Qasim, who was ........,[1] were sent to Taliqan with an army. Apart from the men they killed, they captured four hundred notable men who confessed [to being Qarmatis] and fined them 60,000 dinars. Then they were ordered by royal command to send them to the capital, and some of them were hanged and others were imprisoned for life.

28. When they had finished their operations in Taliqan, Mansur appointed Ishaq Balkhi to go with Bik Arslan to Farghana, and he also sent the scholar Abu Muhammad with them to teach the

[1] Persian *wakīl-i Pārs*: which is surely corrupt.

rebels the religious law. So these men took an army to Farghana and they defeated the rebels. Some were fined; others confessed their folly and repented, and when they were introduced to Islam they accepted it and forsook the other religion. So the army returned to Bukhara bringing much money and booty. The scholar Abu Muhammad was asked, 'What kind of religion do those loathsome people practise?' He said, 'Such that they used not to hide their privy parts from one another, and did not refrain from mutual commerce; when a man was married, their chief was the first to lay hands upon the woman, afterwards the husband; they regarded wine drinking as lawful; they did not wash pollution from their bodies; they made free with their mothers and sisters; they repudiated the duties of prayer, fasting, alms, pilgrimage and holy war.'

29. When this business had been accomplished, The Righteous Amir Mansur had a private meeting with the wazir, the judge and Baktuzun to discover how many of the courtiers, nobles and officials had adopted the Qarmati religion, and to consider how they were to bring about the downfall of Abu Mansur 'Abd ar Razzaq and remove him from the face of the earth, and clear Khurasan, 'Iraq and Transoxiana completely of the Qarmatis. They decided that since the amir of Tus, Abu Mansur 'Abd ar Razzaq, was the most powerful man in Khurasan at the time, because Alptigin had departed from Khurasan and settled at Ghaznain, first of all they must purge the capital, the king's abode, of the Qarmatis. So they appointed Nasir ad Daula [Helper of the Empire] Abu 'l Hasan Simjur as commander-in-chief of Khurasan, and summoned him with the army of Khurasan to the court. When he arrived at the capital they were able with his help to capture all the nobles and officials at the court who had become Qarmatis; they confiscated the whole of their property and then killed them all. After that they sent Abu 'l Hasan Simjur with the Khurasan army to fight and capture Abu Mansur 'Abd ar Razzaq. They sent letters to the border commanders including Washmgir, instructing that the latter should bring his troops from Gurgan, and that the others should join forces with him and surround Tus, capture Abu Mansur, and kill all the Qarmatis they could find.

30. Abu Mansur was sick; when he saw that the armies had

surrounded Tus, he made a sortie in the direction of Gurgan; Washmgir intercepted him on the road, and from breakfast time until afternoon prayer a very fierce battle was fought. Abu Mansur was exhausted with weakness and the pangs of sickness; he dismounted from his horse, laid his head on the bosom of a page, and thereupon expired. His troops then fled. Washmgir ordered his head to be cut off. They continued to chase the fugitives, killing and taking prisoners until the evening prayer. They succeeded in recovering all Abu Mansur's stores and valuables; Washmgir collected all the booty and sent it to the king along with 170 prisoners. Then in one direction Abu 'l Hasan Simjur and in the other direction Washmgir with his son Qabus traversed provinces and districts killing all the Qarmatis they could find. Eventually there remained not a single Batini in all Khurasan and Transoxiana; the religion collapsed completely and its adherents were all forgotten.

### *On the rising of Muhammad ibn 'Ali The Veiled 'Alawi to champion the Batini religion in Khuzistan and Basra with an army of negroes*

31. In the year 255 Muhammad ibn 'Ali The Veiled 'Alawi[1] led a revolt at Ahwaz. For several years he had been deceiving the negro slaves in Khuzistan and Basra with propaganda and promises. He revolted at the promised time and all the negroes joined in league with him. First he took Ahwaz, then Basra and the whole of Khuzistan. All the negroes killed their masters and seized their wealth, wives, houses and farms. Several times they defeated the forces of [the caliph] al Mu'tadid, and for fourteen years four months and six days Muhammad ibn 'Ali ruled like a king over Basra and Khuzistan. In the end he was captured and all the negroes were killed; at the end of the month of Safar in the year 270 he was brought to Baghdad and put to death. His religion was in all respects the same as that of Mazdak, Babak, Abu Zakariyya,[2] the Khurramdins and the Qarmatis.

---

[1] See Minorsky, *Hudud al 'Alam,* 139 s.v. Basra.
[2] See Browne, *Literary History,* I. 359.

### On the revolt of Abu Sa'id Jannabi and his son Abu Tahir in Bahrain and al Ahsa

32. Also in the time of al Mu'tadid was the revolt of Abu Sa'id al Hasan ibn Bahram al Jannabi in Bahrain and al Ahsa. He summoned the people of those parts to the Shi'a, or Batini religion as we call it, and led them astray. He gradually strengthened his position there, and when he had become established, he began to practise highway robbery and pillage the countryside. He also introduced community of property. He continued in this way for some time, and then a servant killed him. After that servants were not trusted in Bahrain and al Ahsa. Abu Sa'id had a son called Abu Tahir. He took his father's place and for a time he lived virtuously. He happened to know something about the doctrines of the Shi'ites; so he sent someone to their missionaries and asked for a copy of their book which they called *Balāghat as Sābi'* [The Eloquence of the Seventh Imam]. They sent him the book. He studied it and became one of those dogs. Then he invited all the men of Bahrain and al Ahsa who were young and fond of arms to join him, saying, 'Come, for I have some hunting for you.' The time of the pilgrimage was near. He gathered a vast crowd of men, marched them off and led them to Mecca, just at the time of the pilgrimage, when pilgrims from all over the world had assembled. He ordered them to draw their swords and kill all they could find, laying hands on the people of Mecca and The Neighbours [of the sanctuary] in particular. They made a sudden attack and began killing. Seeing this the people fled into the sanctuary and protected themselves behind the chests in which the Qurans were kept. The inhabitants of Mecca took up arms and joined battle.

33. At this Abu Tahir sent an envoy to them and said, 'We have come for pilgrimage not to fight. It was your fault for killing one of us without cause and breaking our *iḥrām* [pilgrimage rites], so that we were constrained to take up arms. If the report is spread about the world, that the people of Mecca are arming themselves and killing pilgrims, nobody will be eager to do the pilgrimage any more. The pilgrims' road will then be closed and you will get a bad name. Do not spoil the pilgrimage for us. Allow us to proceed.' The people

of Mecca thought that perhaps he was telling the truth; it was possible that someone had quarrelled with their party, and drawn a weapon and hurt one of them. They agreed that both parties should sheathe their swords, and swear by The Book and with irredeemable oaths that they would not fight again, and that the Meccans would go back and return the Quran-chests to the sanctuary, so that the pilgrims could visit the Ka'ba in safety. The Meccans and the pilgrims both swore oaths and went back and put up their weapons. The Meccans then put the chests back in their place and the pilgrims entered upon the circumambulation of the Ka'ba.

34. When Abu Tahir saw that the armed men had dispersed, he ordered his comrades to take up their arms and fall upon the sanctuary and kill whomsoever they found inside or outside. So they made a sudden rush at the sanctuary, brandishing their swords and killing every one within reach. They killed all The Neighbours and an enormous number of other people lost their lives. In fear of the sword they were throwing themselves into wells and fleeing to the tops of the mountains. The raiders removed The Black Stone from its place, then went up on the roof of the building and tore down the golden gutters, saying, 'Since your god goes to heaven and leaves his house on earth, then let his house be plundered and destroyed.' Then they pulled down the curtains, tore them up and carried them off as plunder, all the while saying in mockery [quoting from the Quran 3. 91], 'And he who entered it was safe,' and [106. 4] 'He saved them from fear.' 'Since you had gone inside the temple, why were you not safe from our swords? If you had had a real god he would have saved you from the fear of our swords'; and suchlike blasphemies they uttered. They took captive the wives and children of the Meccans and led them away. Altogether about 20,000 men were killed apart from those who threw themselves into wells; and they cast the bodies of the slain on top of those [in the wells] so that they too perished. It was impossible to estimate the amount of gold, dirams, dinars, fine linen, musk, aloes-wood, ambergris and other precious things which they took. When Abu Tahir returned to al Ahsa he sent portions of the loot as gifts to his missionaries in various places. This catastrophe for Islam took place in the time of al Muqtadir in the year 317 from the hijra.

35. Abu Tahir sent some gifts to Abu Sa'id in the West, who was a Jewish boy; one of the sons of 'Abd Allah ibn Maimun al Qaddah called Ahmad had married his mother, and brought up the boy; he taught him the liberal arts, provided him with splendid adornments and made him his heir; he instructed him in his propaganda and gave him certain signs. Abu Sa'id arose and went to the West and stayed in the city of Sijilmas; there his affairs prospered and he forced his religion on the necks of the people by the sword. He claimed that he was the Mahdi and of the family of 'Ali; he imposed heavy taxes, made wine lawful, and permitted [commerce with] mothers, sisters and daughters; he openly cursed the Marwanids and 'Abbasids, and if we were to tell of all the innocent blood which he spilt and the wicked practices which he introduced, it would take too long and would not suit this abbreviated account. It is reported in the history books that the present occupant of the throne of Egypt [Fatimid caliph] is descended from him.

36. When Abu Tahir (ibn Abi Sa'id) returned to al Ahsa, he collected all the volumes of the Quran, the Torah and the Evangel that he could find and threw them into the desert, and people defiled them with their ordure. He used to say, 'Three persons have corrupted mankind—a shepherd, a physician and a camel-driver;[1] and this camel-driver was the greatest juggler and the craftiest villain of them all.' He allowed [commerce with] sisters, mothers and daughters; he broke The Black Stone in two, and put the pieces on the two sides of a pit [latrine]; when he squatted over the pit, he put his feet one on each half of the stone; he commanded public cursing of the prophets. But his order that men should have commerce with their mothers was intolerable to the Arabs; many of them ate arsenic and brimstone, and died rather than lie with their mothers; but the people of the West and the more ignorant of the beduin took to this practice quite naturally. He attacked the pilgrim caravan a second time, and again swore false oaths and killed an immeasurable number of people. But when the Muslims of Khurasan and 'Iraq decided to travel by sea as well as land, the bandits were afraid and sent back The Black Stone; one day on entering the Cathedral Mosque at Kufa people unexpectedly saw The Black

[1] viz. Moses, Jesus and Muhammad.

Stone lying there. They picked it up and having mended it with an iron rivet, took it back to Mecca and put it in its place. Then Abu Tahir brought Rakibra the Zoroastrian secretly from Isfahan to al Ahsa and set him up as king; this Zoroastrian set to and killed 700 of their leading men, and he was going to kill Abu Tahir and his brother; but Abu Tahir was apprised of this, and killed him by a trick, so regaining the ascendancy. But if we were to relate all the crimes and all the murders which this dog perpetrated in the lands of Islam, it could not be contained in this brief book. This trouble lasted until the time of ar Radi; and it was in the time of ar Radi that the Dailamites rose to power.

37. This much has been related so that The Master of the World (may Allah perpetuate his reign) may know what the religion of these Batinis is (may Allah forsake them), why their words and oaths are not to be trusted, what crimes and evil works they have done against the Muslims and the lands of Islam whenever they have had the opportunity, what wicked people they are and what enemies of Islam and of the state.

38. Muqanna' [The Veiled] Marghazi[1] also appeared in the lands of Transoxiana at this time. He totally abolished the religious law among his people, and at first he made the same claims as the Batinis, such as Abu Sa'id Jannabi, Abu Sa'id Maghribi, Muhammad The Veiled 'Alawi and their missionaries. Muqanna' and the two Abu Sa'ids lived at the same time and they corresponded with one another. Muqanna' worked a magic spell in Transoxiana and made the likeness of a moon to appear from a mountain; every day at the same time the moon would rise, and all the inhabitants of the district saw it; it lasted for a long time. He took the people of that province out of the bosom of Islam and the divine law. When his position became strong he laid claim to divinity, and then there followed a tale of bloodshed, sedition and crime; armies came from the frontier districts to support him, and for several years the Muslims were engaged in wars against him. If I were to narrate it all, it would come to twice as much as this; and the history of each one of these dogs that I have mentioned would make a large book of itself. This

---

[1] See Browne, *Literary History*, I. 318, and Minorsky, *Hudud al 'Alam*, 356.

much has been told of the story of Muqanna‘ in order that mention of him should not be omitted from our compendium.

39. Whenever the Batinis have appeared they have had a name or a nickname, and in every city and province they have been known by a different title; but in essence they are all the same. In Aleppo and Egypt they call them Isma‘ilis; in Qum, Kashan, Tabaristan and Sabzvar they are called Shi‘ites; in Baghdad, Transoxiana and Ghaznain they are known as Qarmatis, in Kufa as Mubarakis, in Basra as Rawandis and Burqa‘is, in Rayy as Khalafis, in Gurgan as The Wearers of Red, in Syria as The Wearers of White, in the West as Sa‘idis, in al Ahsa and Bahrain as Jannabis, and in Isfahan as Batinis; whereas they call themselves The Didactics and other such names. But their whole purpose is only to abolish Islam and to lead mankind astray.

# CHAPTER FORTY-SEVEN

*On the rising of the Khurramdins
in Isfahan and Adharbaygan*

1. Now your slave will compose a somewhat abbreviated chapter on the subject of the Khurramdins, so that The Master of the World (may Allah perpetuate his reign) may be enlightened concerning them. Whenever the Khurramdins have arisen the Batinis have made common cause with them and strengthened them; and whenever the Batinis appear, the Khurramdins combine with them and assist them with men and resources; for the origin of these two religions is the same and they have but one object—to corrupt the faith.

2. In the year 162 in the days of al Mahdi, the Batinis of Gurgan, known as The Red Banners, that is to say The Wearers of Red, gained great strength and joined forces with the Khurramdins, saying, ‘Abu Muslim is alive! Let us seize the kingdom and give it back to him!’ They made his son Abu ’l Ghara (ibn Abi Muslim) their leader and advanced as far as Rayy. Every unlawful thing they con-

sidered lawful; and they shared their wives with one another. Then al Mahdi wrote letters to the governors of the frontier provinces, ordering them to join forces with 'Umar ibn al 'Ala, governor of Tabaristan, and go to war against the rebels. They attacked and routed them. Later at the time when Harun ar Rashid was in Khurasan the Khurramdins revolted in the Isfahan district, coming from Tirmidin, Kapula, Fabak and other villages. A large mob came and joined them from Rayy, Hamadan, Karaj and Dastaba. Their total number came to more than 100,000. Harun sent 'Abd Allah ibn Malik from Khurasan with 20,000 horsemen to make war on them. They took fright and the various communities went back to their places. 'Abd Allah ibn Malik wrote a letter to Harun ar Rashid saying, 'Abu Dulaf is indispensable to us.' The reply came, 'Take your orders from him.' So the two joined forces. Once again the Khurramdins with the encouragement of the Batinis gathered into a large mob and set their hands to sedition and plunder. Abu Dulaf 'Ijli and 'Abd Allah ibn Malik attacked suddenly and caught them unawares. They killed an enormous number of them and took their wives and children to Baghdad and sold them by auction.

## On the revolt of Babak

3. Nine years after this Babak[1] came out in revolt from Adharbaygan. These Batinis attempted to join him; but they heard that forces had been sent in pursuit of them, so they were afraid and returned and dispersed. Then in the year 212 in the days of al Ma'mun the Khurramdins revolted in the districts of Isfahan, Ravanda and Kapula. A party of Batinis joined them, and they went to Adharbaygan and attached themselves to Babak. Al Ma'mun sent Muhammad ibn Hamid Ta'i to make war on Babak and at the same time to repel the Khurramdins; he ordered him first to engage with Zarir ibn 'Ali ibn Sadaqa, who had revolted and was wandering through Kuhistan and 'Iraq, pillaging the country and robbing caravans. Muhammad ibn Hamid went with speed. He asked for nothing from al Ma'mun's treasury but equipped his

[1] See Browne, *Literary History*, I. 323.

troops from his own resources. He attacked Zarir, captured him and destroyed his followers. For this al Ma'mun gave him Qazwin, Maragha and most of Adharbaygan. Then he made war on Babak and for a period of six months fierce battles took place between him and Babak. In the end Muhammad ibn Hamid was killed. Babak's fortunes rose high. The Khurramdins sent the Isfahani members of their contingent back to Isfahan. Al Ma'mun was extremely vexed at the news of the death of Muhammad ibn Hamid. He immediately nominated ʿAbd Allah ibn Tahir, governor of Khurasan, for the war against Babak and gave him the whole province of Kuhistan and all that had been liberated of Adharbaygan. ʿAbd Allah arose and went to Adharbaygan. Babak was unable to resist him; he fled into a very secure fortress and his army dispersed and with it the mass of the Khurramdins.

4. In the year 218 the Khurramdins of Isfahan, Pars and the whole of Kuhistan and Adharbaygan broke out in revolt because al Ma'mun had gone to Rum. They had determined on a certain night, and having made preparations in all the provinces and cities they revolted on that night; they killed the tax-collectors everywhere, and slaughtered a great many of the peasants, plundering their houses and carrying off the wives and children of the Muslims as slaves. In Pars the Muslims gathered together and defeated the rebels, killing many and taking prisoners; but in Isfahan the Khurramdins banded together under the leadership of a man called ʿAli ibn Mazdak. He mustered 20,000 men outside the gate of the city and went with his brother to Karaj; at that time Abu Dulaf was not there; his brother Maʿqil was at Karaj, and with only 500 horsemen he could not resist; so he fled and went to Baghdad. ʿAli ibn Mazdak captured Karaj, plundered the town and killed all the Muslims he could find; he carried off all the women and children of the ʿIjlis. From there he went to Adharbaygan to join forces with Babak. The Khurramdins flocked to Babak from all sides; their numbers came to 125,000, and they forgathered at a city called Sharistan between Kuhistan and Adharbaygan. There Babak joined them.

5. Then al Muʿtasim sent Ishaq with 40,000 horsemen to fight them; he attacked them suddenly and a battle ensued. In the end he defeated them and Babak fled. Ishaq's army then laid about the

Khurramdins with their swords. When they counted the casualties, those actually killed, apart from those who surrendered, came to 100,000 men. A group [of survivors] made for Isfahan and about 10,000 men under the brother of 'Ali ibn Mazdak plundered the country around Isfahan; they had brought their wives and children with them. The amir of Isfahan, 'Ali ibn 'Isa, was away; the judge, Chaghan, with a party of nobles, mayors and citizens went out to fight them. They came upon them from three directions and massacred them; they took all their women and children and kept them captive; any boys that were come of age they beheaded.

6. Six years after this al Mu'tasim again attended to the matter of the Khurramdins, and he nominated Afshin to make war against Babak. Afshin took troops and set out to meet him. The Khurramdins and Batinis from every place went to Babak's assistance. Altogether they were at war for two years, and several fierce battles were fought between Afshin and Babak, and vast numbers of men were killed on both sides. In the end, when Afshin had failed to capture Babak, he devised a stratagem; he ordered his troops to strike their tents by night, to disperse, retreat ten farsangs and remain there. Then Afshin sent an envoy to Babak saying, 'Send me a wise and experienced man, for I wish to say a few words which are for the benefit of both of us.' Babak sent him a man. Afshin said to him, 'Tell Babak that every beginning has an end; the head of a man is not a leek that it should grow again. Nearly all of my men have been killed; not one tenth remain. I have no doubt that it is the same on your side. Come, let us make peace. You be content with this province which you hold; and dwell here in safety, while I will go back and demand from The Commander of the Faithful another province on your behalf and send you the letters patent. If you do not accept my advice, come, let us contend with one another once for all to see whom fortune favours.' The envoy then left his presence.

7. Now Afshin had concealed 2,000 horsemen and 3,000 foot-soldiers in the mountains and gorges, where they were to lie in ambush as if they were fugitives. The envoy returned to Babak, gave the message, and reported on [what he had seen of] the quantity and quality of the enemy's forces; spies brought back the same report. So they agreed to fight a (fierce) battle after three days. Afshin then

sent a messenger to his troops in hiding, saying, 'On the night before the battle, come and conceal yourselves in the mountains and valleys on the left and on the right at a distance of one and a half farsangs. When I retire in flight and abandon the camp, some of the enemy will pursue me, others will busy themselves with plunder. You will then rush out from the mountains and block the road against them so that they cannot go back into the gorge. Then I will come back and do my utmost.'

8. On the day of the battle Babak brought his troops out of the pass; they were more than 100,000 horse and foot. Afshin's army was contemptible in their eyes, judging from what [the spies] had seen from [Afshin's] camp; and the troops themselves saw no more [than the spies had seen]. Then they joined battle and they fought fiercely on both sides and many men were killed. As the sun was sinking Afshin took to flight and retreated to a distance of one farsang from the camp. Then he said to his standard-bearer, 'Raise the standard!' He drew rein. As his troops arrived at the spot they halted. Babak had told his men not to indulge in plunder so that they might finally dismiss Afshin from their minds. So the horsemen along with Babak went in pursuit of Afshin. However the foot-soldiers fell upon the camp and started to plunder. Then the 20,000 horsemen emerged from behind the mountains to left and to right, and saw all the plain full of the Khurramdin foot-soldiers. They blocked the road against them in the gorge and set about them with their swords. Afshin came back with his troops and Babak was caught in the middle. However much he strove he found no way of escape. Afshin closed in and took him prisoner. They went on charging and killing until nightfall. More than 80,000 men were killed there. Then they took Babak and the other prisoners to Baghdad and led him through the city for a spectacle.

9. When al Mu'tasim set eyes on Babak he said, 'O dog, why did you stir up this trouble in the world and why did you kill so many thousand Muslims?' He made no reply. Al Mu'tasim commanded his hands and feet to be cut off. When they had cut off one hand, he put the other one in the blood and rubbed it on his face making it all red with blood. Al Mu'tasim said, 'Dog, what sign is this?' Babak said, 'There is wisdom in it. You are going to cut off

my hands and feet. Now it is blood that makes men's faces red. When the body loses blood, the face becomes yellow. I am making my face red so that when my body loses blood, people will not say my face has turned yellow from fear.' Then on al Mu'tasim's orders an ox was skinned, and the hide was brought as it was, fresh and with the horns. Babak was then put inside the skin with the horns protruding from behind his ears; and he was sewn up in it, and the skin dried up on him. Then he was hanged alive in that condition and he perished miserably.

10. The complete story of Babak from the beginning of his revolt until his capture is a long one. One of his executioners came to be captured, and he was asked how many persons he had put to death. He said, 'Babak had several executioners, but the number of people that I have executed is 36,000 apart from those the other executioners have put to death.'

11. Al Mu'tasim gained three victories and all three gave strength to Islam—the first was the conquest of Rum, the second was the victory over Babak and the third the victory over Mazyar the Zoroastrian in Tabaristan. If any one of these victories had not been won, it would have been a calamity for Islam.

## The story of al Mu'tasim's three victories

12. One day al Mu'tasim was sitting at a drinking party, and judge Yahya ibn Aktham was present. Al Mu'tasim got up and left the party and went into another room. After some time he came out and drank some wine. Three times he went into three different rooms, and he went to the bathroom and washed himself. He soon emerged and called for his prayer-mat. He performed two *rak'ats* of prayer and went back to the party. He said to judge Yahya, 'Do you know why I said these prayers?' He said, 'No.' He said, 'It was a prayer of thanksgiving for one of God's benefits (to Him be power and glory) which he has vouchsafed me today.' Yahya said, 'O Commander of the Faithful, what benefit was that? If you see fit, please tell us that we too may rejoice.' He said, 'In this hour I have deflowered the maidenhood of three maidens, all of whom were daughters of my enemies; one was the daughter of the king of Rum, the second the

daughter of Babak, and the third the daughter of Mazyar the Zoroastrian.'

13. In the days of al Wathiq the Khurramdins again revolted in the district of Isfahan, and they gave rise to much evil and sedition. They continued their insurrections until the year 300. They pillaged the town of Karaj, killed some people and were later subdued.
........¹ revolted and took refuge in the mountains near Isfahan. The Khurramdins and Batinis gathered about him, and they began to attack caravans and plunder villages, killing old and young, women and boys. He carried on his iniquities for thirty and odd years, and no army was able to resist him. They were powerless against the inaccessible and impregnable fastnesses which he held. At last he was captured and put to death, and his head was hung up in Isfahan. On this victory they sent the glad tidings throughout the lands of Islam. However, if we mention everything, it will take too long. Whoever wishes to know about the revolts and seditions of the Batinis and Khurramdins should study Tabari's History, the History of Isfahan and the History of the 'Abbasid Caliphs, so that it may be known to him.

14. Now the basis of the religion of the Khurramdins is that they avoid all kinds of physical exertion or trouble, and they reject the divine law, renouncing prayer, fasting, pilgrimage, holy war and ablution, while they permit the use of wine and the sharing of wives and property—in fact they discard all obligatory observances. Whenever they hold a meeting or deliberate a matter of importance, they always commence the proceedings by bewailing the death of Abu Muslim Sahib ad Daula and cursing his killer; also they pray for Mahdi Firuz, son of Fatima the daughter of Abu Muslim, whom they call The Learned Boy (and in Arabic [al] Fata 'l 'Alim).

From the foregoing the principles of Mazdak's religion have been made plain, and their identity with the doctrines of the Khurram-dins and Batinis has been demonstrated; the constant object of them all is to overthrow Islam. At first, in order to lure the Muslims, they display themselves as truthful, virtuous and faithful to The Prophet's

---

¹ A proper name is surely concealed in the MS. corruptions *bābar bar shāh* and *bāz bar bādshāh*.

family (upon him be peace). Having gained power and acquired followers, they try to overthrow the divine law. Even infidels shew greater mercy to Muhammad's people (upon him be peace) than they do.

15.\* We have related this account of their deeds and sayings, since at present they are digging a pit, and beating a drum beneath a blanket. There are persons who, having accepted their propaganda, are assisting their purposes, joining in their affairs, and supporting their schemes. Although the whole world belongs to The Master of the World (may Allah perpetuate his rule), and all its inhabitants are his slaves, they have made him greedy for the acquisition of wealth. They are depriving deserving people of their dues, and maintaining that this is economy; but you will never make a whole shirt by cutting off the tail and making it into sleeves. One day The Master of the World (may Allah extend his reign) will recall the words of his slave, when they begin to throw friends and nobles into this pit, when the sound of their drum reaches the ears of all, and when their evil practices and intrigues are exposed; for then will the Muslims suffer calamity, the country will be thrown into disorder, and the religion will descend into the abyss [of heresy]; then will he know that all that his slave said was true, and that he never refused to offer any possible advice or goodwill, and always fulfilled his duties of service and loyalty to The Victorious Empire (may Allah strengthen its pillars). May God Almighty keep the evil eye and the hand of harm far from his life and his empire, may He never permit his enemies to attain their objects and desires, may He keep this court, audience-hall and divan provided with men of true faith until the resurrection, and never let there be any lack of loyal supporters of the dynasty; and may He every day grant new victories, new successes and new glories.

# CHAPTER FORTY-EIGHT

*Concerning treasuries and the procedures and arrangements*
*for looking after them*

1. Kings have always had two treasuries, the capital treasury and the expenses treasury. As revenue was acquired it was usually taken to the capital treasury, and seldom to the expenses treasury, and unless there was urgent necessity they did not allow disbursement from the capital treasury. When they did take anything out, they took it by way of a loan, and put an equivalent sum back later. If care is not taken in this way, the whole income of the state will be dissipated on expenses, and if there comes some unexpected need for money, it will give rise to anxiety and there will be shortcoming and delay in meeting the commitment. It was always the practice that any money paid into the treasury such as revenue from provinces, should not be changed or encashed. Thus expenses were met at their due time, there was no failure or delay in the payment of awards, salaries and presents, and the treasuries were always replenished.

2. I heard that the amir Altun Tash,[1] who was the great amir-chamberlain of Sultan Mahmud, was appointed to be Khwarazm-shah, and was sent to Khwarazm. Now the estimate of the revenue of Khwarazm was 60,000 dinars; while the salaries of Altun Tash's troops amounted to 120,000 dinars. A year after Altun Tash went to Khwarazm a person was sent to demand the revenue. Altun Tash sent his own emissaries to Ghaznain and requested that the 60,000 dinars which were the burden [of taxation] of Khwarazm should be assigned direct to him for the payment of his troops instead of the money being sent from the divan. Shams al Kufat Ahmad ibn Hasan Maimandi was wazir at that time; when he read this letter, he wrote an answer at once as follows, 'In the name of Allah The Merciful, The Clement; be aware that Altun Tash cannot be Mahmud in any respect. Let him take the money which he has collected in taxes, and bring it to the sultan's treasury; having had the gold assayed and weighed let him deliver it and take a receipt. Only then let him ask for the salaries for himself and his troops, and

---

[1] See Muhammad Nazim, *Sultan Mahmud*, 60.

he will be given drafts upon Bust and Sistan;[1] he will then send persons to go and collect the money and bring it to Khwarazm. Thus will be maintained the difference between master and slave, between Mahmud and Altun Tash, because the functions of the king and the responsibilities of the army will be clear and distinct. The Khwarazmshah should refrain from futile talk; as for this request which he has made, either he must regard the sultan with the eye of contempt, or else he considers Ahmad ibn Hasan negligent and incompetent. We did not expect this from the perfect intelligence and sound judgment of the Khwarazmshah. He must apologize for this mistake. It is a grave danger when slaves seek partnership with their masters.'

3. He sent this letter by hand of a *sūbāshī* with ten pages to Khwarazm. So the 60,000 dinars were brought and delivered to Mahmud's treasury, and in exchange drafts upon the provinces of Bust and Sistan were taken from the divan of Ghaznain. Persons went to those places and in return for the drafts took pomegranate skins, oak-apples, cotton and suchlike, and brought them back to Khwarazm.

4. The affairs of the kingdom have always been arranged and managed in this way, for the safeguarding of the interests of the country, for the preservation of the welfare of the peasantry and the prosperity of the treasury, and for the restraining of covetous hands from the revenue of the sultan and the property of the people.

## CHAPTER FORTY-NINE

### *On dealing with complainants, giving answers and dispensing justice*

1. There is always a large crowd of complainants frequenting the court, and even when they receive the answers to their petitions they

---

[1] Compare the well-known story of Nizam al Mulk paying boatmen on the Oxus by drafts on Antioch, as given in *Rahat as Sudur*, 128. 15.

do not go away. Any stranger or envoy, arriving at the capital and seeing this clamorous tumult, will think that at this court gross injustice is done to the people. These doors must be closed to such crowds, and all requests, whether from town or country, should be heard and written down at their place [of origin]; five persons should then come to the court, state their case, explain the circumstances, hear the answer and receive the judgment. Having received the judgment they must go back at once so that there is no more of this unnecessary tumult and groundless clamour.

2. They say that Yazdijird Shahryar sent a messenger to The Commander of the Faithful ʿUmar (may Allah be pleased with him) saying, 'In all the world there is no court more frequented than ours, no treasury more replete, no army more daring; and nobody has such great resources as we have.' ʿUmar replied, 'Yes, your court is crowded, but with complainants; your treasury is replete, but with ill-gotten wealth; your army is daring, but also disobedient; when your fortune is finished, wealth and resources are of no avail. All these facts indicate that your fortune is waning and your empire declining.' And so indeed it was.

3. In order that everyone should practise equity and cease to covet improper and impossible objects, governors must give justice themselves in person, as did Sultan Mahmud.

### The story of Masʿud ibn Mahmud and his debt

4. They say that a merchant came to Sultan Mahmud's court of complaints, and complained against Mahmud's son Masʿud, imploring justice and saying, 'I am a merchant; it is a long time since I came here, and I want to return to my own city. I cannot go because your son has bought goods from me to the value of 60,000 dinars, and he has not given me the money. I request you to send the amir Masʿud with me to the judge.' Sultan Mahmud was vexed at the merchant's words and sent a harsh message to Masʿud saying, 'I desire you either to pay this man his due, or else to go with him to court so that judgment may be given according to the provisions of Muslim law.' The merchant went to the judge's house and a messenger went to Masʿud and delivered the message. Masʿud was at a

loss to know what to do. He said to his treasurer, 'See how much money there is in the treasury.' The treasurer counted it, and said, '20,000 dinars.' He said, 'Take it to the merchant, and for the rest ask for three days grace.' And he said to the messenger, 'Tell the sultan that I have just given 20,000 dinars, and I will pay the rest after three days. I am standing here with my cloak on and my loins girt, waiting for the sultan's command.' Mahmud said, 'Know for sure that you will not see my face until you pay the merchant in full.' Mas'ud dared not say anything further, so he sent people in all directions to ask for loans. By the time of afternoon prayer the 60,000 dinars had been paid to the merchant. When reports of this reached distant parts of the world, merchants from China, Cathay, Egypt and 'Aden set out for Ghaznain bringing all the choicest goods in the world.

5. But as for the kings of this age, if they command the merest servant or groom to be present at the court of law with the civil governor of Balkh or the mayor of Marv, the man will disobey the order and will not care two grains for the king's word.

6. The governor of the city of Homs wrote to 'Umar ibn 'Abd al 'Aziz saying, 'The city wall of Homs is in ruins and it must be built up. What is your command?' 'Umar replied, 'Let the city of Homs be protected by a wall of justice, and let the roads be purged of fear and violence. Then there is no need for bricks and mortar, stones and lime.'

7. God (be He exalted) commands David [Quran 38. 25], 'O David, I have made you a viceroy upon earth; judge between the people with equity.' (Which being translated means: O David, We have made you Our viceroy upon earth, so that you may look after Our servants, and not allow one to do wrong to another; every word that you say, say it with justice; every work that you do, do it with righteousness.) [And the Quran 39. 37 says:] 'Will not Allah suffice His slave?'

8. Muhammad The Elect (may Allah pray for him and give him peace) says [in Arabic], 'He who appoints a governor over the Muslims, knowing that there is amongst the people a better man than that, has betrayed Allah, His prophet and the whole body of

Muslims.' (Which being translated means: Good, pious and honest men should be put in charge of affairs, so that they will not trouble God's servants, but rather have compassion upon them; if a man is appointed who is not so, a treachery will have been committed against God, His prophet and the Muslims.)

9. This world is the journal of kings. If they are good, they are blessed and well remembered; if they are evil, they are cursed and ill remembered—as 'Unsuri says:

If you make the firmament your throne you will be famous;
If you make your girdle of the stars you'll be renowned;
See that when your fame is won that fame is pure and sound;
Take care that when you are renowned your renown is good.

# CHAPTER FIFTY

## *On keeping account of the revenue of the provinces and the method of doing it*

1. Accounts of the revenue of the provinces should be kept, shewing income and expenditure. The advantage of this is that a salutary watch can be kept upon spending; any items which need to be reduced (and the money not spent) can then be cancelled. If someone has something to say concerning income and proposes an increase, his words should be heard, and if what he says has some justification, the money should be raised; thus if it appears that there is any extravagance or waste of money, by this means it can be checked, and the true state of affairs will never remain concealed.

2. Now as regards following a middle course in finance and other affairs, the king must be just, he must practise ancient customs and follow the laws and institutions which good kings have laid down; he must not initiate evil laws, nor assent to heresy. It is obligatory for the king to investigate the actions and transactions of governors, to know about income and expenditure, to look after the revenue,

and to build treasuries and storehouses for the purpose of strengthening the state and resisting enemy attack. He should not be so close-fisted that people will brand him as miserly or worldly; on the other hand he should not squander money on extravagances lest people call him a spendthrift and a wastrel. When giving largesse he should have regard to the rank of each recipient; if ten dinars is a suitable bounty for a man, he should not give a hundred; nor should he give a thousand dinars to one who is fit to receive a hundred; for this is detrimental to the dignity of notable men, and besides people will say that the king is ignorant of men's worth and rank, and is ungrateful for the services and skills of his subjects; then for no cause people will be offended and become less diligent in their work.

3. Furthermore the king should so wage war against his enemies that there remains room for peace; he should so contract friendships that they can be broken, and so break them that they can be mended. He should not drink wine for the sake of intoxication. Let him not be constantly jocular, nor altogether austere. If occasionally he occupies himself with entertainment, hunting, drinking and other worldly pleasures, let him also sometimes devote himself to thanksgiving, almsgiving, nocturnal prayer, fasting and charitable works. Then he will possess both worlds. In all things he should take the middle course, for The Prophet (upon him be peace) said [in Arabic], 'The best of things is the middle of them'. (That is to say: the middle course in affairs is right for it wins the most approbation.) In every work let him observe the portion due to God (to Him be power and glory); then he will suffer no misfortune. Let him be zealous in obeying the commands of The Truth and in the observance of religious duties; then God Almighty will give him sufficient strength for his religious and secular tasks, and cause him to gain his ends in both worlds and attain all his desires.

# EPILOGUE

So ends this book of Rules for Kings. Your humble servant was previously commanded to compile a volume on this subject, and he carried out the command. At the time he composed thirty-nine chapters ex tempore and submitted them to The Lofty Throne (may Allah exalt it). They were found acceptable. However that was merely an epitome. Later he expanded that epitome at his leisure, and wrote chapters and related stories on a variety of subjects, expounding everything in the clearest and simplest language. In the year 485 when we were about to depart for Baghdad, I gave the book to Muhammad Nasikh, the copyist of the royal books, and told him to copy it in a fair hand, and in the event of my not returning from that journey, to offer it to The Master of the World (may Allah perpetuate his reign) so that The Lofty Throne might be roused to vigilance and made duly aware of the fidelity and loyalty of his devoted slave. Let him not listen to what others say, but rather read this book constantly; he will never be wearied by reading this book for it contains advice, wisdom, proverbs, interpretation of the Quran, traditions of The Prophet (upon him be peace), stories of the prophets, memoirs of the saints, and tales of just kings; it tells of the lives of the departed and the deeds of the living; with all its length it is still only a summary, and it deserves the attention of The Righteous Monarch. And Allah knoweth best what is right.

THE END OF RULES FOR KINGS

# INDEX

# Index

Āytāsh, 219

Bābak, 233, 239 ff.
Babdāh, 228
Badakhshān, 147
Baghdād, 6, 13, 15 ff., 52 ff., 80 ff., 120,
  136 ff., 150, 159, 162, 166, 176, 212,
  214, 217, 233, 238–42, 252
Baḥrain, 234, 238
Bahrām Chūbīn, 76–7
Bahrām Gūr (Sāsānian), 24 ff., 178
B'ākhir-āsān, 172
Bakīnak, 228
Abū Bakr, Qāḍī Imām, 167–8
Abū Bakr Nakhshabī, 218
Abū Bakr aṣ-Ṣiddīq (orthodox caliph),
  168, 177–8, 188–9
Baktūzun, 228–32
Balʿamīs, 178
Bālāsāghūn, 170, 220, 224
Balkh, 20, 114 ff., 157–8, 179–82, 187,
  227, 229, 249
Bāmiyān, 116
Barbary (Barbar), 170
Bārbud, 131
Bargiyāruq (Saljūqid), 161
Barmak, 179 n., 180
Barmakids (Barmecides), 178–9
Baṣra, 176, 214, 224, 233, 238
Bīghish, 226
Bik Arslān Ḥamīdī, 229–31
Bikrak, 133
Abū Bilāl (Qarmaṭī), 226–7
Bukhārā, 15, 109 ff., 158, 218–24, 227–
  233
Bulūr, 146
Bust, 247
Buwaihids, see Dailamites
Buzurjmihr, 134, 178, 188, 192
Buzurjūmīd Dīrū, 172

Caesar (Qaiṣar), 61, 79
Cathay (Khiṭā), 155–6, 249
Chāch, 228
Chaghān, 241
China (Chīn), 153, 170, 186, 249
Christians (Tarsāyān), 164, 169, 175,
  195

Chughrī Beg (Saljūqid), 149
Companions of the Prophet, 1, 44, 68,
  126, 167, 188
Constantinople (Qusṭanṭiniyya), 61

Dailamites (Dailamān), 68, 78, 96,
  103–4, 161, 165–6, 217, 237
Dair Gachīn, 67 ff.
Damascus (Dimishq), 180–2
Dānishūmand Ashtar, 100
Darband, 147
Abu 'd-Dardā', 168
Darius (Dārā), 32, 187
Dastaba, 239
David (Dāvud), 249
Abū Dulaf ʿIjlī, 239

Egypt (Miṣr), 128, 170, 236, 238, 249
The Eloquence of the Seventh [Imām]
  (Balāghat as-Sābiʿ), 234
Evangel (Anjīl), 236
Eve (Ḥawwā), 185
Explanation, The Book of (Kitāb al-
  Bayān), 215

Fābak, 239
Faḍl b. Sahl, 132
Abu 'l-Faḍl Sigzī, 74
Abu 'l-Faḍl Zangurz Bardījī, 228–31
Faḍlūmand (mosque at Baghdād), 54
Fakhr ad-Daula, ʿAlī b. Ḥasan (Buwai-
  hid), 172–5, 178
Farāwa, 147
Farghāna, 227–32
Farhād, 187
Fāshābūya, 214, 216
Fāṭima (daughter of Muḥammad and
  wife of ʿAlī), 168
Fāṭima (daughter of Abū Muslim), 244
Fāṭimid caliphs, 17 n., 236
Fīrūz b. Yazdijird (Sāsānian), 203
Fīrūzābād, see Gūl
Frauds of the Prophets (Makhāriq al-
  Anbiyā), 214
Fuḍail b. ʿIyāḍ, 51

Gabriel (Jabra'īl), 12, 95, 202
Ganja, 107

254

# Index

# Index

# Index

257

# Index